Caribbean Literature in English

Longman Literature in English Series

General Editors: David Carroll and Michael Wheeler
Lancaster University

For a complete list of titles see pages vii–viii

Caribbean Literature in English

Louis James

Longman

London and New York

Addison Wesley Longman Limited,
Edinburgh Gate,
Harlow,
Essex CM20 2JE,
United Kingdom
and Associated Companies throughout the world.

Published in the United States of America
by Addison Wesley Longman Inc. New York

First published 1999

ISBN 0-582-49355-2 CSD
ISBN 0-582-49354-4 PPR

Visit Addison Wesley Longman on the world wide web at
http://www.awl-he.com

British Library Cataloguing-in-Publication Data

A catalogue record for this book is available from the British Library

Library of Congress Cataloging-in-Publication Data

James, Louis, Dr.
　　Caribbean literature in English / Louis James.
　　　　p.　cm. — (Longman literature in English series)
　　Includes bibliographical references and index.
　　ISBN 0–582–49355–2. — ISBN 0–582–49354–4 (pbk.)
　　1. Caribbean literature (English)—History and criticism.　2. West
Indian literature (English)—History and criticism.　3. Caribbean
Area—In literature.　4. West Indies—In literature.　I. Title.
II. Series.
PR9205.J36　1999
810.9′9729—dc21　　　　　　　　　　　　　　　98–40621
　　　　　　　　　　　　　　　　　　　　　　　　　　　　CIP

Set by 35 in 10/11pt Mono Bembo
Printed in Singapore (JBW)

Contents

Longman Literature in English Series
General Editors: David Carroll and Michael Wheeler
Lancaster University

Pre-Renaissance English Literature

★ English Literature before Chaucer *Michael Swanton*
  English Literature in the Age of Chaucer
★ English Medieval Romance *W.R.J. Barron*

English Poetry

★ English Poetry of the Sixteenth Century *Gary Waller (Second Edition)*
★ English Poetry of the Seventeenth Century *George Parfitt (Second Edition)*
  English Poetry of the Eighteenth Century, 1700–1789
★ English Poetry of the Romantic Period, 1789–1830 *J.R. Watson*
  (Second Edition)
★ English Poetry of the Victorian Period, 1830–1890 *Bernard Richards*
  English Poetry of the Early Modern Period, 1890–1940
★ English Poetry since 1940 *Neil Corcoran*

English Drama

  English Drama before Shakespeare *Peter Happé*
★ English Drama: Shakespeare to the Restoration, 1590–1660
  Alexander Leggatt
★ English Drama: Restoration and Eighteenth Century, 1660–1789
  Richard W. Bevis
  English Drama: Romantic and Victorian, 1789–1890
★ English Drama of the Early Modern Period, 1890–1940 *Jean Chothia*
  English Drama since 1940

English Fiction

★ English Fiction of the Eighteenth Century, 1700–1789 *Clive T. Probyn*
★ English Fiction of the Romantic Period, 1789–1830 *Gary Kelly*
★ English Fiction of the Victorian Period, 1830–1890 *Michael Wheeler*
  (Second Edition)
★ English Fiction of the Early Modern Period, 1890–1940
  Douglas Hewitt
  English Fiction since 1940

English Prose

★ English Prose of the Seventeenth Century, 1590–1700 *Roger Pooley*
  English Prose of the Eighteenth Century
★ English Prose of the Nineteenth Century *Hilary Fraser with Daniel Brown*

Criticism and Literary Theory

  Criticism and Literary Theory from Sidney to Johnson
  Criticism and Literary Theory from Wordsworth to Arnold
★ Criticism and Literary Theory, 1890 to the Present *Chris Baldick*

The Intellectual and Cultural Context

  The Sixteenth Century
★ The Seventeenth Century, 1603–1700 *Graham Parry*
★ The Eighteenth Century, 1700–1789 *James Sambrook (Second Edition)*
★ The Romantic Period, 1789–1830 *J.R. Watson*
★ The Victorian Period, 1830–1890 *Robin Gilmour*
  The Twentieth Century: 1890 to the Present

American Literature

  American Literature before 1880
★ American Poetry of the Twentieth Century *Richard Gray*
★ American Drama of the Twentieth Century *Gerald M. Berkowitz*
★ American Fiction 1865–1940 *Brian Lee*
★ American Fiction since 1940 *Tony Hilfer*
★ Twentieth-Century America *Douglas Tallack*

Other Literatures

  Irish Literature since 1800
★ Scottish Literature since 1707 *Marshall Walker*
  Australian Literature
★ Indian Literature in English *William Walsh*
  African Literature in English: East and West
★ Southern African Literatures *Michael Chapman*
★ Caribbean Literature in English *Louis James*
★ Canadian Literature in English *W.J. Keith*

★ *Already published*

Editors' Preface

The multi-volume Longman Literature in English Series provides students of literature with a critical introduction to the major genres in their historical and cultural context. Each volume gives a coherent account of a clearly defined area, and the series, when complete, will offer a practical and comprehensive guide to literature written in English from Anglo-Saxon times to the present. The aim of the series as a whole is to show that the most valuable and stimulating approach to the study of literature is that based upon awareness of the relations between literary forms and their historical contexts. Thus the areas covered by most of the separate volumes are defined by period and genre. Each volume offers new and informed ways of reading literary works, and provides guidance for further reading in an extensive reference section.

In recent years, the nature of English studies has been questioned in a number of increasingly radical ways. The very terms employed to define a series of this kind – period, genre, history, context, canon – have become the focus of extensive critical debate, which has necessarily influenced in varying degrees the successive volumes published since 1985. But however fierce the debate, it rages around the traditional terms and concepts.

As well as studies on all periods of English and American literature, the series includes books on criticism and literary theory and on the intellectual and cultural context. A comprehensive series of this kind must of course include other literatures written in English, and therefore a group of volumes deals with Irish and Scottish literature, and the literature of India, Africa, the Caribbean, Australia and Canada. The forty-seven volumes of the series cover the following areas: Pre-Renaissance English Literature, English Poetry, English Drama, English Fiction, English Prose, Criticism and Literary Theory, Intellectual and Cultural Context, American Literature, Other Literatures in English.

David Carroll
Michael Wheeler

Author's Acknowledgements

This study has incurred many more debts of gratitude than I can list here. Ideas and information have been provided by colleagues and students, graduate and postgraduate, in three continents and over thirty years. I hope they will accept thanks no less sincere for being unspecified. Special acknowledgements for help in writing the book are due to Kamau Brathwaite, Stewart Brown, Paula Burnett, Tim Cribb, Jean-Pierre and Carole Durix, Sarah Fulford, Bridget Jones, Bénedicte Ledent, Mervyn Morris, Susheila Nasta, Franchesca Neri and Anne Walmsley. I am grateful to the University of Kent at Canterbury, which has given me generous study leave and encouragement. Thanks are also due to David Carroll, Michael Wheeler and the editorial team at Addison Wesley Longman for their helpful support. Last and first, my gratitude to Lou, for her unstinting encouragement and support. Now that the book is finished, she can have me back.

Publisher's Acknowledgements

We are grateful to the following for permission to reproduce copyright material:

Mrs Phyllis Carter for extracts from the poems 'No madness like this sanity', 'This is the Dark Time my love', 'The Great Dark' by Martin Carter in *Selected Poems*. First published by Demerara Publishers 1989. Revised edition – Thread Press 1997; Faber & Faber Ltd/Farrar Straus & Giroux Inc for extracts from *Omeros* by Derek Walcott. Copyright © 1990 by Derek Walcott & an extract from the poem 'Tales of the Islands' by Derek Walcott in *Collected Poems 1948–1984* by Derek Walcott. Copyright © 1986 by Derek Walcott; Garland Publishing Inc for extracts from *First Poems* by George Campbell 1945; Karnak House for the poem 'Epilogue' by Grace Nichols from *I Is a Long Memoried Woman*. © 1983 Karnak House; New Beacon Books Ltd for an extract from the poem 'Amazon' by Wilson Harris in *Eternity To Season* 1978; Peepal Tree Press for extract from the poem 'Flute' by MaLandai Das in *Bones* 1988; Mrs Joy Scott/University of Pittsburg Press for an extract from the poem 'Portait of an Artist as a Magician' in *Uncle Time* by Dennis Scott. 1973. © Estate of Dennis G. Scott. The author, Derek Walcott for extracts from *Another Life*.

We have been unable to trace the copyright holders of 'Litany' by George Campbell, 'If we must die' by Claude McKay, 'Dan is the Man in the Van' by Slinger Francisco, 'Hawk Heart' by E.M. Roach, and would appreciate any information which would enable us to do so.

On the Arrangement of this Book

Conventional methods of organising such complex material by chronology or theme alone proved unsatisfactory. The following arrangement attempts to gain the benefits of more than one method.

The *Introduction* outlines the peculiar problems of defining Caribbean literature in English, much of which has been written in exile, and which has been often implicated with the writing of other cultures.

Part I examines the two parallel cultures that developed in the Caribbean in the slave era.

Part II outlines the emergence of a common literature from the contrasting regions of the Caribbean.

Part III considers the ways in which a distinctive Caribbean aesthetic took shape.

Part IV uses the West Indian word 'groundation' – meaning a communal discussion and meeting of ideas – to introduce the acceptance of cultures from Africa and India within national cultures.

Part V looks at some of the distinctive contributions made to Caribbean literature by individual writers.

The *Postscript* briefly surveys the role of Caribbean writing in world literature in English.

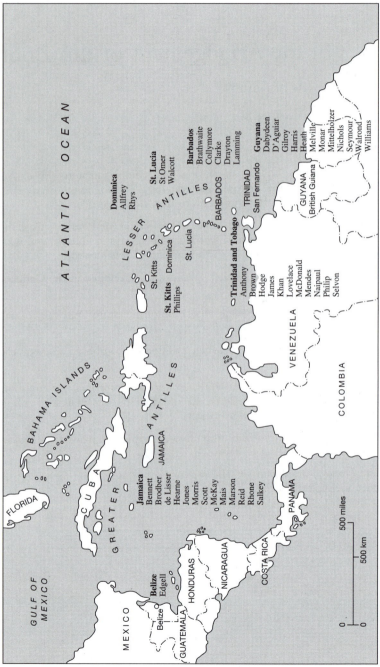

ATLANTIC OCEAN

GULF OF MEXICO

FLORIDA

BAHAMA ISLANDS

GREATER ANTILLES

CUBA

Belize
Edgell

Belize

GUATEMALA

MEXICO

HONDURAS

NICARAGUA

COSTA RICA

PANAMA

Jamaica
Bennett
Brodber
de Lisser
Hearne
Jones
Morris
Scott
McKay
Mais
Marson
Reid
Rhone
Salkey

JAMAICA

LESSER ANTILLES

St. Kitts

St. Kitts
Phillips

Dominica

Dominica
Allfrey
Rhys

St. Lucia

St. Lucia
St Omer
Walcott

ANTILLES

BARBADOS

Barbados
Brathwaite
Collymore
Clarke
Drayton
Lamming

TRINIDAD
San Fernando

Trinidad and Tobago
Anthony
Brown
Hodge
James
Khan
Lovelace
McDonald
Mendes
Naipaul
Philip
Selvon

VENEZUELA

COLOMBIA

GUYANA
British Guiana

Guyana
Dabydeen
D'Aguiar
Gilroy
Harris
Heath
Melville
Monar
Mittelholzer
Nichols
Seymour
Walrond
Williams

500 miles

500 km

0

0

Introduction

*My role, it seems, has rather to do with time and change than
with the geography of circumstances; and yet there is always an
acre of ground in the New World which keeps growing echoes in
my head.*

George Lamming[1]

*For it is certain that the Caribbean basin, although it includes the
first American lands to be explored, conquered, and colonized by
Europe, is still, especially in the discourse of the social sciences, one
of the least known regions of the modern world.*

Antonio Benítez-Rojo[2]

The Caribbean is a region in which the aboriginal communities were virtually exterminated, and replaced by peoples from Africa, Asia and Europe.
Yet it has established a distinctive identity that in turn has contributed to
global cultures, including those of the countries from which its peoples
originally came. This introduction examines the problems of defining the
'Caribbean' and its literatures.

Definitions

'I know of no other area of the world', Janheinz Jahn once wrote of the
Caribbean basin, 'where so many important writers and poets are born in
so small a population'.[3] Yet the region would appear unlikely ground for
literature. It is rural, and economically poor. It is fragmented into islands,
many of them very small, and discontinuous areas on the rim of the American continent. There is no common language. Its countries have inherited
English, Spanish, French or Dutch, modified into Creole forms which are
different within each area. Even in the postcolonial era, territories within

sight of each other remain locked in separate cultural traditions. In terms of topography, language and race, few if any regions of the world are so diverse.

The region has been partly defined by historical accident, and has gone under various names in its history. 'West Indies' was a notorious mistake, made in 1492 when Columbus reached San Salvador, believed he had found the Indies off Cathay, and called the folk he met 'Indians'. The term 'West Indies' became used to distinguish the islands from the 'East Indies', and until recently for English speakers it meant the British territories. The islands were also called the Antilles, and the whole area, the Caribbean. Neither name is precise. The 'Antilles' were a pre-Columbian myth, a land or islands sited somewhere in the Western Atlantic, and although Caribs lived in the area when Columbus arrived, so did Taino Arawaks and Ciboney.

Naming the inhabitants proved as slippery as defining the region. In the first two centuries of European contact the aborigines were hunted like animals, or killed off by slave labour and imported diseases. The Indian population of Hispaniola was in 1492 calculated at between two and three hundred thousand; by 1514, it had shrunk to an estimated fourteen thousand.[4] The original peoples have remained an obstinate presence. Their blood entered the Caribbean racial mix. The last Carib war ended on St Vincent as late as 1797, a Carib settlement still survives on Dominica, and in Guyana and Belize in particular, aboriginal peoples still offer evidence of the pre-Columbian cultural roots surviving in the Caribbean. With the virtual disappearance of the original 'West Indians', however, the huge majority population became one of African descent. This remained invisible to Europe: when Richard Cumberland wrote his play *The West Indian* in 1771, the title referred only to the white planter class. With political independence this changed, and by the mid-twentieth century Kamau Brathwaite could declare that 'when most of us speak of "the West Indian" we think of someone of African descent.'[5] But by now there was a significant presence of 'real' Indians in the south-eastern Caribbean. V.S. Naipaul, one of over a quarter of a million Trinidad Asians, wrote that 'confusion became total' as with the growth of a national identity 'the West Indian East Indians became East Indian West Indians'.[6]

Antonio Benítez-Rojo has argued that the Caribbean, with its conflicting identities, is 'a repeating island', an unstable region suspended between cultures, 'the ultimate meta-archipelago'.[7] It is an area of flux like the 'spiral chaos of the Milky Way', held within contexts of geography, and united by a common history of slavery. The first sixteenth-century Spanish communities grew spices and coffee, and, like the first white Barbadians, farmed small areas. But sugar cane, introduced to Hispaniola in 1522, quickly dominated West Indian life and culture. Its cultivation was labour intensive, and between four and five million African slaves were imported to work the Caribbean plantations:[8] by comparison, the total population of England and Wales in 1701 was calculated at five and a half million. After 1834, when slavery was abolished in British territories, indentured East Indian labourers, together with large numbers of Chinese, Portuguese and Irish, were imported into the still expanding plantations of Trinidad and British Guiana,[9] often living in conditions little better than those of slavery. But the plantation era had set the dominant pattern of subsequent Caribbean society, one in which the power was held by an élite selected not by merit but by colour, while the distinctive culture was created by the disempowered black majority.

The British West Indies by the beginning of the twentieth century comprised some twenty-two territories scattered across two thousand miles. Most lay in or around the Caribbean Sea, although British Guiana (now Guyana) stood outside it on the South American mainland, and Barbados was a flat marine limestone island lying in the Atlantic a hundred miles to the East. Between the two world wars, the British territories moved towards independence, which most achieved in the 1960s. Yet as nations they remained politically insignificant in the shadow of Europe and Northern America. Local economies have become crippled by debts to world banks. Behind the tourist images of the sunny Caribbean lies poverty, unrest and political uncertainty. Walter Rodney, the Radical Guyanese economist murdered in 1980, and Michael Smith, the Jamaican poet stoned to death in Kingston by party thugs in 1983, were but two figures who died speaking out in societies conditioned to violence. The United States, who have controlled Cuba, Haiti and San Domingo for most of the twentieth century, in 1983 invaded Grenada to oust the People's Revolutionary Government there.

Yet while politically powerless, shackled with debt and emasculated by tourism, the Caribbean has continued to produce a remarkable succession of writers, musicians and artists, although much of this has been produced outside the West Indies itself. For Derek Walcott, this weakness can be creative. He has written:

> To begin with, we are poor. That gives us a privilege. . . .
> The stripped and naked man, however abused, however
> disabused of old beliefs, instinctually, even desperately
> begins again as a craftsman.[10]

*   *   *

Context can clarify, but not define, the question, 'What is Caribbean literature?' Historically, the development of West Indian writing has been divisive, for literacy and book learning have been privileges for the élite, and for the mass of the people the profession of authorship meant separation from their cultural roots in an oral tradition. Most West Indians who wished to be writers have emigrated to find education, publishers and a reading public. The first major West Indian novel, Claude McKay's *Banana Bottom* (1933), emerged not from McKay's Jamaica, but from the New York Harlem Renaissance. Nor can West Indian literature be defined as writing set in the Caribbean. Denis Williams's *Other Leopards* (1963) places a Guyanese quest for identity in the African sub-Sahara, while in Naipaul's *The Enigma of Arrival* (1987), an English Wiltshire village focused an Indo-Caribbean exploration of self. Benedict Anderson has argued that 'all communities larger than primordial villages of face to face contact (and perhaps even these) are imagined. Communities are distinguished not by the falsity/genuineness, but by the style in which they are imagined'.[11] Indeed, as we will see, a Caribbean 'style' has emerged. But in literature there was no simple evolution. Robert E. McDowell began his *Bibliography of Literature from Guyana* with Sir Walter Raleigh's *Discoverie . . . of Guyana* (1596). The Trinidadian critic Kenneth Ramchand opened his reader, *West Indian Narrative* (1966), with examples taken from the English writers Aphra Behn, Matthew G. Lewis and Maria Nugent. As we will see, Shakespeare's *The Tempest* (1611), Defoe's *Robinson Crusoe* (1712) and Charlotte Brontë's *Jane Eyre* (1847) are among the European works that have become imbedded in West Indian writing. None of this conflicts with the fact that the basic cultures of the area are rooted in African oral traditions. For the Caribbean has been the site of continual transformation and change.

Intertextuality has been seen as a trope for the Caribbean predicament itself. The Jamaican novelist John Hearne wrote that Antoinette in Jean Rhys's *Wide Sargasso Sea*, trapped in the written framework of *Jane Eyre*, is 'a superb and audacious metaphor of so much of West Indian life'.

> Are we not still, in so many of our responses, creatures of
> books and inventions fashioned by others who used us as
> mere producers, as figments of their imagination; and
> who regarded the territory as a ground over which the
> inadmissible or forgotten forces of the psyche could run free
> for a while before being written off or suppressed?[12]

Naipaul, in his early writing, wrote of West Indian 'Mimic Men'. In his 1967 novel of this title, Ralph Kripalsingh on his island of Isabella feels himself created by images from Europe and America. Walking along the beach, he sees himself on the technicolour island of the Hollywood film, *The Black Swan*; his African schoolfellow, Browne, is locked into a 'world already charted' by stereotypes of the black man.[13]

For other West Indian writers, however, this complicity of cultures has not been a loss, but positive and creative. Addressing the theme of Naipaul's novel, Derek Walcott asserted that 'mimicry is an act of imagination, and in some animals and insects, endemic cunning'.[14] The Guyanese author Wilson Harris has strongly asserted that the diversity of cultures is not imposed onto the Caribbean, but reflects the multiplicity of identities within the Caribbean psyche itself, and as such provides a dynamic nucleus for the creative imagination. He has written:

> What in my view is remarkable about the West Indian
> in depth is a sense of subtle links, a series of subtle and
> nebulous links which are latent within him, the latent
> ground of old and new personalities. This is a very difficult
> view to hold, I grant, because it is not a view which
> consolidates, which invests in any way in the consolidation
> of popular character. Rather it seeks to visualise a fulfilment
> of character.[15]

A recurrent tone in major Caribbean writing has been not mimic, but epic. This sounds within works by St John Perse, Tom Recam and Marcus Garvey in the first half of the twentieth century.[16] It echoes in Derek Walcott's *Drums and Colours* (1961), the play chosen to open the Federation of the West Indies, and reverberates beneath the historical and geographical vistas of Kamau Brathwaite's *The Arrivants* (1973). African beliefs and practices survived the Middle Passage, to become the potent stock onto which were grafted the cultures of three continents. Old World rapacity met a New World humanism. The Caribbean has remained a green place, even if, as Derek Walcott has written, 'the golden apples of this sun are shot with acid'.[17] Between the nightmare of the slave barracoons [barracks], and the vision of Adamic islands, have emerged the imagined worlds examined in this book.

Notes

1. George Lamming, *The Pleasures of Exile* (London, 1960), p. 50.

2. Antonio Benítez-Rojo, *The Repeating Island*, translated by James E. Maraniss (Durham and London, 1996), p. 1.

3. Quoted by Neville Dawes, *Prolegomena to Caribbean Literature* (Kingston, Jamaica, 1977), p. 1. George Lamming estimated the populations of the Caribbean basin as six million, of which '3,000,000 [are] under the rule of Great Britain'. Lamming, *The Pleasures of Exile* (London, 1960), p. 16.

4. Eric Williams, *From Columbus to Castro* (New York, 1970), p. 33. But the figure has been placed higher. See Franklin W. Knight, *The Caribbean: the Genesis of a*

Fragmented Nation, 2nd edition (New York, 1990), p. 7; William M. Denevan (ed.), *The Native Population of the Americas in 1492* (Madison, 1976).

5. Kamau Brathwaite, 'Roots' (1963), reprinted in Brathwaite, *Roots* (Ann Arbor, 1993), p. 40.

6. V.S. Naipaul, *The Overcrowded Barracoon* ([1972] Harmondsworth, 1976), p. 36. Sam Selvon saw himself as an 'East Indian Trinidadian West Indian', 'Epilogue', *Foreday Morning* ([1979] Harlow, 1989), p. 220.

7. Antonio Benítez-Rojo, *Repeating Island*, pp. 1–5.

8. Franklin W. Knight, pp. 112–13.

9. Leo Lowenthal, *West Indian Societies* (London, 1972), p. 213.

10. Derek Walcott, 'The Caribbean: Culture or Mimicry?', reprinted in *Critical Perspectives on Derek Walcott*, edited by Robert D. Hamner ([1974] Washington, DC, 1993), pp. 52, 57.

11. Benedict Anderson, *Imagined Communities* (London, 1991), p. 6.

12. John Hearne, '*Wide Sargasso Sea*: a West Indian Reflection', *Cornhill Magazine* (Summer, 1974), pp. 325–6.

13. V.S. Naipaul, *The Mimic Men* (London, 1967), pp. 112, 134.

14. Derek Walcott, 'Culture or Mimicry?', p. 54.

15. Wilson Harris, *Tradition, the Writer and Society* (London, 1967), p. 28,

16. St John Perse, *Anabase* (1924); Tom Recam, *San Gloria* (1920); Marcus Garvey, *Slavery – from Hut to Mansion* (unpublished, staged 1930).

17. Derek Walcott, 'The Muse of History', in *Is Massa Day Dead?*, edited by Orde Coombs (New York, 1974), p. 5.

PART I

Distorting Mirrors: The Slave Era

*For I am a direct descendant of slaves [the Calibans], too near
to the actual enterprise to believe its echoes are over with the reign
of emancipation. Moreover, I am a direct descendant of Prospero
worshipping in the same temple of endeavour, using his legacy of
language . . .*

George Lamming[1]

The Caribbean in the plantation era acted as a distorting mirror, in which
Europeans imaged desires, prejudices and terrors; and where enslaved
Africans dreamt of ancestral homelands. Yet at times the reflections met
and melded. This section examines in turn two communities, implacably
divided by race, culture and interests, yet bonded by a shared and violent
history.

Chapter 1
Reflections of Europe in the New World

Kamau Brathwaite has observed that in the Caribbean during the slave era 'in the field of literature itself, a great deal of energy was given over to treatises . . . and descriptive and historical works. Some of these . . . may be classed as literary works in their own right, since they reveal the creative eye recording.'[2] Modern concepts of the West Indies first grew out of letters and travelogues, often written by Europeans as acts of Utopian desire. 'In these islands', Columbus wrote on his return to Spain, 'I have so far found no monstrosities, as many expected, but on the contrary all the people are of fine appearance; nor are they negroes as in Guinea, but with flowing hair . . .'[3] Although his letter also mentioned the man-eating Caribs,[4] he portrayed the West Indies as inhabited by child-like, friendly peoples. On his last voyage in 1502, he navigated the South American coast, collecting substantial amounts of gold, and was told by Indians of a wealthy nation ten days' journey into the interior. Subsequent expeditions sought the city of *el hombro dorado*, a ruler who annually covered himself in gold dust and ritually bathed in the centre of Lake Guatavitá in the Andean highlands.[5] One of the last searches for El Dorado was made up the Orinoco in 1595 by Sir Walter Raleigh. His account in *The Discoverie of the Large and Bewtiful Empire of Guyana* (1596) can still enthral today.

> On both sides of this riuer, we passed the most beautifull
> countrie that euer mine eies beheld: and whereas all that
> we had seen before was nothing but woods, prickles,
> bushes, and thornes, heere we beheld plaines of twenty
> miles in length, the grasse short and greene, and in diuers
> part groves and trees by themselues, as if they had been by
> all the art and labour in the world so made of purpose:
> and stil as we rowed, the Deere came downe feeding
> by the waters side, as if they had been vsed to a keepers
> call.[6]

The people

never eat of anie thing that is set or sowen, and as at home they use neither planting or any other manurance, so when they com abroad they refuse to eat of ought, but of that which nature without labor bringing forth.[7]

Politically, and even as exploration, Raleigh's voyage was a disaster. His subsequent 1616 expedition was abortive, and he was summarily beheaded. But the myth lived on. Raleigh's account of his travels encouraged the British settlement of Guyana and Caribbean islands, and even that of Virginia and the Eastern seaboard. Raleigh's account of the Indian as Noble Savage influenced Montaigne's essay 'Of Cannibals', which, in Florio's translation of 1603, helped shape Shakespeare's conception of 'Caliban' (an anagram of Canibal) in *The Tempest* (c. 1611). In turn Caribbean writers such as Césaire and George Lamming were to take Caliban as the European image of the West Indian.[8] The first full account of European settlement in the Caribbean was by the French Dominican priest, Jean Baptiste Du Tertre, *The General History of the French Antilles* (1667–1671). Du Tertre vividly describes a complex society where, in Elsa Goveia's words, 'colonists, free Indians, indentured servants, slaves, buccaneers, Catholics, "heretics", and Jews mingled in a fascinating exoticism under tropical skies'.[9] He had a humane attitude to both Indians and slaves, seeing them not as inferiors but as ill-treated human beings, and his account of Carib life became a main source for Rousseau's *Discourse on the Origins of Inequality* (1754). Another important document was by Père Jean Baptist Labat, who vividly described his encounter with Caribs on Dominica in his *New Voyage to the Islands of America* (1722).[10]

The records of later historians in the area, however, were shaped not by the Enlightenment but by the vested interests of the sugar planters. Richard Ligon's *A True and Exact History of Barbados* (1657) provides a detailed account of everything to do with sugar plantation except the effects of slavery. Nor is this discussed in Bryan Edwards's *History, Civil and Commercial of the British Colonies in the West Indies* (1793), or Edward Long's brilliant and polemical *History of Jamaica* (1774). Although not born in Jamaica, Long was a planter with family on the island, and identified with the island's white Creoles. Up to a point he was a liberal, and his critique of British Imperialism has been compared with that of contemporary revolutionaries in North America.[11] But in his account of Jamaican society as a whole, Long vehemently asserted the 'natural inferiority of Negroes'. His damaged scholarship stands as a monument, Elsa Goveia noted, to 'the power of all societies to mould and often to warp, the minds and hearts of individuals that the social order may be preserved'.[12] Yet time had one ironic revenge. To demonstrate Africans' lack of intelligence, Long transcribed a Latin poem by one Francis Williams, including his own contemptuous translation. Williams was a freed Jamaican slave, brought to England in 1711 by the Duke of Montague, and educated at Cambridge in order to discover whether, properly educated, 'a Negro might not be found as capable of literature as a white man'. Distinguished in mathematics and classics, Williams was evidently also an accomplished poet. The only surviving example of his verse is one cited by Long, a Latin ode written in 1759 to George Haldane, the new Governor of Jamaica. If it inevitably flattered Haldane, Williams's Latin was witty and elegant, and addressed his own racial situation, asserting that 'virtue and prudence, established by a powerful hand, themselves know no colour (for creating God gave the same soul to every being, nothing forbidding)'.[13] Williams's application for Government office was blocked, and instead he became a teacher in Spanish Town. Nevertheless, Long had unwittingly established Williams as the first published black West Indian poet.

The brutalising effect of the slave system permeated West Indian society as a whole. Lady Nugent's account of Jamaica in 1802 has often been quoted.

> It is extraordinary to witness the immediate effect that climate and habit of living in this country have upon the minds and manners of Europeans, particularly of the lower orders. In the upper ranks, they become indolent and inactive, regardless of every thing but eating, drinking, and indulging themselves, and are almost entirely under the dominion of their mulatto favourites.[14]

Yet the society itself was complex. The lavishly entertaining major land-owners in their Great Houses enjoyed a gracious lifestyle reminiscent of Faulkner's South. Below them were a class of professionals and small plantation owners, and these were usually the most racist elements in the society, including *petits blancs*, overseers and book-keepers.[15] Each had their own level of involvement in plantation life. The private diaries of Thomas Thistlewood, a small landowner in Western Jamaica from 1750 to 1786,[16] give a vivid account of the harshness of plantation discipline, its obscene punishments, and the routine sexual abuse of black women. Thistlewood continually faced non-cooperation and physical violence from his slaves. Yet he also evokes a shared intimacy in which fear and hate could mingle with dependency and even loyalty. Central to the diaries is Thistlewood's chequered but enduring relationship with Phibbah, a slave cook on a neighbouring estate who was a woman of intelligence and moral stature. Through her, he had some access to the black community. Phibbah bore him a son, and the largest bequest in his will was to buy her her freedom.

Away from the squalor of the slave barracoons, white Creole communities created the amenities of an expatriate culture. Touring companies of actors, often en route from Europe to America, performed alongside amateur groups and some local professional actors in venues ranging from small playhouses to candle-lit barns. The first theatre was opened in Jamaica as early as 1682, in Barbados in 1792, and by 1820 Port-of-Spain in Trinidad had three.[17] Most plays were European, with Shakespeare's the favourite, although some were written locally.[18] Theatre-going was largely the privilege of the white élite, but segregation was not absolute as has been sometimes claimed. Servants were often allowed in the gallery, and writing of Jamaica, Errol Hill noted 'that it is fair to say that by the beginning of the nineteenth century the . . . theatre catered to a broad cross section of the public, if indeed it had been exclusive before that time'.[19] Newspapers also fostered local culture. *The Weekly Jamaican Courant*, established in 1718, was the first of many journals that carried local news, comment and satirical squibs. Small presses, set up to print journals, published pamphlets and even books. The anonymous *Whole Proceedings of Captain Dennis's Expedition* was printed in Jamaica in 1718; John Singleton's more substantial verse travelogue, *A General Description of the West Indian Islands* (Barbados, 1767), followed. With local publication came the beginnings of a West Indian literary tradition. Better known than Nathaniel Weekes's poem *Barbados* (1754), James Grainger's *The Sugar-Cane* (1764) was an ambitious four-part 'West Indian Georgic' that, in investigating agriculture, created new poetic images from the island's topography. Grainger was a Scots medical doctor who settled and died in St Kitts, wrote a medical handbook on the care of slaves, and had a professional interest in plantation life that can animate the ponderous Miltonic pentameter of his verse.

> On festal days; or when their work is done,
> Permit thy slaves to lead the choral dance,
> To the wild banshaw's melancholy sound.
> Responsive to the sound, head feet and frame
> More awkwardly harmonious; hand in hand
> Now link'd, the gay troop circularly wheels,
> And frisks and capers with intemperate joy.
> Halts the vast circle, all clap hands and sing;
> While those distinguish'd for their heels and air,
> Bound in the centre, and fantastic twine.[20]

Grainger in general described a working landscape, although even medical advice on slave housing appears dependent on aesthetic considerations.

> It much imports to build thy Negroe-huts
> Or on the founding margin of the main,
> Or on some dry hill's gently-sloping sides
> In streets, at distance due . . .[21]

Writers and painters saw the Caribbean through Europe-tinted spectacles. In *A Description of the Island of Jamaica* (1790) Jamaican-born William Beckford presents tropical landscapes as 'finer than Matlock and Dove-Dale',[22] and considers the trees and shrubs 'singular for the richness of their tints, the depths of their shadows, and the picturesque appearance they make'.[23] Within this, the slave gangs present a 'picturesque appearance among the shrubs and ferns',[24] and even 'the blackness of the negroes faces' serves to enhance the whiteness of the cotton.[25] It was not until William Hosack's *The Isle of Streams; or the Jamaican Hermit and other Poems*, published after emancipation in 1876, that black people became acknowledged as the inhabitants of the landscape rather than its decoration.

Controversy sparked creative literature. The story of Inkle and Yarico had been told by Ligon in 1657. Yarico, an Indian girl on a Caribbean island, was said to have rescued and saved Inkle, a British sailor, when his foraging party had been attacked by tribesmen. Falling in love, she accompanied Inkle to Barbados, only to be promptly sold by her lover into slavery. The story went through several metamorphoses. By 1711, when Addison used the story in *The Spectator* no. 11, Yarico's tale had become a sentimental idyll; in May 1734, an anonymous poem 'The Story of Inkle and Yarico' appeared in the *London Magazine*. Here Yarico was African, 'a negro virgin', part of the anti-slave iconography. George Coleman the Younger's popular stage version *Inkle and Yarico* (1787) returned the story to Barbados, and gave it a happy ending, with Yarico released by the benevolent Governor and reunited with a repentant Inkle.[26] The story still lives on, and forms the subject of *Inkle and Yarico* (1996), a recent novel by the Guyanese author Beryl Gilroy.

If the passive suffering of the Caribbean slaves was imaged in Yarico, their rebellion found an icon in the eponymous hero of Aphra Behn's *Oronooko* (1688). Oronooko, an African prince, and his lover, Imoinda, were sold separately into slavery as punishment for rejecting the grandfather's amorous claims on Imoinda. By chance the two met in Surinam, and when Imoinda bore Oronooko's child, Oronooko raised a rebellion in which the lovers escaped. Recaptured and beaten by Byam, the craven deputy governor, Oronooko resolves revenge; he kills the consenting Imoinda to save her from Byam, and himself faces death by torture, stoically smoking his pipe. The story may have a basis in fact. Aphra Behn claimed that 'I was myself an Eye-witness to a great part of what you will find here set down',[27] and she could well have visited Surinam prior to 1670. The administrators are historical figures; the names 'Oronooko' and 'Imoinda', long thought exotic inventions, have Yoruba roots.[28] The novella was constantly reprinted, and, dramatised by Thomas Southern in 1695, became after *Jane Shore* the most frequently produced English play of the eighteenth century. Its popularity exemplifies British double-think on racial issues. Oronooko's harangue to the rebels might appear to be the first black power speech in English literature:

> And why (said he) my dear friends and fellow–sufferers, should we be slaves to an unknown people? Have they vanquished us nobly in fight? Have they won us in honourable battle? . . . And shall we render obedience to such a degenerate race, who have not one vertue left, to distinguish them from the vilest creatures?[29]

Yet Oronooko speaks as a 'Noble Savage', not a slave. He becomes disgusted by the behaviour of the rebellious 'ordinary Negroes' and is 'ashamed of what he had done, in endeavouring to make those free, who were by nature slaves, fit to be used as Christian tools . . .'[30] Oronooko, as a royal Prince, had slaves himself. A more Radical version of Oronooko appears in the black hero of John Fawcett's *Obi; or Three-Fingered Jack*, played at the Theatre Royal, Haymarket, London, in 1800, later transferring to Covent Garden. Obi, whose story is told in B. Moseley's *Treatise on Sugar* (2nd edn, 1800), was a Jamaican slave who escaped into the interior and waged war on the white planters with the aid of 'obeah' in the 1770s. He was treacherously killed by two fellow slaves for a ransom and the promise of their freedom. In London in 1831 the part of Obi was played by Richard John Smith at the Coburg Theatre with such elan that he was ever after-wards known as 'O' ('Obi') Smith. Fawcett made Obi a romantic villain/hero, like another of Smith's sensational roles, the Monster in a stage version of *Frankenstein*. Both were ambivalent icons of rebellion in a revolutionary era. *Obi* was performed in Glasgow as late as 1843, with the name-part played by the black American actor Ira Aldridge, and briefly, even in Jamaica. Although a marked contrast to William Barrymore's racially hostile drama *The Foulahs* (1832), *Obi* was no anti-slave tract, and while the opening chorus laments the cruelties of slavery, it also praises good masters. When a truly sympathetic account of a black revolutionary appeared on the British stage, it was the hero of George Dibdin Pitt's *Toussaint L'Ouverture* (1846) at the working-class Britannic Theatre, Hoxton.

Controversy intensified as slave emancipation came nearer. *Jamaica: a Poem in Three Parts* (London, 1776), by an anonymous eighteen-year-old resident of Jamaica, expresses horror at plantation life:

> Lo! tortures, racks, whips, famine, gibbets, chains,
> Rise on my mind, appall my tear-stained eye,
> Attract my rage, and draw a heart-felt sigh[31]

J.B. Moreton's *West India Customs and Manners* (1793), which also made a stand against slavery, was to become an important source of Jamaican work songs and dances. Moreton took a genial attitude to the moral laxity of West Indian society as a whole, attributing it mainly to the effect of the climate. A more Romantic approach appears in James Montgomery's long historical and geographical poem *The West Indies* (1809). Although Montgomery himself had not visited the Caribbean, it expressed his missionary concerns, and became a popular Abolitionist text. On the other hand, *Manley; or a Planter's Life in Jamaica* (1828) was written by 'a Slave Driver', who 'exchanged his whip for his pen' to write a viciously racist eulogy of slavery. In 1832, in the heat of the emancipation debate, playgoers in Barbados could watch the anonymous drama, *The Fair Barbadian and the Faithful Black*, where attempts to separate the (white) lovers are frustrated by a black servant called Hampshire. Hampshire is terrified of being liberated, crying 'Gee me free! wha I want with free? If massa lub Hampshire, he no trow he way upon the world!' His owner promises him his servitude.

The novel *Hamel, the Obeah Man* (1827) was set in Jamaica. The anonymous author evidently had first-hand experience of the island, and the story opens with a vivid panoramic scene of a storm in the ravine of the Rio Grande. Roland, a white Methodist minister, finds refuge in the cave of Hamel, an Obeah man, in a subterranean network used by runaway slaves. Hamel is 'at least sixty' years old, small in stature, but with impressive composure.[32] He defends Obeah as traditional African religion, older than and as legitimate as Christianity: 'we say nothing against your religion, nor your God.'[33] When captured, he vows vengeance on the whites for his sufferings as a slave:

> There is justice upon the earth, though it seems to sleep;
> and the black men shall, first or last, shed your blood, and
> toss your bodies into the sea![34]

Yet, like Oronooko, Hamel also reviles the rebellious slaves, led by Combah, as brutal savages who would make Jamaica 'ten times worse than my own country [Africa] was ever made by war, and fighting, and robbery and murder'.[35] The real villain of the novel, however, is Roland, a missionary with all the brooding evil of a Gothic monk. *Hamel* in fact emerges as a violent tract against the Methodists, whose sympathy for the blacks was bitterly resented by Jamaican planters. In the end Roland dies a Gothic agony of guilt, while Hamel escapes, sailing north-eastward towards Haiti.

Michael Scott's *Tom Cringle's Log*, serialised in *Blackwood's Magazine* 1822–33, was based on Scott's life as a plantation overseer in Jamaica, and the book alternates romance with factual description. After swashbuckling adventures with smugglers, hostile Spaniards, and a black pirate chief who turns out to be a native of Edinburgh, 'Tom Cringle' lands in Jamaica and observes its life and manners, landscape and climate.[36] He joins in a rowdy ball in Kingston, watches a black 'John Canoe' festival [the main Christmas celebration of the Jamaican slaves], and an obeah ceremony for the dead. He includes circumstantial detail, and Jamaican words such as 'nyam' [eat], 'backray' [white man], and 'duppy' [ghost]. But he remains the paternalistic overseer. Watching black people dancing in neat clothes down country paths to a country festival 'in all the anticipation of a good dinner', he comments

> And these are slaves, . . . *and this is West Indian bondage!*
> Oh that some of my well-meaning anti-slavery friends were here, to judge from the evidence of their own senses![37]

Other writers had been on naval exercises in the Caribbean. Frederick Marryat cruised there, serving in the Royal Navy from 1806 to 1820, and drew on this experience in writing certain of his novels. In *Peter Simple* (1834) he caricatures the black islanders, but *Percival Keene* (1842), written on slave emancipation, is remarkably different. Percival is captured by Vincent, a noble black pirate bent on revenging himself against the slavers. Percival actually blackens himself in order to become one of his crew. In the end, Vincent blows himself up to elude capture, while Percival escapes.

Women writers, both expatriates and Creole, made a particular contribution to early West Indian writing. Mrs Carmichael's *Domestic Manners and Social Conditions of the White, Coloured and Negro Population of the West Indies* (1833) was for information; other works, like Mrs Lynch's *The Family Sepulchre: a Tale of Jamaica* (1848) or *Years Ago: a Tale of West Indian Domestic Life of the Nineteenth century* (1865), were fiction. As Evelyn O'Callaghan in her study of this literature[38] notes, women's writing reveals aspects of domestic and family life omitted from male accounts. White women, themselves sexually vulnerable, tended to be more sensitive to the moral degeneracy of the slave system than the men. The frail heroine of romance bore little relation to the West Indian reality. Lady Nugent, who cropped her hair and rode intrepidly across Jamaica on horseback, may have been exceptional, but life in the tropics demanded courage and resilience, even for those with servants. Even more remarkable than Lady Nugent's *Diary* was the autobiography *The Wonderful Adventures of Mrs. Seacole in Many Lands* (1857). Mary Seacole was a Jamaican Creole woman, born the 'brown' child of a free black boarding house keeper and a Scottish officer. She acknowledges that 'energy and activity . . . are not always found in the Creole race', and that her own vigorous nature may be partly due to her Scottish blood. However, she equally valued her mother's traditional African skills in herbal healing, and saw nothing inferior in being black. She notes wryly that Europeans in the West Indies are blessed in that Nature predisposes the Creoles to care for them when they are sick and feeble.[39] Widowed, she went first to Panama, then served as a nurse in the Crimean War with such good effect that she received French, Turkish, and probably English military decorations.[40] She found colonial Jamaica restrictive, and settled finally in England, a female 'Ulysses' whose career looks forward to future generations of West Indian emigrées

As the Victorian age progressed, anti-West Indian prejudice deepened in Britain. Robert Young has demonstrated that 'race became the fundamental determinant of human culture and history: indeed it is arguable that race became *the* principle of academic knowledge in the nineteenth century'.[41] The Jamaican Morant Bay Rebellion of 1865, and the Indian Mutiny of 1854, reinforced by the pseudo-scientific theories of race surrounding Darwin's *On the Origin of Species* (1859), turned leading British intellectuals, including Carlyle, Ruskin, Tennyson and Dickens, against the West Indian Creoles. Racial prejudice sold travel books. In *The West Indies and the Spanish Main* (1860), Anthony Trollope described West Indian Creoles as a degenerate race belonging neither to Africa nor to Europe, with no language but 'their broken English'. The black West Indian possesses exceptional physical endurance, 'but he is idle, ambitious as to worldly position, sensual, and content with little'. A happy, careless people, 'a little makes [black people] happy and nothing makes them permanently wretched'.[42] The subtitle of James Anthony Froude's *The English in the West Indies; or the Bow of Ulysses* (1887) referred to the bow of authority, that Froude believed could only be drawn by the British. He contrasted the excellence of English administration with the revolutionary bloodbath of Haiti. The patronising tone of Froude's travelogue caused even greater offence in the Caribbean than its content.

These hostile attitudes in Britain created a new self-assertion in the West Indies. In Trinidad, Froude was answered by *Froudacity* (1889) by the brilliant, largely self-educated black schoolmaster, J.J. Thomas. Thomas systematically rejected Froude's claims to white racial superiority. He devastated Froude's methods of research, which were based on 'drives about the town and neighbourhood',[43] and demonstrated that British rule, far from being a benefit, was riddled with ignorance and deliberate maladministration. Thomas ended with a stirring plea for West Indian independence, part of a growing educated class that were beginning to define and defend its culture. Canon Nelson Huggins, a St Vincentian living in Trinidad, also illustrated this new historical consciousness. His long poem *Hiroona* celebrates the rebellion of the St Vincent Caribs against the British in 1795, attributing their defeat largely to European corruption of their culture. Warrimou, the defeated Carib chief, attacked the English forces in stirring tones

I tell you, white man, to your teeth
No less than robbers, pirates ye,

And plunderers by land and sea.
What restless greed would make you roam
Has England no waste lands at home?[44]

Understandably, Huggins could find no one to print his epic in his lifetime, and it had to wait until 1930 for publication.

Notes

1. George Lamming, *In the Castle of my Skin* (London, 1960), p. 15.

2. 'Creative literature of the British West Indies during the period of slavery', [1970], reprinted in Kamau Brathwaite, *Roots*, pp. 128–9.

3. Christopher Columbus, *Letter* (1493), quoted in Peter Hulme and Neil L. Whitehead (eds), *Wild Majesty* (Oxford, 1992), p. 14. See also John Michael Cohen (trans.), *The Four Voyages of Christopher Columbus* (Harmondsworth, 1969); Robert F. Fuson (trans.), *The Log of Christopher Columbus* (Camden, Maine, 1987).

4. John Michael Cohen, *Four Voyages*, p. 121.

5. The El Dorado expeditions are described in Robert Silverberg, *The Golden Dream* ([1967, 1985] Athens, Ohio, 1996).

6. *The Discoverie of the Large and Bewtiful Empire of Guyana by Sir Walter Raleigh* ([1928] London, 1928), p. 42.

7. Ibid., p. 38.

8. See George Lamming, *Pleasures* (London, 1960), pp. 95–159; Aimé Césaire, *Une Tempête* (Paris, 1967, trans. Richard Miller as *A Tempest* (New York 1986)); Roberto Fernández Retamar, 'Caliban, notes towards a discussion of culture in America', *Massachusetts Review* (Winter–Spring 1974), pp. 11–16; Albert A. Vaughan, 'Caliban and the Third World . . .', *Massachusetts Review* (Summer 1988), pp. 289–313; Robert Nixon, 'Caribbean and African appropriations of . . . The Tempest', *Critical Inquiry* 13 (Spring 1987), pp. 557–8.

9. Elsa V. Goveia, *A Study on the Historiography of the British West Indies* (Tacubaya, Mexico, 1956), p. 20.

10. Père Jean-Baptiste Labat, *New Voyage to the Islands of America* (1722), reprinted in Hulme and Whitehead, pp. 155–68.

11. Elsa V. Goveia, *Historiography*, p. 59.

12. Ibid., p. 62.

13. Translation by Locksley Lindo, 'Francis Williams – a "free" Negro in a Slave World', *Savacou* 1, 1 (June 1970), p. 77.

14. *Lady Nugent's Journal*, edited by Philip Wright, fourth edition ([1801–6] Kingston, Jamaica, 1966), p. 98.

15. Gad Heuman, 'The Social Structure of Slave Societies', in *The General History of the Caribbean* (London, 1997), edited by Franklin W. Knight, vol. III, pp. 138–68.

16. *In Miserable Slavery. Thomas Thistlewood in Jamaica, 1750–86*, edited by Douglas Hall (London and Basingstoke, 1989).

17. Errol Hill, 'The Emergence of a National Theatre in the West Indies', *Caribbean Quarterly* 18, 4 (Dec. 1972); Kole Omotoso, *The Theatrical into Theatre* (London, 1982), p. 23.

18. See Errol Hill, 'The First Playwrights of Jamaica', *Carib* (Kingston, Jamaica, 1986), no 4, pp. 16–34.

19. Errol Hill, *The Jamaican Stage, 1655–1900* (Amherst, 1992), p. 10.

20. James Grainger, *The Sugar-Cane* (London, 1764), book IV, ll. 583–59. Quoted by Kamau Brathwaite, 'Creative Literature of the British West Indies . . .', *Savacou* 1 (June 1970), pp. 54–5. [A banshaw is a primitive guitar.]

21. Ibid., book IV, ll. 554–7.

22. William Beckford, *A Description of the Island of Jamaica* (London, 1790), p. 18.

23. Ibid., p. 31.

24. Ibid., p. 227.

25. Ibid., p. 319.

26. See Wylie Sypher, *Guinea's Captive Kings* (New York, 1942), pp. 111–37.

27. Aphra Behn, *Oronooko and Other Stories*, edited by Maureen Duffy ([1688] London, 1986), p. 27.

28. 'Introduction', ibid., pp. 89.

29. Ibid., p. 83.

30. Ibid., p. 88.

31. Reprinted in Burnett, *Caribbean Verse*, p. 111.

32. Anon., *Hamel, the Obeah Man* (London, 1827), I, p. 26.

33. Ibid., I, 42.

34. *Hamel*, II, p. 157. Edward Brathwaite claims it as 'probably the first Black Power speech in our literature', 'Creative Literature of the British West Indies', *Savacou*, 1, 1 (June 1970), p. 71.

35. Ibid., vol. I, p. 179.

36. Michael Scott, *Tom Cringle's Log* ([1932] London, 1984), p. 570.

37. Ibid., p. 161.

38. See in particular Evelyn O'Callaghan, *Woman Version* (London: Macmillan, 1993). Novels by women she notes include Henrietta Camilla Jenkin, *Cousin Stella; or Conflict* (London, 1859); Anne Marsh-Caldwell, *Adelaide Lindsay: a novel* (London, 1850); and Ethel Maude Symonett, *Jamaica: Queen of the Carib Sea* (Kingston, Jamaica, 1895).

39. *Wonderful Adventures of Mrs Seacole in Many Lands* with an Introduction by William L. Andrews ([1857] New York, 1988), p. 60.

40. Ibid., p. xxxiii.

41. Robert C.J. Young, *Colonial Desire* (London, 1995), p. 93.

42. Anthony Trollope, pp. 58–60.

43. J.J. Thomas, *Froudacity. West Indian Fables by James Anthony Froude* ([1889] London, 1969), p. 94.

44. Canon Horatio Huggins, *Hiroona* (Trinidad, Port-of-Spain, 1930), pp. 341–2. See also Paula Burnett, *Caribbean Verse*, pp. 126–9, 399–400.

Chapter 2
The Dark of the Mirror: Slave Communities

'The half', says Ole African in Erna Brodber's *Myal* (1988), 'has not been told'.[1] The life of early black communities in the West Indies is still relatively undocumented. Unlike North American slaves, who worked in a predominantly white society with printed records, slave communities in the Caribbean were majority cultures that took shape in isolation from towns and books. These settlements began from a trauma so extreme that sociologists have compared it to the psychic experience of death.[2] It is hard to conceive the horror of the 'middle passage' from Africa, even in a brutal age when whites were subjected to the Australian penal settlements, and the press gang. Voyages from the Bight of Benin to the Caribbean lasted between five and twelve weeks; in the years 1680–8 the Royal Africa Company recorded that 23.7 per cent of the slaves died, although the proportion dropped to 10 to 15 per cent.[3] Men, women and children were chained down in dark galleries two to three feet high, five foot by three wide, wet with excrement and vomit. They were allowed on deck briefly for feeding, or, if the weather was bad, not at all. Those that survived lost their names, their families, their religion and their language, and a strange identity was forced on them. Any infringement of plantation rules brought flogging, mutilation, the most intimate indignities, torture and execution. In one respect only was the lot of black slaves better than that of white convicts: it was in the slave master's interest to keep his valuable property in good working order.

Unlike the United States, the Caribbean produced almost no narratives by the slaves themselves. *The Interesting Narrative of the Life of Olaudah Equiano* (1789), has been claimed as both African, West Indian, and freed black. Equiano, an Ibo captured with his sister at the age of ten, was sold as a slave in Barbados, bought by a benign English Captain and soon freed. The vivid quality of Equiano's prose can be caught in this account of the slave ship's arrival off Barbados, where the boarding merchants and planters deftly reverse the stereotype of Africans as cannibals.

> We thought by this we should be eaten by these ugly men,
> as they appeared to us; and when soon after we were all

put down under the deck again, there was much dread and trembling among us, and nothing but bitter cries to be heard all the night from these apprehensions, insomuch that at last the white people got some old slaves from the land to pacify us. They told us we were not to be eaten but to work, and were soon to go on land where we should see many of our country people.[4]

A rare account of the life of a domestic slave has survived in *The History of Mary Prince*, published in 1831,[5] the story of her efforts to work out her manumission, culminating in her escape in London in 1828. While edited as an Abolitionist tract, the simple narrative offers insights not only into her courageous personality, but the conflicting attitudes of her owners, who liked her, yet fiercely resented her independent spirit.

Other evidence of this period has come through the witness of communities founded by slaves who escaped into the forested interiors, and were called 'Maroons' or 'wild cattle', after the Spanish term 'cimarrón'. Here they established independent communities, and, more at home in the tropical terrain than Europeans, became a feared fighting force. In Jamaica they held the British to treaties in 1739 and 1795, and later provided mercenaries for their militia. Maroon communities survive to be an important source of knowledge of West Indian African-based customs, music and beliefs.[6] One account of Maroon life is *The Autobiography of a Runaway Slave* by the hundred-year-old Esteban Montejo, published in 1965.[7] This may be compared to Milton McFarlane's historically based stories in *Cudjoe the Maroon* (1977). As interesting as either is *Black Albino* (1961) by the Jamaican Namba Roy (born Atkins). Set in a Jamaican Maroon community in the eighteenth century, the novel recounts the struggle between the warrior leader Tomaso and his sinister rival, Lago, for leadership of the village. Kisanka, Tomaso's spiritually radiant love, bears Tomaso an albino son, Tamba. Lago uses this disgrace to oust Tomaso, and causes Kisanka's death. Without Tomaso's leadership, the Maroons are defeated by the British. Led by the spectral voice of Kisanka, however, Tomaso returns to defeat the invaders. At the story's close, Tamba is chosen leader of the Maroons. The novel is splendid historical melodrama. But in writing it, Roy was continuing the traditions of his father and grandfather, both of whom had been story-tellers and wood-carvers in a Maroon community, and his fable not only contains a wealth of detail about the Maroon way of life,[8] but its heroic and spiritual concerns reflect its ethos. It has interesting affinities with Achebe's novel of Ibo life, *Things Fall Apart* (1960), published a year earlier. It also contains a parable. By ending with the chieftainship of the 'black albino', Roy signals that the heroism of the Maroon past was available for a modern multiracial Jamaica.

Roy's novel recounts of the secret links between the Maroons and the plantation slave communities. Here, in spite of the slave-owner's attempts to demoralise and segregate, a distinctive culture rapidly evolved, as historians have demonstrated.[9] Slave societies found their visionaries and healers, story-tellers and organisers of resistance. A network of complex blood ties was formed. Plantation work created hierarchies in which skilled slaves supervised menial workers. Women, with a lower status than men, became field labourers, domestic servants, and children's nannies.[10] An important aspect of slave life was the small-holdings, given to enable slaves to feed themselves. These developed into a source of trade and barter, deepening a bond between them and the land that was to persist into the twentieth century, when George Lamming was to claim that the West Indian sensibility remained essentially 'peasant'.[11] Caribbean food and cooking, an index of cultural diversity, based as it was on West African yam, coconut, ackee and bananas, Indian mangoes, and breadfruit from the South Seas, became a significant element in West Indian cultural identity. Spiritual traditions survived from Africa. Where slaves lacked physical strength, they turned to religious practices, and popular religion featured prominently in all rebellions. Although punished when discovered, often by death, the cults of obeah, shango, myalism, pocomania and vodoun were central to slave culture, and they remain a dynamic force in the Caribbean today. Ancestor worship maintained spiritual contact with the past, and a 'Spirit Messenger' or 'Kumina Queen' interviewed in the mid-twentieth century expressed her unbroken communion with Africa.[12] Animism survived the middle passage from the Old to the New World, and for the Barbados shango cult, the Yoruba god of war and ironwork emerged in the power of the steam engine.[13] European Christianity met African beliefs, melded, and was transformed. Torn from their homelands, Africans identified with the exiled Children of Israel. For the Rastafarians in Jamaica and Shouter Baptists in Trinidad, the prophesies of Daniel and Isaiah condemned the white and brown worshippers of Mammon, and the Book of Revelations promised their apocalyptic demise.

Denied tribe and name, slave communities found their identity above all in music. As early as 1722 Père Labat identified distinctive rhythms as the common characteristic of the whole Caribbean area, noting in particular that the drum-based 'Calenda' dance, evidently originating in Guinea, was popular with both black and white Creoles in the West Indies. Other accounts confirm this central importance of distinctive, African-based, music to black West Indian culture. Rhythm embodied the spirit of the community, and in Lamming's *Season of Adventure* (1960), the police destroy the spirit of the villagers by piercing Gort their leader's drum. In both Trinidad and Jamaica drumming was intermittently prohibited as 'too much inciting them to rebellion'.[14] African tribal society is organised around ritual and celebration, and slave communities in the New World seized any opportunity to hold a festival. Kole Omotoso[15] notes their variety – locally devised masquerades like that of Papa Diable, and the Roses and the Marguerites, in St Lucia; African-based[16] Jonkonnu parades in Jamaica and the Bahamas; the Christian-influenced Crop-over festivities of Barbados, and the annual Trinidadian Carnival, which embodied everything. Such festivities continuously evolved with the addition of new and often, to white observers, mysterious characters. The exact origin of the Jamaican Jonkonnu (or John Canoe) dance is unknown, though the name has been associated with that of an African king, and also with the Ewe words 'dzono' [sorcerer], and 'kuno' [deathly], suggesting a religious ceremony.[17] Performed in the Christmas break between growing season and croptime [harvest], the masquerade combined elements of African ancestor worship and fertility rituals, English Morris dancing and Mumming, and French set-dancing. In the early nineteenth century, Michael Scott described a costumed band of over fifty, surrounding a Jonkonnu figure in military uniform, Janus-faced black and white, who danced on the back of a gigantic figure in bullock's hide and skull. In 1826 the lead dancer carried not horns but the now traditional model of a house on his head.[18] A later 'Jonkonnu' procession even included Queen Victoria.

Such traditions were essentially forms of street theatre, uninhibited by the restrictions of formal production. As the young Derek Walcott was to note, watching the poorer St Lucians parading the streets on Sunday nights, poverty released them into a spontaneous 'theatre where everything was possible, sex, obscenity, absolution, freedom . . .'.[19] The underprivileged, possessing only their imaginations, and the rhythms and language of the body, created drama out of 'an oral culture of chants, jokes, folksongs and fables'. This thriving popular tradition of theatre existed in the Caribbean centuries before the emergence of its written form.[20] From the eighteenth century, troupes of black players performed for specific public events. On New Year's Day, 1816, Monk Lewis saw slave actors expertly perform scenes from Nicholas Rowe's *The Fair Penitent* (1703) and John Home's *Douglas* (1756); other reports describe (farcical) performances of *Richard III*.[21] Such sophistication supports a reassessment of a performance that has previously been treated as a bizarre extravaganza. On Christmas Day 1801, Lady Nugent, the wife of the newly arrived Governor of Jamaica, watched a band of masqueraders performing a play in their honour.

> All dance, leap and play a thousand antics. Then there
> are groups of dancing men and women. They had a sort
> of leader or superior at their head, who sang a sort of
> recitative, and seemed to regulate all their proceedings; the
> rest joining at intervals in the air and the chorus. The
> instrument to accompany the song was a rude sort of drum,

made of bark leaves, on this they beat time with two sticks, while the singers do the same with their feet.[22]

This culminated in an elaborate play in which a child, dressed, Lady Nugent was told, as Henry IV of France, stabbed the children of Tippoo Sahib, Sultan of Mysore. The interpretation was specific if arcane. As Henry IV brought peace after decades of civil war, the slave community hoped Lord Nugent would curb the excesses of the local plantocracy. Nugent was engaged in friendly negotiations with Toussaint, the black leader of the newly independent San Domingo, who was in turn threatened by Napoleon and the French. The French were encoded as 'the children of Tippoo Sahib', for Napoleon was allied to the demonised Tippoo before the British killed him at Serangapatam in 1799, two years before the present masquerade. The performers were offering a graceful compliment to Nugent as the new Governor, and asking for his sympathetic intervention. But it was lost on the observers; 'What a mélange', snorted Lady Nugent.

Carolyn Cooper has considered how far Creole performance emerged as a *conscious* alternative to the culture of the master by examining a Jamaican song first recorded by the book-keeper J.P. Moreton, 'Me Know no Law, Me Know no Sin'. In this, a black slave laments her changing status as the 'Massa's' mistress, first wooed with blandishments and clothes, but when pregnant, beaten and sent to work in the fields with the child on her back. When she has a white child, she is beaten by the Master's wife. Flogged when she resists sex, flogged when she consents, in consequence she becomes freed from European law and morality.

> Me know no law, me know no sin,
> Me is just wat ebba them make me;
> This is the way dem bring me in;
> So God nor devil take me![23]

It is clear that the planters feared the subversive potential of the black oral tradition. By 1817, the English Radical journal *The Black Dwarf* noted the 'simple but beautiful songs' of the slaves, whose militant strains caught the nervous attention of the West Indian magistracy.[24] Moreton in 1790 recorded a work song:

> If me want for go in a Ebo [Iboland, Africa],
> Me can't go there!
> Since dem tief me from a Guinea,
> Me can't go there!
>
> If me want for go in a Congo,
> Me can't go there!

Since dem tief me from my tatta [father],
Me can't go there!

If me want for go in a Kingston [the Jamaican capital],
Me can't go there!
Since Massa go in England,
Me can't go there![25]

Caribbean folklore was creating its own tradition. A chorus recorded in
Jamaica by Monk Lewis in 1817 runs

'Take him to the Gulley! Take him to the Gulley!
But bringee back the frock and board'. –
'Oh! massa, massa! me no deadee yet'! –
'Take him to the Gulley! Take him to the Gulley!
Carry him along'.[26]

Lewis takes this to refer to an incident when a notorious Jamaican
slave-owner called Bedward, as was his wont, had a sick slave carried on
a board to be thrown down a steep gulley to die: the slave survived and
later encountered Bedward in Kingston. Evidence suggests, however,[27]
that what Lewis heard was an adaptation of a still earlier Jamaican folk-
song about Anancy the Spiderman, who persuades Fowl-hawk to have
'Dry-head' (Death) carried on a board and thrown down a gulley. If this
is so, it was not the event that created the song, so much as an existing
folk-lore that shaped and preserved the historical narrative.

On mainland Guiana and British Honduras, aboriginal cultures continued their magical creation stories and myths, providing a rich source
for later writers, as we will see. On the islands, especially in Jamaica, folk-
tales have been associated with 'Anancy' the trickster spider.[28] In origin,
Anancy was probably associated with the Ashanti trickster deity, Anansi
Krokoko, who becomes secularised in the Caribbean tradition, although
often retaining powers to change himself into other forms. 'Each Nancy
story', noted Lewis, 'must contain a witch, or a duppy [ghost], in short,
some marvellous personage or other'.[29] He gave, as an example of the
Jamaican 'Nancy story', a long tale which has nothing to do with Anancy,
concerning virtuous and wicked girls, a woman without a head, and
magic eggs that reward the good and punish the bad. Rattray also noted
that among the Ashanti, 'anansesem, i.e. ananse asem, lit. stories about a
spider' is a generic term for all folk-tales.[30] The Jamaican 'Anancy stories'
collected by Walter Jekyll, however, are all animal fables, many of which
feature Anancy the Spider, perhaps because Anancy, physically weak but
surviving by trickery, is an anti-hero particularly relevant to slaves who
often had to play stupid to outwit their masters.

As Helen Tiffin has pointed out, however, Anancy represents all aspects of plantation life.[31] He is resilient and resourceful, but also boastful, greedy and often cruel. He can take the role of the slave, but as in the story already quoted, where he orders Hawk to throw Dry-head down the gulley, he personifes the white Master. Louise Bennett, who as a girl was nightly delighted by Anancy tales told by her grandmother, attributed the phrase used to end them, 'Jack Mandora, me no chose none', as a protest to 'Jack Mandora, the doorman at Heaven's door' that the listeners didn't really agree with Anancy's 'wicked ways'.[32] Pride is his nemesis. In 'Anancy an Common Sense',[33] he puts all the wisdom of the world in a calabash and tries to carry it up a tree tied to his stomach. He is so annoyed when a child laughs at him for not tying it to his back that he throws the calabash down, where it breaks, common sense is blown all over the world, 'an everybody get a lickle bit'. Yet his resourcefulness typically triumphs. In 'Anancy an Ass-head', for instance, Anancy wins a prize for capering on Jackass whom he has made drunk, solving the problem of how to combine the liberation of alcohol with the control of a sober head. Anancy was also the creator of traditions, and provides the John Canoe dance with its hobby-horse.

> An so seh; so done. Po Jackass was too shame fi dance afta
> dat, so every year somebody dress up like Jackass an call
> himself Ass-head. Is Anancy meck it.[34]

Some Anancy stories have a darker note, in particular when Anancy comes in contact with the menacing Dry-head [skull]. In 'Brother Anancy and Brother Death' Anancy and his family are trapped in the rafters by Death and drop, one by one, into his jaws. Anancy himself, however, persuades Death to place a 'barrel of flour' below him so he will land dusted all over and oven-ready. But the flour is quicklime, and Anancy pushes Death's face into it, blinds him, and escapes.[35] A spider who asserts dignity, a lisping story-teller with a cleft palate, resourceful yet fallible, Anancy embodies resilient humanity in a dangerous world. In their universality, Anancy stories have come to represent the persistence of popular traditions in the Caribbean. As Kamau Brathwaite was to write

> memories trunked up in a dark attic
> he stumps up the stares
> of our windows, he stares, stares
> he squats on the tips
>
> of our language
> black burr of conundrums
> eye corner of ghosts, ancient his-
> tories . . .[36]

Trinidad, eight hundred miles to the south-east, also had its rich folk-lore, but its popular culture has been most closely associated with Calypso and Carnival. The origins of Trinidad Carnival[37] have been traced back to the three-day *Felice Loco* (Happy Mad) celebration held between the Caribs and the Spanish on their conquest of Trinidad in 1498. It was not always a folk festival. Throughout the eighteenth century it appears slave emancipation Carnival was celebrated chiefly among the white and free coloured population, where it allowed a masked release from the restrictions of élite society. In the years immediately before emancipation, however, masked slave bands were organised by the self-styled King Beggorat, a quadroon slave owner from St Lucia,[38] and after 1834, Carnival became dominated by the freed blacks, with their masquerade celebrating slave emancipation, 'Canboulay' ('cane-burning'). The subversion and confrontation of the festival continued into the post-slave era, where rival stick-fighting groups engaged in verbal and physical combat, setting a model for the later 'calypso' contests. Carnival provided the basis for street theatre. Elaborately costumed Kings and Queens were elected to preside over troupes of dancers, and the Wild Indians, miming a tribe of aboriginal Indians from the Orinooco Delta who had visited Trinidad in 1848, were the first of the street bands that vied for supremacy in the crowded streets.

By the end of the nineteenth century the music, words and spectacle of Carnival had become a focus for the emerging national identity. If the Anancy story preserved traditions of the African past, Carnival celebrated a forward-looking ferment of cultures on an island which included Spanish, British, East Indians, Africans and South Americans, people holding Catholic, Protestant and African-based beliefs. Its spirit continued to be subversive. In his 1963 calypso 'Dan is the Man in the Van', the Calypsonian Mighty Sparrow was to rubbish the English reading of a colonial education:

> Peter Peter was a pumpkin eater
> And the Lilliput people tie Gulliver
> When I was sick and lay abed
> I had two pillows at my head
> I see the Goose that lay the golden egg
> The Spider and the Fly
> Morocoy with wings flying in the sky
> They beat me like a dog to learn that in school
> If my head was bright I woulda be a damn fool.[39]

His 'stupidity' had become his escape from the confines of a British education into the creative possibilities of the Trinidadian popular culture.

Notes

1. See Edward [Kamau] Brathwaite, *The Development of Creole Society in Jamaica, 1770–1820* (Oxford, 1971); Melville J. Herskovitz, *Life in a Haitian Valley* (New York, 1971).

2. See Orlando Patterson, *Slavery and Social Death* (Cambridge, Mass., 1982).

3. See Colin A. Palmer, 'The slave trade, African slavers and the demography of the Caribbean to 1750', in *General History of the Caribbean* (London, 1997), edited by Franklin W. Knight, pp. 9–44.

4. *Equiano's Travels*, edited by Paul Edwards ([1789] London, 1967), p. 31.

5. *The History of Mary Prince*, edited by Moira Ferguson with a Preface by Ziggi Alexander ([1831] London, 1987).

6. See Sylvia W. de Groot *et al.*, 'Maroon communities in the circum-Caribbean', *A General History of the Caribbean*, pp. 169–93; Richard Price (ed.), *Maroon Societies: Rebel Communities in the Americas* (New York, 1973).

7. Esteban Montejo, *The Autobiography of a Runaway Slave*, translated by Miguel Barnet ([1968] London and Basingstoke, 1993).

8. Mervyn Morris, 'Introduction' to *Black Albino* ([1961] Longman Caribbean, 1986).

9. Elsa Goveia, *Slave Society in the British Leeward Islands at the End of the Eighteenth Century* (New Haven, 1965); Edward Brathwaite, *The Development of Slave Society in Jamaica, 1770–1820* (London, 1971); Orlando Patterson, *The Sociology of Slavery* (London, 1967).

10. Barbara Bush, *Slave Women in Caribbean Society, 1650–1838* (London, 1990).

11. George Lamming, *The Pleasures of Exile* (London, 1960), p. 45.

12. Maureen Warner Lewis, 'The Nkuyu: Spirit Messengers of the Kumina', *Savacou* no. 13 (Gemini, 1977), pp. 57–78.

13. See Kamau Brathwaite, *Barabajan Poems* (New York, Kingston and Mona, 1994), pp. 189–202; 369–76.

14. Errol Hill, *The Jamaican Stage*, p. 219.

15. Kole Omotoso, *The Theatrical into Theatre* (London, 1982), chapter 2.

16. Richardson Wright, *Revels in Jamaica*, rev. edition ([1937] Kingston, Jamaica, 1986), p. 239.

17. See Frederick G. Cassidy, *Jamaica Talk* (London, 1961), pp. 242–62; Sylvia Wynter, 'Jonkonnu in Jamaica', *Jamaica Journal* (June 1970), pp. 34–48; Errol Hill, *Jamaican Stage*, p. 236.

18. Cynric R. Williams, *A Tour through the Island of Jamaica* (London, 1826), quoted in Cassidy, p. 257.

19. Derek Walcott, 'What the Twilight Said', in *Dream on Monkey Mountain* (London, 1972), p. 22.

20. Errol Hill, 'The Emergence of a National Drama in the West Indies', *Caribbean Quarterly*, 18, 4 (1972); Martin Banham, Errol Hill and George Woodyard (eds), *The Cambridge Guide to African and Caribbean Theatre* (Cambridge, 1994), pp. 195–248.

21. Errol Hill, pp. 237–8.

22. *Lady Nugent's Journal* (25 Dec. 1801), p. 48.

23. *Voices in Exile* (Tuscaloosa and London, 1989), edited by Jean D'Costa and Barbara Lalla, p. 14.

24. *Black Dwarf* (18 June 1871), p. 336. Quoted by S.O. Osein, 'The "Protest" tradition in West Indian Poetry', *Jamaica Journal* 6, 2 (June 1972), p. 40.

25. Recorded J.B. Moreton, *West India Customs and Manners* (London, 1873). Quoted by Burnett, *Caribbean Verse*, p. 3.

26. M.G. Lewis, *Journal of a West Indian Proprietor* (London, 1834), p. 322. 'Carry him along' is probably Lewis's anglicised version of 'Carry him long', meaning 'Carry him a long way off'.

27. Walter Jekyll, *Jamaican Song and Story* ([1902]; repr. New York, 1966), pp. 48–51; H.P. Jacobs, 'Old Bedward of Spring Garden', *Jamaica Journal*, 6, 2 (June 1872), pp. 9–13.

28. Laura Tanner, *Jamaican Folk Tales and Oral Histories* (Kingston, Jamaica, 1984); Walter Jekyll, *Jamaica Song and Story* ([1907] New York, 1966); Maria Warren Beckwith, *Jamaican Anansi Stories* ([1924] New York, 1969); Philip Sherlock, *Anansi the Spider Man* (London, 1959); Louise Bennett on disc, *Anansy Stories* (Federal Records, FRM 129).

29. M.G. Lewis, *Journal of a West Indian Proprietor* (London, 1843), pp. 259–301.

30. R. Sutherland Rattray, *Ashanti Proverbs* (Oxford, 1952), p. 73.

31. Helen Tiffin, 'The Metaphor of Anancy in Caribbean Literature', in Robert Sellick (ed.), *Myth and Metaphor* (Adelaide, 1984), pp. 20–2.

32. Jekyll, p. ix.

33. Louise Bennett, *Anancy and Miss Lou* (Kingston, Jamaica, 1979), p. 67.

34. Mervyn Morris, 'Introduction' to *Anancy and Miss Lou*, p. ix; 'Anancy and Ass-head' is on pp. 55–8.

35. Jekyll, pp. 31–4.

36. Edward [Kamau] Brathwaite, *Islands* (London, 1969), p. 6.

37. Errol Hill, *The Trinidad Carnival* (Austin, Texas, 1972), chapters 1–5.

38. Mitto Sampson, 'The Origins of the Trinidad Carnival', in Arts Council of Great Britain, *Masquerading* (London, 1986), pp. 30–4.

39. 'The Mighty Sparrow' [Slinger Francisco], 'Dan is the Man', quoted in Stewart Brown, Mervyn Morris and Gordon Rohlehr (eds), *Voiceprint* (Harlow, 1986), p. 130.

Part II

Anancy's Web: The Caribbean Archipelago

No Barbadian, no Trinidadian, no St Lucian, no islander from the West Indies sees himself as West Indian until he encounters another islander in a foreign territory. It was only when the Barbadian childhood corresponded with the Grenadian or the Guianese childhood in important details of folk-lore, that the wider identification was arrived at. In this sense, most West Indians of my generation were born in England.

George Lamming[1]

I am the archipelago hope
Would mould into dominion . . .

E.M. Roach[2]

To write of a single West Indian literature can be misleading, for much of it is essentially regional, and in comparing a text from continental Guyana with one from a small island like St Lucia, the differences may be more significant than any common 'Caribbean' character. However, a West Indian identity has evolved within a cultural web which, like that of Anancy, is strong though sometimes tenuous. The chapters that follow place Caribbean writing into the varied contexts from which it emerged, ending with the 'final passage' to the island that was in turn to be colonised by West Indians – Britain.

Chapter 3
Barbados and the Lesser Antilles

The first West Indian island either English or African voyagers were likely to encounter was Barbados, a flat marine limestone island lying out in the Atlantic. It was the earliest West Indian territory to be taken by Britain in 1627, and it remained exclusively British until independence in 1966, the only main West Indian territory to do so. Its plantocracy was renowned for its conservatism. Although small, only a twenty-fifth of the size of Jamaica, it fostered the joke told in Marryat's *Peter Simple* (1834), and repeated in George Lamming's *In the Castle of my Skin* over a century later, where a black Barbados toastmaster declares 'All di world fight against England, but England nebber fear; King George nebber fear *while Barbadoes stand stiff!*'[3] This does not deny the vitality of a Bajan black popular culture. The lively verse sketches in Edward A. Cordle's *Overheard* (1903) taken from the local *Weekly Recorder* were among some of the earliest published examples of Creole writing in the West Indies. Bruce St John later developed the writing of poetry in Barbadian Creole, giving Cordle's humour a political edge,[4] while the variety of Barbadian village life was recreated with humour and panache in the short stories of Timothy Callender.[5] The most trenchant postwar critics of the West Indian colonial establishment – George Lamming, Austin Clarke and Kamau Brathwaite – were all Barbadian.

Yet a moving force in the island's culture for half a century was a genial schoolmaster actively disinterested in politics. Frank [Appleton] Collymore was a linguist, painter and actor. He wrote verse both serious and whimsical, and his accomplished short stories show an unexpected gift for the macabre and the Gothic.[6] But his greatest gift was his ability to encourage local talent. From 1910 to 1963 he taught at Combermere School, Bridgetown, and during his lifetime most of the island's writers became indebted to 'Colly'. In 1942 he co-founded *Bim* [the local name for a Barbadian], the little magazine with which he was to be identified for over thirty years. By its tenth number it had contributors from across the West Indies, including George Lamming, Sam Selvon, A.L. Hendriks, Derek Walcott and A.J. Seymour, and almost all West Indian writers of any note at some point published in *Bim*. It was strictly non-political. An editorial in number fifteen (1951) stated that 'a literature, the product of tradition, is not brought into being by blue-prints. A literature needs the right climate of ideas . . .'[7] Collymore's genial eclecticism however proved Radical in effect, opening the way to unfettered innovation in West Indian writing.

One of Collymore's pupils was George Lamming. Lamming cut his literary teeth as an early contributor to *Bim*. His later agency for the magazine in Trinidad gave him valuable contact with fellow West Indian writers, before he moved to the still broader intellectual world of Britain. Yet *In the Castle of my Skin* (1953), begun when the author was barely twenty-three and homesick in London, is an intensely local novel. When Kamau Brathwaite read it, he felt 'everything was transformed'. It was his imaginative repossession of his own childhood. 'Here breathing to me from every pore of line and page, was the Barbados I had lived. The words, the rhythms, the cadences, the scenes, the people, their predicament. They all came back'.[8] No previous work had evoked the island's village life with such immediacy. It opens on the ninth birthday of G. in the estate village of Creighton. It is raining, as on his previous birthdays, and the fragility of the island existence is reflected in the connected images of birth and flood, for the rain brings life to the small limestone island, but is also washing it away. In the night the mother sings out to her neighbour and others answer 'until the whole village shook with song on its foundation of water'.[9] Secured by the sounds of community, G.'s consciousness focuses on the spluttering flame of the lamp his mother lights, and 'for memory I had substituted inquiry'. The closeness with his mother is counterpointed against his sense of isolation. Father forgotten, his mother's relatives dispersed, 'my birth began with an almost total absence of family relations'. Families are like the village itself, crumbling down the unstable hillside, shifting and merging. 'There was difference and there was no difference'. The 'Ma and Pa' of the novel are not G.'s relatives, but the oldest couple, the repository of Creighton village's history and its present consciousness.

An early episode identifies the claustrophobic intimacy of village life. G. is naked, being washed down by his mother, and neighbouring boys crowd on the fence to watch; G. feels humiliated, the fence sags and breaks, snapping the pumpkin vine. The consciousness of the book expands, involving Bob, his mother, and other villagers. Thirty years later, Lamming with hindsight commented:

> The book is crowded with names and people, and although
> each character is accorded a most vivid presence and force
> of personality, we are rarely concerned with the prolonged
> exploration of an individual consciousness. It is the
> collective human substance of the Village, you might say,

which is the central character . . . It is this method of
narration, where community, and not person, is the central
character, things are never so tidy as critics would like.
There is often no discernible plot, no coherent line of
events with a clear causal connection.[10]

The focus takes in the school on Empire Day, Queen Victoria's birthday. Marshalled in squads below the Head Teacher and the Inspector,
their individuality locked in rote learning and discipline, the boys form
a figure of their ancestors packed in slave ships. But the amnesiac ritual
has expunged the slave past. Slavery 'had nothing to do with people in
Barbados. No one there was ever a slave, the teacher said. It was in
another part of the world that those things happened'.[11] They are given
pennies, but the boys are confused. Whose face is on the coins, validating
them? Had anyone known or seen him? Perhaps 'there was a shadow
king who did whatever a king should do . . . The shadow king was a
part of the English tradition. The English, the boy said, were good at
shadows'.[12]

In the community all authority is precarious. The Headmaster flogs a
pupil in uncontrollable rage, himself the victim of the boy's knowledge
that he, the Headmaster, is beaten by his wife. G.'s own identity is
vulnerable. 'The eye of another was a kind of cage. When it saw you the
lid came down, and you were trapped. It was always happening'.[13] The
two oldest inhabitants of the village, Ma and Pa, express a communal
consciousness, yet they, too, have no security. The island is in a crisis of
change. The war brings the cutting down of the woods, and the destruction of the railway intimates a wider breakdown of communications.
With the ending of colonialism, the islanders are exploited from within.
The schoolmaster Mr Slime cuckolds his Head, then cheats the villagers
by setting up a Penny Bank while secretly selling the land from under
their shacks. At the beginning of the book Mr Foster floats away on his
house in a flood, and is rescued by a rope. At the end the shoemaker,
dispossessed of his land by Slime, tries to move his house, but it collapses
in ruins. Ma dies, and Slime has Pa sent to the workhouse.

G. has been intellectually precocious. At school his literary talent is
encouraged by a schoolmaster, a figure based on Collymore, but education cuts him off from his emotional roots, and his knowledge of 'big
words' both protects and alienates.

Nothing would ever go pop, pop, pop in your head.
['Pop-pop' in Barbadian speech connotes a cataclysmic
upheaval.] You had language to safeguard you. And if you
were beginning to feel too strongly, you could kill the
feeling, you get it out of the way by fetching the words

that couldn't understand what the feeling was all about. It was like a knife.[14]

G. remains ambivalent about his intellectual acquisition, and his account of later encouragement by his schoolmaster (the unnamed Collymore) may be compared with Austin C. Clarke's brilliantly hostile account of Barbadian education in *Among Thorns and Thistles* (1965), and his autobiographical *Growing up Stupid under the Union Jack* (1980).

While G. went into education, his friend Trumper left the island for the United States, where he discovered his identity as a black man. 'He had found what he needed and there were no more problems to be worked out. Henceforth his life would be straight, even, uncomplicated'.[15] But G. is suspicious. 'Suppose I didn't find it. This was worse, *the thought of being a part of what you could not become'*.[16] Trumper had always been a rebel, growing up in a reform school: his discovery of an identity in America was a further alienation from his home village. Separated by his education, G., before leaving to teach in Trinidad, returns to his mother for what is, in more senses than one, a 'last supper'. The evocative smell, touch and taste of lovingly cooked flying fish and cuckoo [okra], a dish that draws on both the African past and Barbadian present, intimates the richness of the community G. is losing. When he leaves

> The earth where I walked was a marvel of blackness and I
> knew in a sense more deep than simple departure I had said
> farewell, farewell to the land.[17]

Lamming's novel was the first of a long succession of West Indian novels of childhood, one of which, also set in Barbados, is Geoffrey Drayton's *Christopher* (1959). Here the boy is white and his father, like Lamming's Creighton, is one of the planter class facing diminishing status and wealth as sugar prices fall with the effects of the war. Christopher's family is part of the old plantocracy caught between a new thrusting commercial class, and the black poor, whose hostility is imaged in a beggar, 'his face gaunt and hideous with sores'[18] spitting hate at him through the car window. Christopher is artistic, and much of the book's charm is the evocation of an island beauty irrelevant to the hard life of Lamming's Creighton village. Yet the two different works curiously overlap. Christopher is also isolated within the skin of his racial identity. He is drawn to the black folk culture of the tenantry in the village below the gully, its spiky agaves carved with sexual mysteries by the village boys. His effective mother is black, his nurse Gip. 'He could not, in fact, conceive of a world without Gip. She was as much part of his life as school and holidays, food and play'.[19] When Gip dies, Christopher has to be prevented from leaping into her grave after her, and held in his (white) mother's embrace, realises that this is 'the last of his childhood'.[20]

In its topography, the flat, Atlantic-bound Barbados is an anomaly among the Antilles. Growing up there, Lamming looked westwards towards 'the curve of dots and distances continuing for nearly two thousand miles from the coast of Florida to the northern tip of South America', the outer Antilles. Along this rim, even the smaller islands produced their writers and musicians. From Montserrat came the poet Archie Markham; from St Vincent, 'Shake' (Ellsworth McGranahan) Keane, jazz musician and poet; from Antigua, Jamaica Kincaid; from St Kitts, Caryl Phillips. Grenada was the birthplace of Merle Collins and Dione Brand. The two islands in the Antilles most distinguished for literature are Dominica and St Lucia. Both are dramatically different to Barbados. Dominica is under three hundred square miles in area, yet rises to over four thousand feet. In Jean Rhys's words, it is 'all crumpled into hills and mountains as you would crumple a piece of paper in your hand – rounded green hills and sharply-cut mountains'.[21] Inaccessible to European settlement, a refuge for the Caribs who controlled the island until the sixteenth century and for escaped slaves, its history is as untamed as its 'boiling lake', an intermittent geyser cradled among the interior peaks. If the flat, open landscape of Barbados evoked one island sensibility, the rugged, intensely green world of Dominica created another. Jean Rhys, who as the sixteen-year-old Gwen Williams landed at Southampton in August 1907, recorded the shock of arriving in England in her first-written novel, *Voyage in the Dark* (1934).[22]

> It was as if a curtain had fallen, hiding everything I had
> ever known. It was almost like being born again. The
> colours were different, the smells were different, the feelings
> things gave you right down inside were different. Not just
> the difference between heat, cold; light, darkness; purple,
> grey. But a difference in the way I was frightened and the
> way I was happy.[23]

The main protagonist, Anna Morgan, comes from an island identified by position if not by name as Dominica. She sings as a chorus girl, works in a shady 'manicure' parlour, has a sexual liaison, is deserted, and has an abortion. But the 'voyage' of the title is not between countries, but between the experiences of England and her Caribbean island. In a seedy London apartment, Anna dreams of

> the walls of the Old Estate house, still standing, with moss
> on them. That was the garden. One ruined room for roses,
> one for orchids, one for tree-ferns. And the honeysuckle all
> along the steep flight of steps that led down to the room
> where the overseer kept his books.[24]

The island stands not only for a sensual beauty absent from England, but for humanity destroyed by race. In a loveless act of sex in England, she remembers a servant, Maillotte Boyd, who was raped in an alien Caribbean house, also eighteen, like her a half-caste.[25] She yearns for her black childhood friend Francine. But her colour intervenes. In a remembered masquerade, the black dancers thrust out pink tongues at her through masks of white or pink-painted wire mesh, a racial nightmare that returns when, in England, her agonised convulsions in abortion merge with the contortions of the remembered Carnival. She tries to ride into the high, moonlit hills, but falls. Waking, she hears the doctor say, 'She'll be alright . . . Ready to start all over again in no time, I've no doubt'.[26]

Kenneth Ramchand, in his anthology *Tales of the Wide Caribbean* (1985),[27] has vividly demonstrated how central Jean Rhys's Dominican childhood was for her early short stories, and later she returned to it when, after over twenty years in obscurity, she wrote *Wide Sargasso Sea* (1966), retelling Charlotte Brontë's *Jane Eyre* from the point of Rochester's mad wife. Rhys's novel opens on Coulibri estate. The emancipation of the slaves has broken the plantation life, leaving Antoinette Cosway and Annette, her mother, 'marooned' and ruined. Neither black nor expatriate white, they have no role in the new society, dooming Antoinette's attempt at friendship with the black girl Tia. Their one support is the black servant Christophine, tall, intensely dark, emotionally strong, yet independent, a practitioner of obeah. Rhys did not know Jamaica, and Coulibri is drawn from her experience of her grandmother's ruined estate on Grand Bay, Dominica, right down to the stone mounting step, which remains today. Coulibri (humming bird) was the name of their neighbour's property. But Rhys choses the largest and second oldest British possession, to epitomise the effects of British slavery and imperialism, with its materialism embodied in Mr Mason and in the weak, predatory 'Rochester', although Rhys does not humanise him with a name. Jamaica, an Eden ruined by colonialism, is contrasted with Grandbois, the honeymoon island to which Antoinette takes her young husband. Again, although the place is unnamed, Rhys drew on Dominica: the house is modelled on her father's holiday cottage, and 'Massacre' – the village where the couple land – is a fishing hamlet there, although the name was probably chosen more for its ominous associations than for its topography. But Rhys invokes the national divisions of colonialism to dramatise the novel's psychic conflict. If Rochester is associated with the British tradition, then Antoinette, Annette and Christophine are part of the French, and, beyond this, have an instinctual rapport with elemental Caribbean. An inruption from another, northern isle, 'Rochester' feels threatened by a place so sensuous, intensely green, 'sacred to the sun'.[28] When a malicious letter impugns Antoinette's character and motives, he reads it almost with relief. Desperate to keep his love, Antoinette begs an obeah love potion from Christophine, but such practices are not for 'Béké' [whites] and it goes disastrously wrong. In an insane rage, 'Rochester' attempts to obliterate the object of his deepest desire and terror. As slaves had their identity erased with names given by their masters, he makes Antoinette 'Marionetta', 'Bertha',[29] and steals her spirit. Ironically, he himself enacts the 'obeah' he fears; both he and Antoinette in effect become 'zombies', the walking dead.

The novel questions the substance of reality itself. When Antoinette conjectures, 'a big [English] city must be like a dream', 'Rochester' thinks of the tropical island, 'No, this is unreal and like a dream'. In her final imprisonment, Antoinette glimpses another England of 'grass and olive-green water' behind the 'cardboard' walls of her emotional repression.[30] Questioning turns to assertion. She discovers her red dress, worn in the Caribbean, still smelling of the islands. 'The smell of vertivert and frangipanni, of cinnamon and dust and lime trees when they are flowering. The smell of the sun and the smell of the rain'. Escaping onto the battlements she sees the sky. 'It was red and all my life was in it'. Sensually reborn, she is instinctively drawn into the cycle of Caribbean history. In a vision she sees her one time black childhood friend Tia, who at the burning of Coulibri had rejected her and wounded her with a stone. Now Antoinette calls out to Tia, and sets out to fire Thornfield Hall, at one with the rebellious freed slaves who burnt Coulibri. The novel however ends not with the fire, but with Antoinette carrying the candle down the dark corridor. It almost goes out. 'But I shielded it with my hand and it burned up again to light me along the dark passage'.[31] Rhys's superb closure draws the reader away from Antoinette's revenge and self-destruction to the act's inner significance, that of survival and psychic liberation.

The place of the novel in a Caribbean 'canon' has been debated. Kenneth Ramchand[32] and Evelyn O'Callaghan[33] have located Rhys's work alongside other writing by white Creoles, seeing this as an integral part of the total Caribbean experience. For Kamau Brathwaite, however, Antoinette could not reach out to Tia, for white Creoles had not creatively shaped Caribbean society,[34] while in an influential article Gayatri Spivak has protested that Jean Rhys 'rewrites a Canonical English text within the European novelistic tradition in the interest of the white Creole rather than the native'.[35] Wide Sargasso Sea, however, is not socio-history. It is a work of imagination and intuition, one which cannot be identified with a single character, exploring an experience of alienation that is not confined to one racial group or even to the Caribbean itself. Its fragmented narrative, which contains unexplained gaps and silences, deliberately deconstructs a single authorial point of view. 'There is always the other side', says Antoinette, 'always'.[36] Peter Hulme, in his survey of criticism on the novel, sees that 'perhaps on one level what is "West Indian" about Wide Sargasso Sea is the struggle to find a narrative form that is not − cannot be − the self-confident bildungsroman of Jane Eyre, a struggle that is analogous to that [of] the novel's protagonist to put together the fragments of [a] disintegrating world'.[37]

In an earlier novel, *The Orchid House* (1953), by Rhys's friend and compatriot Phyllis Shand Allfrey, the story is narrated by Lally, the black nursemaid to the three white Creole daughters of L'Aromatique, the old Great House. Lally is an outsider, 'fresh from Montserrat in my middle years, and being an English Negress and proud of my skin', a Methodist, 'not Frenchy and Catholic' like another Christophine, the family servant.[38] She is both of and outside the family. Loyal to L'Aromatique, she carries a tumour, echoing the book's image of the white establishment as a bromeliad, a parasite growing on the tree of island life, 'sapping it like a disease'.[39] Yet if instinctively conservative, Lally's attitudes to the island change through the book, and her shifting vision allows the story to have different viewpoints.[40] At the centre of the novel stands the old Great House of L'Aromatique, with its exotic orchid conservatory, its languorous scents intimating beauty and decay. The master of the house, who has been shell-shocked fighting in Flanders, escapes into opium, extending the metaphor of the island's heavy perfumed atmosphere. 'Beauty and disease, beauty and sickness, beauty and horror: that was the island'.[41] The tuberculous Andrew prefers 'to cough my own blood out . . . in a scene of beauty',[42] to treatment abroad. The story opens at the moment when the Master comes back to L'Aromatique, and the novel is structured by the successive returns of his three daughters. Stella, the eldest, is passionately drawn to the physical beauty of the Caribbean. Impatient, she kills Mr Lillipoulala, a vampire-like opium trader from Haiti. But her action is potentially disastrous: the Master cannot live without drugs. Joan is the objective 'scientist',[43] loving 'these marvellous small things, their amazing vividness. I could give up all the grandeur of the world for a thing like that humming-bird'.[44] Brash Natalie flies in from Trinidad with her rich playboy partner, the voice of new, American-centred Caribbean capitalism. She forces her father to leave the island, but he dies of terror on the flight. The island's future lies with the island Jesuits, and the politics orchestrated by Joan through her crippled husband, and her son Ned. One of the most sensuously evocative island novels is also one of the most political. Phyllis Allfrey herself came back to the Caribbean and co-founded the Dominican Labour Party to organise the exploited fruit labourers. Elma Napier, who wrote novels as Elizabeth Garner, was brought up on Martinique, but in 1932 also settled in Dominica which she made the setting for two novels *Duet in Discord* (1935) and *A Flying Fish Whispered* (1938) – both tragic love stories strong on atmosphere and setting – besides a number of shorter pieces. Like Allfrey, Napier became involved in island politics, and was elected to the Dominican legislature in 1940.

To the south, the volcanic island of St Lucia is only relatively less mountainous than Dominica. But where Dominica's hostile coastline

ensured its isolation, St Lucia's magnificent harbour shaped its very different history. The 'Helen' of the Antilles – a prize fought over and fortified
by the French and British from 1650 until 1814 – it changed national-
ities some thirteen times. The St Lucian culture evolved as a turmoil of
African, French and English influences that underlie cultural achievements
prodigious for an island of a hundred thousand inhabitants. St Mary's
College, Castries, produced two Nobel Prize winners, Derek Walcott and
the economist Sir Arthur Lewis, besides the distinguished novelist Garth
St Omer. Its painters include Harold Simmons and Dunstan St Omer.
Garth St Omer's distinctive vision is to some extent encapsulated in his
early novella, 'Syrop', published in 1964.[45] This is set in a fishing village,
located between hill and sea, separated from the main town by canals
stagnant with ooze and sewage. To buy breakfast for a brother coming
out of jail, Syrop dives for a coin thrown from a tourist liner, and is
sucked into the propeller and beheaded. His tragedy has an inevitable
logic on an island circumscribed by poverty, Catholic ritual and guilt,
and claustrophobic family relationships. St Omer's vivid use of the
island setting and meticulous concern with literary form, which link his
work with the James Joyce of *Dubliners*, provides the basis for his succession of finely crafted novels: *Shades of Grey* (1968), *A Room on the Hill*
(1968), *Nor any Country* (1969) and *J-, Black Bam and the Masqueraders*
(1972).

The island has also been remarkable for its theatre. The initiative was
taken by Derek Walcott and his twin brother Roderick (Roddy). In
1950, Derek, with Maurice Mason, founded the St Lucian Arts Guild in
the island capital, Castries, staging his own historical play *Henri Christophe*
there. When Derek left with a scholarship for the University of the West
Indies in Jamaica, the Guild continued to prosper under Roddy. St Lucian
theatre became a creative force throughout the West Indies: five prizes at
the 1957 Jamaica Drama Festival went to Roddy Walcott's enduringly
popular comedy, *The Harrowing of Benjy* (1957). The achievement of the
Walcott twins drew on a broad range of the island's cultures. Their
parents had African and British blood on both sides of the family, and
were of a 'genteel, self-denying Methodist poverty', which set them apart
from the predominantly black, Roman Catholic and peasant island population. Derek was to write of how, as 'two pale children', he and Roderick
watched on Sunday nights the dancing crowd below from an upstairs
window, unable to join in 'because they were not black and poor'. Yet
he was instinctively drawn to this other world, and from his earliest
writing found that 'the rhythms of the street itself were entering the
pulse-beat of the wrist'.[46] Not yet twenty, funded by a gift from his
mother, he privately published *Epitaph for the Young* (1949), a long poem
that was to form the basis of *Another Life* (1973). In both, childhood in St
Lucia, and growing into art and literature, form one experience.

Walcott entitles the first section of *Another Life* 'The Divided Child'. This refers not to racial division, but to conflicting perspectives of artistic vision. It begins with a meditation on the light that mediates human awareness.

> But which was the true light?
> Blare noon of twilight
> 'The lonely light that Samuel Palmer engraved'
> or the cold
> iron entering the soul, as the soul sank
> out of belief.[47]

The warm twilight invokes a golden glow of memory, and the image in turn fixes the past, 'a landscape locked in amber'. It is also the light of a provincial world, the dusk of empire, the 'whiskey-coloured light' where colonels sit watching the sunset of the British Empire. The sun goes down, and dark is followed by the moon, radiant as a flash bulb, which like the poet's creative memory at once reveals and transfixes, a photographic negative, the cold reflex of life. The first book evokes Walcott's experiences of early boyhood, the family house in Castries, where the nervous tensions of family life are held in balance by mother's sense of order. At school, the boy looks on the town community through the eyes of his reading, making a comic epic alphabet in which a stamping cart-horse becomes A for Ajax, and Jamey, the town's one clear-skinned whore, H for Helen of Troy. Darker forces are glimpsed in obeah practices ('One step beyond the city was the bush. One step behind the churchdoor stood the devil'),[48] and in the tale of Manoir, merchant by day and werewolf by night. In his fourteenth year, Walcott was possessed by an overwhelming sense of poetic vocation, at once to his art and to the island people, for 'something still fastens us forever to the poor'.[49]

Walcott's early youth was spent painting with his close friend Dunstan St Omer (Gregorias), drunk on rum and beauty. In the Eden of an island where 'no one had yet written of this landscape/ that it was possible',[50] they revel in 'Adam's task of giving things their names'.[51] Gregorias's spiritual insight spontaneously transforms reality into a painted fresco in the Catholic church of Gros Islet. But Walcott turns from art to words as his chosen medium for exploring the complexities of St Lucian identity. Light became a blaze in the 1948 catastrophe which virtually destroyed Castries. Rebuilt in ugly concrete, a 'cement phoenix', Walcott's childhood landscape had forever changed. That same year he left school, and found first love with 'Anna', the sixteen-year-old Andreuille Anceé. But returning twenty years later, the 'simple flame' has gone: Anna has become all women, in both life and literature, that he has loved.

so every step increased that subtlety
which hoped that their two bodies could be made
one body of immortal metaphor.
The hand she held already had betrayed
them by its longing for describing her.[52]

Separated from the past, the 'landscape locked in amber' was replaced by
the colder metaphor of a ship in a bottle, 'sealed in glass'.[53] He must leave.

For the final book, Anna is Walcott's Beatrice, conducting him through
Inferno. Harry Simmons, a long-standing family friend, had been an
implicit presence in the earlier poem, the art teacher of both Walcott and
Gregorias. Painting the island directly, with natural affection for the lives
of the poor, Simmons had been Walcott's inspiration. 'People entered
his understanding/ like a wayside country church,/ they had built him
themselves'.[54] But in 1966, unrecognised in the Caribbean and culturally
isolated, Simmons killed himself. His death gave a new meaning to being locked in the past, and Walcott turns his rage on those who perpetuate
the humiliation of slavery:

> Those who peel, from their own leprous flesh, their names,
> who chafe and nurture the scars of rusted chains,
> like primates favouring scabs, those who charge tickets
> for another free ride on the middle-passage,
> those who explain to the peasant why he is African . . .
> they measure each other's sores
> to boast who has suffered most,
> and their artists keep dying . . .[55]

But Simmons's art had made Walcott aware of the sanctity of true simplicity. Walcott can now pair his objectivity with the transfiguring vision
of Gregorias, and the poem ends with an assertive, humanist reprise of the
earlier question, 'But which was the true light?'

> Gregorias listen, lit,
> we were the light of the world![56]

Notes

1. George Lamming, *Pleasures*, p. 214.

2. E.M. Roach, *The Flowering Rock* (Leeds, 1992), p. 128.

3. Frederick Marryat, *Peter Simple* (London, 1834) ch. xxxi.

4. Bruce St John's published collections include *Bambatuk* I (Bridgetown, Barbados, 1982).

5. Timothy Callender, *It so Happen* ([1975] Oxford, 1991).

6. Frank Collymore, *The Man who Loved Attending Funerals and Other Stories* (Oxford, 1993).

7. Cited by Edward Baugh, 'Frank Collymore the Miracle of *Bim*', *New World*, Barbados Independence Issue (1966/7), p. 132.

8. Edward Brathwaite, 'Timehri', *Savacou* 2 (September 1970), p. 35.

9. George Lamming, *In the Castle of my Skin* ([1953], London, 1970), p. 11.

10. George Lamming, '*In the Castle of my Skin*: Thirty Years After' [1983], reprinted in *Conversations, George Lamming*, ed. Richard Drayton and Andaiye (London, 1992), p. 47.

11. George Lamming, *Castle*, p. 57.

12. Ibid., pp. 54–5.

13. Ibid., p. 73.

14. Ibid., p. 154.

15. Ibid., p. 299.

16. Ibid., p. 299.

17. Ibid., p. 303.

18. Geoffrey Drayton, *Christopher* ([1969] London, 1972), p. 60.

19. Ibid., p. 37.

20. Ibid., p. 192.

21. Jean Rhys, *Voyage in the Dark* [1934], in *Jean Rhys: the Early Novels* (London, 1984), p. 23.

22. Ibid., p. 23.

23. Ibid., p. 17.

24. Ibid., p. 46.

25. Ibid., p. 48.

26. Ibid., p. 128.

27. See also Teresa F. O'Connor, *Jean Rhys: the West Indian Novels* (New York, 1986); Carole Angier, *Jean Rhys* (London, 1990).

28. Jean Rhys, *Wide Sargasso Sea* ([1966] Harmsworth, 1968), p. 109.

29. Ibid., pp. 121, 127.

30. Ibid., pp. 67, 150.

31. Ibid., pp. 151, 155, 156.

32. Kenneth Ramchand, *The West Indian Novel and its Background* (London, 1970), pp. 230–6.

33. Evelyn O'Callaghan, 'The Outsider's Voice', *Journal of West Indian Literature* I, i (1986), pp. 74–85.

34. Kamau Brathwaite, *Contrary Omens* (Mona, Jamaica, 1974), pp. 33–8.

35. Gayatri Chakravorty Spivak, 'The Women's Texts and a Critique of Imperialism', *Critical Inquiry* 12 (Autumn 1985), p. 253.

36. *Wide Sargasso Sea*, p. 106.

37. Peter Hulme, 'The Place of *Wide Sargasso Sea*', *Wasafiri* 20 (Autumn 1994), p. 10.

38. Phyllis Shand Allfrey, *The Orchid House* ([1953] London, 1982) p. 4.

39. Ibid., p. 178.

40. Ibid., pp. 8, 86.

41. Ibid., p. 75.

42. Ibid., p. 69.

43. Ibid., p. 137.

44. Ibid., p. 161.

45. *Introduction 2: Stories by New Writers* (London, 1964), [no editor given], pp. 139–87.

46. Derek Walcott, 'What the Twilight Said', in *Dream on Monkey Mountain* (London, 1972), p. 22.

47. Derek Walcott, *Another Life* (London, 1973), p. 43.

48. Ibid., p. 25.

49. Ibid., p. 43.

50. Ibid., p. 53.

51. Ibid., p. 152.

52. Ibid., p. 94.

53. Ibid., p. 108.

54. Ibid., p. 134.

55. Ibid., pp. 127–8.

56. Ibid., p. 152. See also Edward Baugh's essential 'Derek Walcott. Memory as Vision: "*Another Life*"' (London, 1978).

Chapter 4
Jamaica

Jamaica was by far the largest of the British West Indies, and its size has created a literary sensibility quite different to that of the smaller islands. At four thousand square miles it is twice the area of Trinidad, the next largest island. Wrested by Britain from Spain in 1655, its population, which reached a million by 1920 and then more than doubled by 1990, is predominantly African in origin, with a significant brown and white middle class, stratified by both class and colour.[1] It has a dramatically varied landscape. Across the Blue Mountains to the north lie the coral beaches of the rugged coast, cooled by the 'Doctor' wind; to the south-east stretch the black sands of Morant Bay. To the west are the high lush pastures of Mandeville, and the fertile plains of Black River and Negril. The extreme wealth and poverty of cosmopolitan Kingston contrasts with villages whose Africa-centred culture was lovingly evoked in Claude McKay's *Banana Bottom* (1933),[2] and in the moonscaped Cockpit country, an isolated Maroon community preserves African traditions from the eighteenth century. By 1900, middle-class Jamaicans felt themselves a nation, a proud part of the British Empire. The brutal repression of the 1865 Morant Bay Rebellion had effectively crushed popular opposition, and the Governor from 1907 to 1913 Sir Sydney Olivier, a founder-member of the Fabian Society, actively encouraged the development of an independent Jamaican culture.

Local writing had been fostered by local newspapers, notably *The Gleaner*, established in 1834. The first Jamaican literary magazine, significantly titled *The Victoria Quarterly*, appeared in 1883. A contributor was 'Tom Redcam' (the reversal of his name, Thomas Henry MacDermot), who was to be celebrated as the 'father' of Jamaican literature, and posthumously named Jamaica's first Poet Laureate in 1933. His poems, bearing titles such as 'My Beautiful Home', described the island's flora and landscapes for a readership whose poetic ear had been tuned by Keats, Tennyson and Browning.

> There slumbers the Mango in gloom,
> There flings the Marengo its snows

And dark where Convolvuli bloom,
Slow-motioned, the deep river flows.[3]

J.E. Clare McFarlane noted that 'Redcam's "Jamaica Marches On" has been sung countless times to the tramping feet of little children, and "We are Marching to Conquer the Future" is, I believe, known to every school boy in Jamaica – and every school girl, too'.[4]

Redcam broke new ground with his interest in Jamaican history. In 1889 *Jamaica*, a long Tennysonian poem strikingly sympathetic to the common people, appeared by 'T.R. a Jamaican', indicating Redcam. His later verse mourned the massacred Arawaks, and praised the 1895 Cuban revolutionaries 'whose mutual love is known/ but may not yet be shown'.[5] His poetic drama on Columbus, *San Gloria* (first published in 1920), was not written for the stage, but nevertheless looks forward to the dramatic epics of C.L.R. James and Derek Walcott.[6] His light colour and middle-class status separated him from the effects of the slave era and the lives of the Jamaican poor, and his experiments with dialect verse lacked conviction. Yet he was an important innovator whose work helped create the literary audience for which J.E. McFarlane founded the Jamaica Poetry League in 1923. From 1899, Redcam's editorship established *The Jamaica Times* as the leading Jamaican literary periodical. He also started the first West Indian novel series in 1904, the *All Jamaican Library*, published cheaply at a shilling for local readers. It included E.A. Dodd's *Maroon Medicine* (1905), a collection of short stories which introduced the figure of an obeah trickster into West Indian fiction, and two titles by Redcam himself, *Becka's Buckra Baby* (1904) and *One Brown Girl and –* (1909). *Becka*, a curious story of a young black girl who dies under a tram while trying to save her white doll, alone sold two thousand copies, but the series ended after four issues, perhaps because Redcam could not find suitable material.

From 1904 Redcam's genial patriotism was challenged by an edgier, thrusting young talent. H.G. de Lisser, self-educated from the age of fourteen, fought his way up from an impoverished Afro-Jewish background in rural Jamaica, came to Kingston, and in 1903 became, at twenty-six, editor of *The Gleaner*, which he rapidly established as the most influential paper on the island. His views could be contradictory. He championed J.H. Froude's views in *The English in the West Indies* (1888) that West Indian societies were irredeemably degenerate, and to his death in 1944 he campaigned against Jamaican self-government. Yet for forty years he made *The Gleaner* a driving force in Jamaican politics and culture, and actively promoted local writing both in *The Gleaner* and in the annual *Planter's Punch* (1921–44), where he first published most of over twenty novels that he wrote himself. An intelligent observer of all levels of island life, he was encouraged by his patron Olivier to write *Jane* (serialised in

1912, retitled *Jane's Career* in 1914), which Kenneth Ramchand claimed as 'the first [novel] in which the central character, the one whose feelings and thoughts are described in depth, is a Negro'.[7] In it Jane Burrell, born into a large impoverished family in a mountain village, is hired as a maid by Mrs Mason, a mulatto living in downtown Kingston. She finds the city a startling new world.

> ... the electric-cars, all lighted up now and moving swiftly
> on their lines with a constant clanging of warning gongs;
> the hubbub, the incessant movement of hundreds of people,
> the sound of religious singing which pierced its way
> through all the other noises; and then the market itself, that
> market to which Jane's mother had come occasionally to
> sell her goods, and which to Jane's wondering eyes looked
> as though it contained all the food that could be grown in
> a whole year in all the villages she had ever seen - all this
> filled her with unspeakable delight.[8]

But Mrs Mason lives with her deeply unlovely children amid the decorative clutter of middle-class Kingston pretensions. Jane is seduced by Cecil, Mrs Mason's nephew, a casual incident for which she extorts money, while keeping out of his reach. Rather than submit to Mrs Mason's domineering, Jane's experience awakens her independent spirit. When Cecil's attentions become irksome, she decamps and works in a factory, where the overseer's sexual attentions throw her onto the protection of Vincent Broglie, a type-setter with 'respectable' prospects. As one who 'did not allow even the immediate future to trouble her much . . . [but] lived in the day and for the day', Jane has been dubbed a romanticised stereotype of the Jamaican peasant.[9] But her extrovert vivacity is convincing. She is instinctively good, and if she extorts money from the predatory Cecil, she leaves the intolerable Mrs Mason without asking for her wages, or stealing in lieu. When Broglie loses his job, it is her disinterested faithfulness that wins him to propose. 'It doan' matter to me if y'u don't have anyt'ing now. It is not because you have or you doan't have a job that I like you Mr Vin. If I love you an' you love me, it's all right. I doan't mind for anything else'![10]

Jane's authenticity owes much to De Lisser's accurate rendering of the registers of Jamaican speech, the basis for the success of Ernest Cupidon's stage version of 1933. The novel ends with Jane's white wedding to Broglie and her establishment in Kingston bourgeois society, triumphing over Mrs Mason. Ironically, with her white wedding Jane succumbs to the middle-class world of the Masons which she had so held in contempt. De Lisser never wrote another *Jane*, and he is chiefly remembered in Jamaica for his sensational historical novel, *The White Witch of Rosehall*

(1926), based on the reputed obeah practices of the slave owner Annie Palmer. But his range was impressive.[11] In works like *Morgan's Daughter* (1931) he expounded his (reactionary) attitudes to Jamaican race and history, and *Triumphant Squalitone* (1917) illustrates considerable skill in political satire.

De Lisser would have had little sympathy for two contemporary Jamaicans who were to make a major impact on Jamaica, although both lived largely in exile. Marcus Garvey, born in 1887 in rural St Anne's Bay, began life as an apprentice printer before travelling the Caribbean as a journalist campaigning for black-worker rights. Returning to Jamaica from London in 1914, he founded the Universal Negro Improvement Association (UNIA) to 'establish a Universal Confraternity among the race'[12] which, with headquarters in Harlem, became the first mass black activist movement in history. Garvey knew little of Africa, which he never visited, but a good deal of the Bible, and his flamboyant pulpit rhetoric struck a chord in the religious consciousness of the Jamaican masses. Both condemned as maverick and revered as a prophet, Garvey electrified his audiences by proclaiming that Africa was superior to Europe. Styling himself the 'Provisional President of Africa', he called on the black peoples of the world 'to pledge our manhood, our wealth and our blood to [Africa's] sacred cause'.[13] In Jamaica in 1930 the UNIA presented three epic plays on a public stage in Eidelweiss Park, Kingston, dramatising Jamaica's African past, their history and their aspirations across the world. Ignored by the middle-class public, these evangelical pageants had a powerful impact on the island's black mass public, in the process exposing sources of local theatrical talent including Ranny Williams, the Jamaican playwright and comedian who became Manager for Garvey's productions. The Jamaican establishment ridiculed and harassed Garvey, and he spent much of his life in the United States, where he established his headquarters and published his routinely banned newspaper, *The Negro World*. His grand projects for West Indian repatriation to Africa failed, he was arrested for alleged fraud, and in 1935 he left Jamaica for England, where he died in obscurity. But he had sown the seeds of the Jamaican Rastafarian Movement, and in *In the Castle of my Skin* Lamming has his Shoemaker, away in Barbados, declare, 'An from the time the Great Marcus Garvey come down an' tell us that the Lord ain't drop Manna in we mouths I start to think'.[14]

Claude McKay was a Jamaican contemporary of Garvey. A happy childhood in the large family of a Jamaican hill farmer gave him an enduring affection for black rural life, and its story-telling and popular beliefs instilled a sense of continuity with the African past. Life in Kingston, where he went aged sixteen and briefly (and painfully) served in the police, brought him into sharp contact with the urban poor. He also met the English folklorist Walter Jekyll who had based his own groundbreaking

anthology *Jamaican Song and Story* (1907) on research in McKay's home
area. Jekyll lent McKay books, and encouraged him to experiment with
writing dialect poetry. He helped McKay publish *Songs of Jamaica* (1912),
followed in the same year by the urban *Constab Ballads*. The two volumes
formed a landmark in Caribbean literature. Although he knew British
'dialect' poets such as Burns, McKay started from the experiences of the
Jamaican peoples, using Creole to animate dramatic tableaux in verse, a
form richly developed by later artists such as Louise Bennett.[15] McKay
had no sympathy with Garvey's messianic vision of African repatriation.
Nevertheless he chafed at his own isolation in Jamaica and, against Jekyll's
advice, at the age of twenty-four sailed for the United States. Racial per-
secution in the South shocked him from sympathy into outrage, and his
protest verse was later to inspire Radical West Indian poets like Martin
Carter in Guyana, and George Campbell in Jamaica.

> Though far outnumbered let us show us brave,
> And for their thousand blows deal one deathblow!
> What though before us lies the open grave?
> Like men we'll face the murderous, cowardly pack,
> Pressed to the wall, dying but fighting back![16]

McKay wrote the best-selling novels *Home to Harlem* (1928) and *Harlem
Shadows* (1922) out of his American experience, where he became a major
figure in the Harlem Renaissance. He also travelled throughout Europe,
championing black and workers' rights, experiences that informed *Banjo*
(1929). He never again saw Jamaica, though he was to return there
imaginatively in his posthumous *My Green Hills of Jamaica* (1975), in the
four Jamaican stories in *Gingertown* (1932) and, in particular, in *Banana
Bottom* (1933).

McKay wrote this novel at the end of a life in exile, and into the main
character Bita he projected his own glowing memories of childhood,
while his relationship with his patron Walter Jekyll appears in Squire
Gensir, the white scholar who befriends Bita. Bita who, like de Lisser's
Jane, embodies the vitality of the Jamaican folk, is adopted by the missionaries Malcolm and Priscilla Craig. When at thirteen she has sex with
the light-headed village musician, Crazy Bow, they send her to England
to get a 'respectable' education. On her return, her intended spouse is
Herald Newton Day, a smug theological student the Craigs are grooming
to be their black assistant. But Bita is too vital to fit into their plans. She
embodies McKay's ideal of black self-respect; warm and impulsive, she
belongs only to herself.

> I thank God that although I was brought up and educated
> among white people, I have never wanted to be anything

but myself. I take pride in being coloured and different, just
as any intelligent white person does in being white.[17]

The book's title denotes a place, and Bita's personality is inseparable from
the hill community of her birth. The origins of Banana Bottom are multi-
racial. Adair, a Scots emigré to Jamaica in the 1820s, had bought up the
estate, liberated the slaves, married the blackest of them, and sold them his
land in small holdings. In Banana Bottom and its village, Jubilee, McKay
vividly evokes the traditional Jamaican lifestyle with its rituals, festivals,
choir festivals and dances. Music is a major if implicit theme in the novel.
The Craigs' one positive gift to Bita is to teach her Western music, and on
her return from schooling abroad, her first public act is to play the piano
for the Black Choristers in the chapel. But McKay portrays an alternate,
folk tradition in the village 'tea meetings' dances to fiddle and drum, and
in the inspired playing of Crazy Bow. Crazy Bow, the grandson of Adair,
is a light-headed genius who can play all instruments and embodies the
music at the heart of the community.

> He made the people weep, recreating again the spirit of
> ancient martyrdom that still haunted the crumbling stones
> and rusted iron of many a West Indian plantation.[18]

It is his playing that seduces Bita in the 'rape' for which she is sent for
education abroad. Squire Gensir teaches her that art transcends cultural
boundaries and that Mozart and Jamaican folk music come together, just
as 'some of our famous European fables have their origin in Africa'.[19]
However, when the drum rhythms tilt a Christian revivalist meeting into
a Pocomania spirit ceremony, Bita is swiftly snatched away to safety.
Reason must be preserved, and obeah, too, is shown as a dangerous
delusion.[20] Gensir's balanced attitude is contrasted with the Craigs' exclus-
ivity. Their pious intentions crumble when their protegé Newton Day is
discovered fornicating with a goat, ending their marriage plans for Bita.
Bita herself settles for life on a small-holding, marries the carter Jubban,
and the village choir sing 'Break Forth into Joy' as an epithalamion under
the couple's window.[21] McKay does not disguise the cultural difference
between the couple, and at the end Bita turns to Pascal's *Pensées* for 'a
golden thread of principle to guide her through the confusion of life'.[22]

The vitality of the Jamaican hill culture shapes the very different work
of Eileen Bliss, born in Jamaica in 1903, later calling herself 'Eliot' after
the writers George and T.S. She recreated her childhood as the daughter of
an officer in the West Indies regiment in her novel *Luminous Isle* (1934).
The young Em grows up in a repressive white Roman Catholic world.
Leaving the island for education in England, she discovers that Jamaican
colours, scents and, above all, the mountains haunt her sensibility. At the

age of nineteen, she returns. 'Inevitably and imperceptively one does travel towards somewhere – perhaps towards the place one had determined upon long ago'.[23] Escaping from two white suitors,[24] she finds herself drawn towards the forbidden world of the black community, where people 'move at the source of life. They are part of life and not outside it. They accept, absorb and recreate'.[25] In the Blue Mountains Em twice meets the woman Rebekka, a tall, independent black hill farmer. Although the meetings are brief, their immediate bonding gives Em the strength to set off on her own into an unknown future in England. Like the fiction of Jean Rhys, the novel was significantly written outside the male-orientated world of the West Indies itself.

By the 1930s, however, the scene was also changing in a Caribbean increasingly shaken by economic depression, riots and strikes. Out of this turmoil comes the work of Una Marson. Born in 1905 in a well-to-do Jamaican family, Marson trained as a social worker, and her later career, shuttling between Jamaica and London, was a continuous round of public service. She edited the first Jamaican magazine devoted to women's writing and interests, *The Cosmopolitan* (1928–31), and in 1935 was the only black woman speaker at the Twelfth International Alliance of Women Congress in Istanbul. In London, she became assistant secretary to the League of Coloured People, and, later, assistant secretary to the exiled Haile Selassie. She encouraged local Jamaican writing, founded the Kingston Drama League in 1938, and in 1949 helped found the Pioneer Press which published affordable local literature.[26] Her most influential achievement was to edit from 1938 the BBC programme that developed into *Caribbean Voices*, which was to play a major role in West Indian writing in the 1950s and 1960s. Marson published three books of verse, *Tropic Reveries* (1930), *The Moth and the Star* (1937) and *Towards the Stars* (1945). She felt ill at ease with poetry, as she herself recognised, and in her restless search for a personal style, wrote much that was immature. Yet she developed, and her later work restrained sentiment within a taut, staccato form. Following Langston Hughes, she experimented with Afro-American rhythms, as in 'Kinky Hair Blues' where the black girl sings that nobody loves 'me black face/ and me kinky hair':

> So I'se gwine press me hair
> And bleach me skin.
> I'se gwine press me hair
> And bleach me skin.
> What won't a gal do
> Some kind a man to win.[27]

At a time when West Indian women poets typically eulogised tropical landscapes, Marson turned to the everyday conflicts of a black woman's life. In one poem she forbids her eighteen-year-old daughter to go to the movies, because Hollywood makes 'cinema eyes', a striking image for the vision that sees black people with contempt.[28] She introduced a personal woman's voice into West Indian poetry, and brought an edgy fluency to bear on issues of race and gender.

Una Marson was also a pioneer as a playwright and actor. *At What a Price*, a one-act comedy co-written with Horace Vaz, became in 1933 the first Jamaican play to be staged in London. In Kingston, Jamaica, *Pocomania* was the theatrical sensation of 1938. This still unpublished drama[29] focuses on the spiritual crisis facing Stella Manners, the frail, attractive daughter of a stern Baptist Deacon, bored by the narrow respectability of her life. Her father is campaigning against Pocomania [a Jamaican cult featuring spiritual possession], which he sees corrupting his flock. However, depressed by a death in the family, Stella is drawn to their emotive, drum-based Ninth Night ceremony, in which the dead return to make their peace with the living. The stirring climax of spiritual possession becomes a riot when the musicians demand rum, and Stella, disillusioned, turns to marriage and middle-class life with her doctor suitor, David. In spite of its anticlimactic ending, the play confronted its middle-class audience with a contemporary moral issue. It was also the first of many that exploited the power of popular ritual on stage.

Louise Bennett also made her professional debut in 1938. On the death of her father, her mother at great sacrifice kept her at school, giving her a simultaneous experience of English education and the oral culture of the Jamaican folk which was to inspire her 'dialect' poems. These first appeared in the Jamaican *Sunday Gleaner*. She recited them with panache on radio and resplendently dressed as a village woman, 'Miss Lou', at local festivals. But her work was too popular to be taken seriously in the cultural climate of the 1930s. 'And of course [at school] we all recited Louise Bennett's poetry', recalled Olive Senior, 'but we did not recognise Louise Bennett's work as "literature"'.[30]

The year 1938 also saw the emergence of the People's National Movement (PNM) under the socialist leader Norman Manley. This changed both the political and cultural scene. The movement encouraged Radical plays such as Frank Hill's *Upheaval* (1939) and Roger Mais's *Hurricane* (1943), and the Little Theatre Movement (LTM) formed in 1941. The LTM folk pantomime, featuring Louise Bennett, and Ranny Williams as Anancy the Spider Man, became a major annual event on the island, while the Caribbean Thespians, founded in 1946, marked the expansion of local theatre. *Focus* (1943–60), an occasional annual edited by Edna Manley, also fostered the Jamaican arts. The PNM weekly, *Public Opinion* (1938–), covered both politics and literature, and a list of its contributors reads like a 'who's who' of the island's talent, including Roger Mais, John Hearne, Louise Bennett, V.S. Reid and George Campbell. Campbell's

First Poems, privately published in 1945, contained simple, strong verse that moved the young Derek Walcott on St Lucia, who read his lines

> Holy be
> the white head of the Negro.
> sacred be
> the black flax of a black child.

and found they 'matched the exhilaration [of] their reader'.[31] Campbell also wrote resonantly political verse in the tradition of McKay:

> Negro aroused! Awakened from
> The ignominious sleep of dominance!
> Freedom! Off with these shackles
> That torment, I lift my head and scream to heaven
> Freedom![32]

Although privately printed, his verse was read and made an impact not only in Jamaica, but also in Britain and the United States.

In 1944 Jamaica gained self-government under Crown supervision, an event celebrated by V.S. Reid with his novel, *New Day* (1949). Written throughout in a modified Jamaican Creole, the novel revisions seventy years of history through the consciousness of Johnny Campbell, now eighty-seven years old, remembering when, aged eight, he was present at the 1865 Morant Bay Rebellion. The event was pointedly chosen, for the Rebellion had been taken by British intellectuals to show that Jamaicans were unfit to govern. The rhythmic prose, with its apostrophes to the reader, recreates the stance of the community story-teller, and evokes the experience of a Morant Bay farming family, its hardships and simple pleasures - drought; mangoes, hot sun and cool water, birdsong and mountain scents. Its idiom, with its Biblical echoes, intimates a religious consciousness, and ranges from lyricism to epic.

> Fire has got to conchs' tails. [Conch = sea-shell blown as
> a rallying call.] They come a-seek cooling wind. See them
> come, Shepherd Bogle? See them coming from the fire into
> the cool where you are?
> *Brethren — the Lord hath delivered the Philistines into we hands!*[33]

The drama of the stoning of the Morant Bay courthouse and its violent sequel is seen by a child: when the father is shot down defenceless by the British Redcoats, it is also the death of Johnny's innocence. Part Two of the novel traces the establishment of an independent political order, engineered through the political skills of Campbell's grandson Garth, a thinly disguised persona for Michael Manley. Reid ignores the fact that the 1865 Rebellion set back the cause of Jamaican independence by half a century, and his focus on a 'brown' middle-class family neglects the importance of 'black' populist movements.[34] Yet his ambitious novel grounds Jamaican identity in the island's soil and language, and gives an epic dimension to its political evolution.

Roger Mais's work also came out of the ferment surrounding the emergence of the People's National Movement. A restless, pugnacious figure, middle class by birth but militantly working class in sympathy, from 1938 to 1944 Mais regularly contributed Radical sketches and short stories to *Public Opinion*. He also wrote drama, including his own version of the Morant Bay Rebellion, *George William Gordon* (printed 1976). His journalism culminated in a famous attack on the Churchill government, 'which permits the shameless exploitation of those colonies across the seas of an Empire upon which the sun never sets'.[35] He was jailed in Spanish Town, charged with sedition. In 1953 he drew on his prison experience in *The Hills were Joyful Together* (1953). The novel marks Jamaican literature coming to terms with the experience of the underprivileged majority.[36] Cut for publication, the published version omits Mais's original sections set in the Jamaican countryside: as a novel exclusively focused on Kingston, its title becomes bitterly ironic, for the serene mountains, evoked when the cultists sing from Psalm 98, 'let the floods clap their hands: let the hills be joyful together', look down on the horrors of urban slums. The 'dancing hills' had yet another meaning on an island that had known earthquakes, and Rema, the central woman character, crazed by the loss of her lover Surjue, sees the hills shake again. 'They would trample me to death, you know? The hills'.[37] The novel shocked middle-class readers with its revelations of a Jamaica of routine beatings, murder, rape and incest, degradation made all the more appalling by flashes of instinctive goodness evident in even the most depraved of its characters.

Kamau Brathwaite has seen in Mais's method the 'rhythmic, thematic and structural features' of a West Indian 'jazz' aesthetic.[38] The story is set out as a drama – '*The scene is a yard in Kingston, Jamaica. Time: Today*'.

> The yard counted among its ramshackle structures an old shaking-down concrete nog [timber-frame] building with the termite-ridden wood frame eaten away until only a crustacean shell under the dirty white cracked and blistering paint remained.[39]

There are twenty-five characters. In an early passage, the community celebrates at a fish-fry, where the singing becomes a dance, and the dance enacts crossing a river, like the Israelites crossing the Jordan, but perhaps, too, Africans negotiating the Middle Passage.

Woy-oh, Ah glad you come over,
Woy-oooh, Ah glad you come o-o-over!

And Zephyr in the simulated and real excitement of the
moment, put her arms up around Lennie's neck and let her
face down against his chest, as though she wanted to tell
him before them all how glad she was he had come across
the swollen river safely.

And they all laughed, and bright tears stood in the eyes
of some, to witness that they still understood the meaning
of miracles.[40]

The yard-dwellers form a chorus of the Kingston poor. Ironically only
Zephyr, the generous-hearted prostitute, has a relatively assured living.
Ras, who is learning to read and write, works a hand-cart, but most are
unemployed with crime the only alternative. Surjue with his love for
Rema provides the core of the book. With no outlet for his ambitions, he
sees life as a lottery, and taking a chance with the petty criminal Flitters,
is abandoned during a robbery, and gaoled. The final sections of the book
alternate between Surjue's life behind prison walls, and the poor of the
yard, themselves immured by poverty. The two come together. Rema
burns herself alive in crazed grief for Surjue the same moment that
Surjue, under the cover of a prison fire, attempts to escape and is shot
against the prison walls, arms apart as a crucified Christ, 'staring up at the
silent unequivocal stars'.[41]

Brother Man (1954) is Mais's 'Christ in Kingston'. Its main character,
John Power, a shoemaker of simple and charismatic humanity, becomes a
preacher and healer, living with Minette, a girl he has rescued from the
streets. His goodness provokes the emotionally unstable Cordelia to betray him by planting counterfeit coins in his room, and later he is wrongly
suspected of murder for his bearded appearance. The crowd attacks him
in the street and leaves him for dead. Mais's title indicates Power's link
with the Rastafarians, in 1954 feared and ostracised in Jamaican society,
but he has left the cult, representing an all-embracing humanity. Minette
nurses him back to life, and the book ends at dawn, with her candle
lighting his room. Mais's imprisonment had made him a national hero,
but as a person he became increasingly depressed. In 1952 he left Jamaica
for England, taking with him the manuscripts of the three novels which
were to make his name. His last novel, *Black Lightning* (1955), examined
the tensions within his own life as both social activist and creative writer.
Jake carves a life-size statue of blind Samson with whom he identifies, a
parallel confirmed when he himself is blinded in a freak electric storm.
Art becomes an impulse to lonely self-destruction, and Jake is seduced
by the Delilah of his craft. Jake's drift to suicide is contrasted with his

extrovert friend Amos who finds happiness in caring for Jake and serving his community. Mais himself died of cancer in 1954, leaving an unfinished manuscript *In the Light of this Sun*, a reading of the tragic love of David for Jonathon.

John Hearne was a close friend of Roger Mais, and his fellow-traveller through Europe. Less involved with Jamaican folk, his writing expresses the tension between politics and personal relationships facing the island's middle class. In his accomplished first novel, *Voices under the Window* (1955), Mark Lattimer lies dying in a slum room. A light-skinned mulatto lawyer supporting the Workers' People's Party in a riot in downtown Kingston, he had been cut down by a ganja-smoking labourer. In flash-backs, he revisions the aspirations and betrayals of his life, and his death, watched over by his black mistress and an Indian social worker, is an ambi-valent summation of his self-discovery. In his subsequent novels Hearne created the imaginary island of 'Cayuna', closely based on Jamaica, and the gracious lifestyle of Brandt's Pen recreates that of the old plantation Great Houses. Politics and self-sacrifice are the central issues in *Stranger at the Gate* (1956), which ends when the lawyer Roy MacKenzie dies ramming a police car to allow Étienne, a Communist ex-President of a neighbour-ing island, to escape: in *The Faces of Love* (1959), Rachel throws herself in the way of a bullet intended for her lover Michael. *The Land of the Living* (1961) considers the emergent Rastafarian movement with Marcus Hennekey as the leader of the 'Sons of Sheba'. The love affair between his daughter Bernice and Mahler, a Jewish expatriate university lecturer, becomes a compassionate exploration of human relationships within a turmoil of politics and race.

Mahler reflects the growing impact of the University of the West Indies on the island from the first opening of its Mona campus in 1949. It drew together talent from across the Caribbean. In 1953 Derek Walcott was among the first of its succession of graduating writers and scholars, which was to include Jean D'Costa, Gordon Rohlehr, Wayne Brown and Victor Chang. The campus also provided an intimate theatre, music facilities, and a broadcasting unit. The Trinidadian Errol Hill joined the Extramural Department from 1953, and by writing and directing plays such as *Man Better Man* (1957), based on stick-fighting rituals, developed new directions in local drama. From 1955 he edited the series *Caribbean Plays*, making cheap locally written playscripts available throughout the region. In 1965 Trevor Rhone returned to Jamaica from Rose Bruford College, England, and with the Jamaican actress and producer Yvonne Brewster addressed Kingston's cultural 'desert'.[42] They transformed the Brewster family's private garage into the 150-seat Barn Theatre. In 1971 Rhone's satirical *Smile Orange*, written throughout in the Jamaican idiom, touched the nerve of an island increasingly weary of tourist exploitation. Set entirely behind the scenes of a seedy north coast hotel, the tragic-comedy exposed a way of life where self-respect and honesty came second to dollar tips or the chance of an American visa. Running a record 245 nights, it confirmed the commercial viability of local drama.

Rhone's *Old Story Time* (1979) achieved even greater success world wide, and was as tender as *Smile Orange* was acerbic. Members of a village community take various parts in a drama covering forty years of social change, orchestrated by the genial story-teller Pa Ben. At the centre is the conflict between Ma, representative of the old village values, and her son Len, the modern generation of college-educated Jamaican, who marries the smart black girl Lois, although Ma wants him to have a 'nice brown girl with hair down her back'. The situation is exploited by the unscrupulous George, representing the commercial dishonesty undermining contemporary Jamaica. Unpretentiously religious, the play closes in a moving assertion of reconciliation between the generations. Rhone's dramatic range was confirmed by *Two Can Play* (1982), an accomplished two-hander in which a Jamaican wife's sexual liberation in the United States challenges, and finally emancipates, her husband. In 1972 Rhone became the father of Jamaican film as well as theatre when, with Perry Henzell, he co-scripted the first full-length Jamaican film, *The Harder They Come*, and in 1976 directed the film of his own *Smile Orange*. Jamaica was now part of the international theatre scene, and Barry Reckord's *A Liberated Woman* (1970) and *In the Beautiful Caribbean* (1972) were produced in both Jamaica and London.

Jamaica was recognising the resources of its island culture. Robert le Page, David de Camp and Frederic Cassidy at the University at Mona were researching and transcribing Jamaican Creole, and Cassidy's *Jamaica Talk* (1961) prepared the way for Louise Bennett's collection of poems in Creole, *Jamaica Labrish* (1962). This was published by Sangsters, a Kingston bookshop, with a preface by the university staff tutor and dance director Rex Nettleford. From the early 1970s, annual arts festivals aroused interest in the Jamaican cults of pocomania, kumina, and customs such as Jonkonnu. This provided a basis for Sylvia Wynter's play *Maskarade* (1973) and Marina Omowale Maxwell's experimental 'yard theatre'.[43] Louise Bennett performed traditional Jamaican Anancy stories, and the spider trickster became the hero of political satire in the LTM pantomimes.

The 1970s were good years for Jamaican poetry. *Seven Jamaican Poets* (1971), edited by Mervyn Morris, included work by Dennis Scott, Anthony McNeill and Mervyn Morris himself. As the title of his *Shadow-boxing* (1979)[44] indicates, Morris's precise poetic identity can be hard to hit. His poems impact a significance out of all proportion to their characteristic brevity. His subjects range from black awareness, false consciousness, to social issues,[45] and the four quatrains of 'I am the man' say more than most longer protest poems. In poems like 'To a Crippled Schoolmaster', Morris shows depths of compassion and sensitivity; in others he shows

wisdom salted with wry humour. *On Holy Week* (1976) movingly reinter-
prets Christian faith in the light of his work as a university hostel warden.
If there are common characteristics in his work, they are his scorn for
pretension and his intelligence defined by literary craft. As he writes in
'Question Time':

> Sometimes a poem
> is a mask
> to ritualize
> connection[46]

Dennis Scott's verse is more theatrical, and reflects his roles as dancer,
actor, cultural critic and Brechtian dramatist. His verse is performance, a
dialogue with the reader or with himself. 'Portrait of the Artist as Magician'
begins

> He painted the ball
> first, balancing on it himself
> a pale boy soft as young thorns,
> and in his hand mirrors.
> In these he observed
> a delicate equilibrium.[47]

Concern for the Jamaican poor is transformed by his imagination, the
'prism . . . the jewel hooked at the mind's edge', fusing with a private
dread, where his wit 'ratchets, roaming the hungry streets/ of this small
flesh, my city . . .'.[48] In the work of a third Jamaican poet, Anthony
McNeill, panache becomes the taut, fragmented voice of nightmare,
'generated by the tension between brain and gut'.[49] In the poems of *Reel
from 'The Life Movie'* (1972), an intense desire for the 'Other' coexists
with terror that the unknown may prove the void indicated in the title of
his collection *Hello Ungod* (1971), and the poet's pain will be 'a clown's
crucifixion'. *Credences at the Altar of Cloud* (1979) brings a marked shift, as
words are recognised as the craft in which he can navigate the dark seas of
unknowing:

> poem be open
> and bless
> whoever you touch[50]

Women's writing also flourished. Sylvia Wynter's powerful if somewhat overwritten account of a revivalist group in a Jamaican village, *The
Hills of Hebron*, had been published in 1962, but it was the depth of
Jamaican women's poetry that emerged most notably from the anthologies *Jamaica Woman* (1970), edited by Mervyn Morris, and *From Our Yard*.

Jamaican Poetry Since Independence (1987), edited by Pamela Mordecai. Lorna Goodison's locally published *Tamarind Season* (1980) introduced her best-known poem, 'I am Becoming my Mother', a deeply felt recollection of her mother's humanity, 'brown/yellow woman/ fingers smelling always of onions', which at the same time was an affirmation of her daughter's cultural identity. Goodison's seminal place in Caribbean women's writing will be considered later,[51] yet her work is immediately accessible outside categories of gender, race or nationality. Each of her poems emerges as a creation from within a specific, felt experience. Her work creates an organic fusion of meaning, sound and spirit in a standard Jamaican form, with linguistic complexity that can assimilate Rastafarian terms and local nuances. Strongly rhythmic and written to be heard, its incantatory form brings it closer to meditation than to 'performance poetry'. Goodison's other talent is painting, and her poems create images at once specific and universal: 'your trees dripping blood-leaves/ and jasmine selling tourist-dreams' ('Jamaica 1980'); 'I'll open the curtains and/ watch the lightning conduct/ your hands' ('Keith Jarrett – Rainmaker'). The poems of 'I am Becoming my Mother' (1986) and 'Heartease' (1988) move through aspects of the Jamaican identity towards individual self-fulfilment. But, as Edward Baugh has pointed out, there are island villages called Heartease, and the word suggests both a state of mind and a place, intimating a hard-won objectivity that makes self and community merge into one consciousness:

> Believe, believe
> and believe this
> the eye know how far
> Heartease is.[52]

Goodison's short stories, exploring women/men relationships with sometimes painful sensitivity, are collected in *Baby Mother and the King of Swords* (1990).

The poems of Goodison's Jamaican contemporary, Olive Senior, first collected in *Talking of Trees* (1985), show the narrative and descriptive rather than mystical insights, which combine to create her sharp and innovative short stories. Senior's childhood was divided between village and city, and she brings a finely tuned observation to bear on a wide spectrum of Jamaican society, familar from within. Her stories are in the popular Jamaican story-telling tradition, energised by a sharp ear for idiomatic speech, an unpatronising fascination with the comedy and tragedy of everyday life, and a brilliant sense of timing. Many of her best stories are seen through the eyes of a child, often a girl, who is trying within a family or group to 'create self-identity out of a chaotic personal and social history'.[53] A characteristic 'epiphany' occurs in 'Confirmation Day',[54] where the desolate aftermath of the empty church ritual turns into exultation, as *self*-confirmation brings release from a life stifled by a class-bound Anglican ethos. The fine story 'Ballad' counterpoints the self-conscious narrative of a young middle-class girl against the emancipating life force of the outrageous, illiterate, Miss Rilla. The apparent ease of Senior's style is deceptive. Once editor of the Jamaican *Social and Economic Studies*, she writes stories that explore with precision Jamaican issues that range from the position of women in society, to historical change. In the title story of *Arrival of the Snake-Woman* (1989), the coming of 'Miss Coolie' acts as a catalyst for the rural Mount Rose community, challenging prejudices and forging new loyalties, sketching the emergence of a multi-racial society in Jamaica prior to independence. The husband Philip in 'The Tenantry of Birds' represents the new breed of politician who in the pursuit of his career loses touch with rural and personal loyalties.

Senior's work is sensitive to the background developments in Jamaican society from the 1960s onwards, in which a major force was the Rastafarian movement. Rooted in the earlier preaching of Marcus Garvey, which looked to a return to Ethiopia under the divine kingship of Haile Sellassie, the cult's popularity flourished, particularly in the deprived areas of Kingston, and in 1954 this caused public alarm when Pinnacle, a Maroon-like Rastafarian community led by Leonard Howell, was stormed by police. By 1960, when a largely sympathetic report on the movement by members of the university was published, its wide support among the underprivileged masses began to become clear. Two years later came Jamaican independence, and the Rastafarians, with their dreadlocks and distinctive lifestyle, offered a highly visible alternative to the Western models that the leaders of the new nation seemed all too eager to adopt. The movement began to attract interest from Radical intellectuals. N.D. Williams's *Ikael Torass* ['from Ikael to Rasta'], published in 1976, is a lively *bildungsroman* tracing the career of Ikael, a young middle-class Jamaican, through education abroad to life in a Rastafarian community. Other writers were more circumspect. In Orlando Patterson's *The Children of Sisyphus* (1981), the cultists, though sympathetically portrayed, are trapped in the helpless squalor of the 'Dungle' (the Jamaican slums), and in McNeill's poem 'Ode to Brother Joe', the jailed cultist fills his cell with 'power/ and beauty of blackness,/ a furnace of optimism', but 'the door is real and remains shut'.[55] Yet Rastafarianism had arrived to stay, with an impact increasingly felt throughout the Caribbean, and then around the world. Their lifestyle and vision were promulgated through the music of Bob Marley, artists like Ras Daniel Heartman, and performance poets including Mikey Smith, Mutabaruka and Oku Onuora, whose subjects range from neo-colonialism and political corruption to love songs and the environment.[56]

The urban deprivation out of which the Rastafarian movement came also created the cult of urban violence. This was dramatised in the film by

Trevor Rhone and Perry Henzell, *The Harder They Come* (1972), the reggae-inspired saga of Ivan Rhygin, a Kingston gunman and song-writer of the 1950s. In 1980 Michael Thelwall turned the film into an accomplished novel, placing the story firmly in the context of Jamaica's shift from rural to urban life, with the establishment of a gang and gun culture. The theme recurs. Neville Dawes followed his political novel *The Last Enchantment* (1960), set in the 1940s, with *Interim* (1978) which reflects the increasing American pressure on Jamaica. In the first, a country boy goes through an élitist education only to be faced with the failure of nationalist hopes: the second ends with the violence of a crushed revolution. But the Jamaican countryside remained a central focus. Olive Senior's collection of poems, *Gardening in the Tropics* (1995), goes back, literally, to the roots of Caribbean life, finding in the earth the history of its peoples, their hardships, beliefs and regeneration. Evan Jones's wonderfully relaxed, objective novel, *Stone Haven* (1993), begins when Grace Neville comes to Jamaica from America as a Quaker missionary and, against opposition from her church and family, marries the Jamaican hill farmer Stanley Newton. The couple's roots in the community, its customs and the land, create a symbiosis echoed in the name of their house, and the book's title. The Newton family saga covers the years from 1920 to an ambivalent ending in the violence and changes of the post-independence years. After Grace's death, Stone Haven remains, obstinately surviving the indignities of change, but now shuttered by louvres, 'producing a curious effect, as if the house shut its eyes and ceased its observation of the sea'.[57]

Notes

1. Leo Lowenthal, *West Indian Societies* (London, 1972), p. 78.

2. See below, pp. 50–1.

3. Tom Redcam, 'My Island Home', in J.E.C. McFarlane (ed.), *Voices from Summerland* (London, 1929), p. 265.

4. J.E.C. McFarlane, *A Literature in the Making* (Kingston, Jamaica, 1956), p. 4.

5. 'Cuba', reprinted in *Caribbean Verse*, edited by Burnett, p. 132.

6. C.L.R. James, *The Black Jacobins* (1976); Derek Walcott, *Drums and Colours* (1958).

7. *Jane's Career* (1972), p. ix.

8. H.G. de Lisser, *Jane's Career* (1914; with an introduction by Kenneth Ramchand, London, Caribbean Writers Series, 1972), p. 39.

9. Glyne A. Griffith, *Deconstruction, Imperialism and the West Indian Novel* (Kingston, Jamaica, 1966), p. 26.

10. *Jane's Career*, p. 188.

11. See Rhonda Cobham, *The Creative Writer and West Indian Society; Jamaica 1900–1950*, PhD thesis, Univ. of St Andrews, 1981.

12. See J.H. Clarke (ed.), *Marcus Garvey and the Vision of Africa* (New York: Vintage Books, 1974) pp. 38–70.

13. Marcus Garvey, *The Negro World* (2 August, 1919) quoted by Adolph Edwards in *Marcus Garvey* (London, 1967), p. 11.

14. George Lamming, *In the Castle of my Skin* (Trinidad and Jamaica, 1970), p. 102.

15. See below, pp. 123–50.

16. 'If We Must Die', reprinted in Burnett (ed.), *Caribbean Verse*, p. 144.

17. Claude McKay, *Banana Bottom* (New York, 1933), p. 169.

18. Ibid., p. 258.

19. Ibid., p. 124.

20. Ibid., p. 250.

21. Ibid., p. 306.

22. Ibid., p. 314.

23. Eliot Bliss, *Luminous Isle* ([1934] London, 1984), p. 49.

24. Ibid., p. 152.

25. Ibid., p. 342.

26. Erika Sollish Smilowitz, '"Weary of Life and All my Heart's Dull Pain": the Poetry of Una Marson', in *Critical Issues in West Indian Literature*, edited by E.S. Smilowitz and R.Q. Knowles (Parkersburgh, 1994), pp. 19–32.

27. Una Marson, *The Moth and the Star* (London, 1937), p. 91.

28. Ibid., pp. 87–8.

29. Manuscript in the Institute of Jamaica. I am grateful to Dr Delia Jarrett-Macauley for access to a copy.

30. Anna Rutherford, 'Interview with Olive Senior', in *Hinterland*, edited by E.A. Markham (Newcastle-upon-Tyne, Bloodaxe Books, 1989), p. 215.

31. Derek Walcott, *Another Life*, p. 7.

32. George Campbell, *First Poems* (Kingston, Jamaica: privately printed, 1945), p. 28.

33. V.S. Reid, *New Day* (New York, 1949), p. 139.

34. The issues are well summarised in Mervyn Morris, 'Introduction' to the Caribbean Writers Series edition of *New Day* (London, 1973).

35. Roger Mais, *Public Opinion*, 1 July 1944.

36. Edward [Kamau] Brathwaite, introduction to *Brother Man* ([1954] London, 1974), p. ix.

37. Ibid., p. 207.

38. Kamau Brathwaite, 'Jazz and the West Indian Novel', reprinted in Brathwaite, *Roots*, pp. 93–106.

39. Roger Mais, *The Hills were Joyful Together* ([1953]; reprinted in *The Three Novels of Roger Mais* (London, 1966)), pp. 7, 9.

40. Ibid., p. 52.

41. Ibid., p. 288.

42. Mervyn Morris, 'Introduction' to Trevor Rhone, *Old Story Time and Smile Orange* ([1981] Harlow, 1987), pp. v–xx.

43. Kole Omotoso, *The Theatrical into Theatre* (London, 1982), p. 84; Judy S.J. Stone, *Studies in West Indian Literature: Theatre* (London, 1994), p. 73.

44. Other titles by Morris include *The Pond* (1973) and *Examination Centre* (1992).

45. Pamela C. Mordecai, 'Mervyn Morris', in Daryl Cumber Dance, *Fifty Caribbean Writers* (Westport, Conn., 1986), pp. 341–56.

46. Mervyn Morris, *Examination Centre* (London, 1992), p. 11.

47. Dennis Scott, *Uncle Time* (Pittsburg, 1973), p. 10.

48. 'No sufferer', ibid., p. 53.

49. Dennis Scott, introduction to Tony McNeill, *Reel from 'The Life Movie'* (Mona, Jamaica, 1972), p. 12.

50. Anthony McNeill, *Credences at the Altar of Cloud* (Kingston, Jamaica, 1979), p. 118.

51. Chapter 18.

52. Lorna Goodison, *Heartease* (London, 1988).

53. 'Interview', *Callaloo* 11, 3 (1988), p. 481.

54. Olive Senior, *Summer Lightning* (Harlow, 1986), pp. 80–4.

55. *'Life Movie'*, pp. 40–1.

56. *Dub Poetry: 19 Poets from England and Jamaica*, edited by Christian Habekost (Neustadt, 1986).

57. Evan Jones, *Stone Haven* (Kingston, Jamaica, 1993), p. 409.

Chapter 5
Trinidad

The Republic of Trinidad and Tobago, some three hundred miles south of Barbados, comprises two islands sixteen miles apart, separated from South America by the narrow gulf of Paria. Trinidad, the larger, was named by Columbus in 1498, and it remained Spanish until seized by the British in 1797, although its plantations were developed mainly by the French. The origin of the population is African and Asian, with a significant admixture of Chinese and Portuguese. Labourers emigrating to Venezuela and Panama, and the presence of American military bases during the Second World War, have given Trinidad a continental American flavour. With an industrial base in bitumen and later oil, its culture has escaped the worst consequences of tourism suffered by Barbados and Jamaica. Although under two thousand square miles in area, with a population that only reached a million in the 1970s,[1] Trinidad is the most cosmopolitan of the Anglophone West Indies.

In the late 1920s, the Marxist Radical group associated with the *Beacon* periodical met in Port-of-Spain to discuss the overthrow of bourgeoise colonialism. Its members included Albert Gomes, Alfred H. Mendes, Ralph de Boissière and C.L.R. James. Their discussions were strenuously intellectual. James was to note that 'I didn't learn literature from the mango-tree, or bathing on the shore and getting the sun of the colonial countries; I set out to master the literature, philosophy and ideas of Western civilization'.[2] James used the local library, but personally subscribed to some thirteen periodicals, including *The Times Literary Supplement*, the *Criterion*, the *New Republic*, *Le Mercure de France* and the *Gramophone*. The intention was to understand metropolitan culture, not to comply with it, but to defeat the colonial mentality. James later declared:

> We are members of this civilization and take part in it, but
> we come from outside. . . . And it is when you are outside,
> but can take part as a member, that you see differently from
> the ways they see, and you are able to write independently.[3]

The group published two journals, *Trinidad* (annually in 1929 and 1930) and *The Beacon* (1930–3). Its editorials savaged what they saw as literary chatter passing for cultural advancement, and gleefully declared that 'stepping on corns' was a far more just and honest procedure than 'patting on backs'. For 'the very atmosphere of the "literary club" reeks of an unctuousness, a stupid formality and hypocrisy, from which any man or woman of true artistic sensibilities would flee in disgust'. First in the line of fire was imitative literature. Gomes wrote:

> It is important, moreover, that we break away as far as possible from the English tradition; and the fact that some of us are still slaves to Scott and Dickens is merely because we lack the necessary artistic individuality and sensibility in order to see how incongruous that tradition is with the West Indian scene and spirit.[4]

For Gomes, even McKay's evocation of Jamaican rural life in *Banana Bottom* smacked of self-indulgent primitivism.[5]

The most prolific writer of the Beacon group was Alfred H. Mendes, a Portuguese Creole with socialist convictions, who wrote over fifty short stories and two novels. The most personal and moving of these is *Pitch Lake* (1934), set in the strata of Trinidad society Mendes knew best. It is seen through the consciousness of Joe da Costa, a first-generation Portuguese Creole who fights his way up from his father's rum-shop into affluent Port-of-Spain society. Caught in the moral morass intimated in the book's title, he seduces Stella, an inexperienced Indian servant girl, while courting the lively heiress Cora Goveia, who embodies all his social ambitions. When Stella becomes pregnant, threatening his prospects with Cora, he murders her in a frenzy of frustration and anger. The novel is given life by Joe's strongly realised inner turmoil, and the spendidly vivacious, bob-haired Cora. Mendes's second novel, *Black Fauns* (1935), is less effective. Based on Mendes's research into the yard communities in a poor area of Port-of-Spain, the novel remains a sociological tract in which five women characters reflect on black working-class attitudes towards politics, colour, money, class and sex.

The dominating genius of the *Beacon* group was C.L.R. James. James was a Renaissance man, a talented writer of fiction, drama and criticism, besides being an informed and original thinker on politics, economics, history, and popular culture.[6] His short story, 'La Divina Pastora', published in the *Saturday Review* in 1927 and selected for *The Best British Short Stories of 1928*, was the first Caribbean short story to receive international notice. The plot is slight. Anita Perez, a poor cocoa worker, wishes to marry Sebastian, but after two years he shows no sign of doing so. She is anxious for marriage because 'in that retired spot' it was 'the sweet perfection of a woman's existence' and because 'feminine youth and beauty, if they exist, fade early in the hard work of the cocoa plantation'.

So she makes a pilgrimage to the shrine of La Pastora to ask the Madonna's
help, and leaves her only valuable possession, a gold chain. Subsequently
Sebastian shows some signs of romantic interest. On her return to her
room, she collapses senseless: her gold chain is there back in its cigarette
tin. The mastery of the story lies in its silences. At the end, stepping back
as narrator, James disclaims judgement: 'of my own belief in the story I
shall say nothing'. It stands as an early example of Caribbean 'magical
realism',[7] leaving the reader with only the logic of Anita's faith.

With his novella 'Triumph', published in *Trinidad* (1929), James shocked
the repectable classes with the life of the barrack yards.

> Each street in Port-of-Spain proper can show you
> numerous examples of the type: a narrow gateway leading
> into a fairly big yard, on either side of which run long
> buildings, consisting of anything from four to eighteen
> rooms, each about twelve feet square. In these live, and
> have always lived the porters, prostitutes, carter-men,
> washer-women and domestic servants of the city.[8]

James contrasts the short, dark, voluptuous and easy-going Mamitz with
her lighter-skinned, wiry friend Celestine, who has a policeman for a
lover. James's freedom from class or colour prejudice allows him to
unpretentiously recreate the theatre of yard life.

> 'Married!' said Celestine with fine scorn. 'Me married to a
> police! I wouldn't trust a police further than I could smell
> him. Police ain' have no regard. A police will lock up 'is
> mudder to get a stripe. An' besides I wan' want to married
> nobody. If I married I go'n' have the man in the house all
> the time, he go'n' want to treat me as 'e like. I go'n be a
> perfect slave. I all right as I be.[9]

Their common enemy is Irene, who is jealous of Mamitz's lovers. They
frustrate her attempts to persuade Nathan, a jealous and menacing butcher,
of Mamitz's infidelity, and finally Mamitz throws open her door to show
the humilated Irene an interior papered with Nathan's money.

C.L.R. James researched for *Minty Alley* (1936) by actually living in the
Port-of-Spain slums, and sixty years later the reader is still startled by its
fresh authenticity. On the death of his mother, the twenty-year-old Haynes
finds cheap lodging in a yard mortgaged to Mrs Rouse, who also runs a
small bakery. The novel was the first of many to use the 'yard' as a natural
theatre for the interaction of class and colour. Mrs Rouse, 'brownish' in
complexion, lives with Benoit, an African with a trace of Indian blood;
Maisie, her niece, is African with a hint of European. Her servant Philomen

is East Indian; the Nurse, whose status is second only to Mr Haynes, is to all appearances white. Although Minty Alley was 'not two hundred yards' from his home, Haynes finds himself living as in a different world, dominated by physical and emotional violence, sexual infidelity, and by 'science' (obeah). James's fine novel reverses the convention of a servant girl seduced by her social superior: here a respectably educated male, Mr Haynes, is initiated into sex by a working-class girl. Maisie, Mrs Rouse's black niece, is vital, intelligent, and bored with yard life, drawn to Haynes with his education, his books and gramophone. She is younger but emotionally mature, coming from a tough yard culture alien to that of the protected Haynes. With tact and affection she teaches him respect and self-assertion. James never blurs the cultural gap that separates Haynes from the yard-dwellers with their poverty and physical violence. At the novel's climax, Mrs Rouse and Maisie viciously confront each other, throwing each other's clothes into the muddy yard. Maisie emigrates to find her fortune in America, while Haynes returns to the limited certainties of bourgeois life. It was some twenty years before the Jamaican Roger Mais would write of a West Indian black community with such unromanticised understanding.

In 1932 James, finding he had no place as a black man in Trinidad politics, emigrated to England. He left behind a Trinidad caught in the waves of strikes and social disturbance that were beginning to sweep the British Caribbean. In 1937 a strike of oilfield workers led to a general strike, and riots during which a black policeman was burnt alive. With James's absence, the member of the Beacon group most directly caught up in these events was the light-skinned son of a solicitor, Ralph de Boissière. De Boissière had abandoned a secure career, taking a series of casual jobs that brought him into contact with common people, including baker's delivery to 'little shops and hovels and stinking alleys' across the island.[10] Out of this experience came *Crown Jewel* (1950). The novel, indebted to Tolstoi and Gorki, covers a grand canvas, from yard rooms to colonial style mansions, from the unemployed Luna Popo to the wealthy Syrian town councillor Jo Elias. The central political debate is conducted between Benjamin Le Maître, an intellectual black Radical, and Cassie, a serving girl, who overcomes her natural timidity to emerge as a leader in the political movement. Cassie's development as a person lies at the centre of the novel, and she humanises and finally marries le Maître. De Boissière himself may be seen in the middle-class André de Coudray, whose conflicting affections for the English socialite Gwenneth Osborne, and a coloured dress-maker, Elena Henriques, symbolise divided political loyalties. The novel builds up to a stirring climax in the oilfield riots, and André commits himself to the life of the people, marrying Elena. The thinly veiled *roman à clef* was too politically sensitive to be published in either Trinidad or Britain, appearing first in Australia, with an English edition in 1980.

The political activities of the 1930s had left a vacuum. In 1941 an Anglo-American agreement permitted United States bases to be set up on the island. The American lifestyle broke down old colonial conventions of colour and class, and the power of the 'Yankee dollar' reigned supreme. Trinidadian politics reached a nadir. Elections, held with full adult suffrage in 1946, 1950 and 1956, lacked coherent political programmes, and independent candidates pandered to the prejudices of a largely unprepared electorate. The scene is reflected in De Boissière's *Rum and Coca-Cola* (1956), a sequel to *Crown Jewel*, which mourns the failure of Trinidad's hard-won freedom. Le Maître is imprisoned under war-time restrictions, while radicalism loses André his job. In 1947, De Boissière himself was forced to leave the island for America, then Australia.

With the suppression of the Beacon movement, Radical dissent passed to the people. As Gordon Rohlehr has demonstrated in detail,[11] although vigorously censored by the authorities, from the 1930s calypso became the most vital medium for popular opinion on the island. Local drama was also developing. The modern era of Trinidad theatre began in 1946 when the Whitehall Players was founded by Errol John and Errol Hill. Two years later, a national arts festival attracted some five hundred entries, and Beryl McBurney opened the Carib Theatre to promote local dance-drama. The 1950s saw productions of Walcott's *Henri Christophe* (1950) and *The Sea at Dauphin* (1954), and in 1958 a spectacular production of his epic drama, *Drums and Colours*, marked the inauguration in Trinidad of the West Indies Federation. Playwrights increasingly drew on the resources of popular culture. Errol Hill's ground-breaking play *The Ping Pong* (1954) was set in a Carnival steel band competition, where the tuning of the drums on stage enacted the group's social harmony. One player wrongly suspects the leader of stealing his woman, and untunes his 'pan', forcing him out of the Carnival competition. Yet this becomes the occasion for members of the band to discover their individual self-reliance, and they win without him. Trinidad's Premier Eric Williams enthused about the play, 'these are the creators of our Caribbean music, the characters of our Caribbean drama, the voters of our Caribbean democracy'.[12] But he did not note the play's message, which was not to be too dependent on a charismatic leader.

In 1959 Walcott founded the Trinidad Theatre Workshop, presenting plays by himself and by his talented twin, Roddy Walcott, whose *Harrowing of Benji* (1956) was to remain a staple comedy in West Indian drama repertoires. The Workshop also became a cradle for local writing and acting, and the West Indian showcase for contemporary theatre from around the world, including plays from France and Africa. West Indian drama was itself finding an international audience. Walcott's *Henri Christophe* (1950), Errol Hill's *Man Better Man* (1957) and the Jamaican Barry Reckord's *Della* (1954) were all produced in London in the 1950s. It was, however, Errol John's *Moon on a Rainbow Shawl*, premièred in 1959, and the winner of the 1957 London *Observer* playwriting competition, which did most to establish a worldwide audience for West Indian drama. Like C.L.R. James's novel *Minty Alley*, the play used a West Indian 'yard' of shanty houses grouped around a communal space as a natural theatre, and made the life of the common people its drama. Within this boundary, aspiration is also circumscribed by poverty and human weakness. The young Rosa loves Ephraim, but is sexually harassed by Old Mack, her landlord; the raucous Mavis yearns for marriage, but poverty traps her in prostitution. The strongly drawn cast of yard folk is dominated by the matriarchal figure of Sophie Adams, whose hopes for escape to a better life are ruined when her partner Charlie is arrested for stealing money, ironically to enable their daughter Esther to take up a scholarship to High School. Errol John's lyrical use of the folk idiom, which moves with deceptive ease between joy and grief, is reminiscent of the Irish dialogue of O'Casey, a playwright he admired, and whose *Moon for the Misbegotten*[13] is echoed in his title. The use of the 'yard' as a natural arena, however, was distinctively West Indian.

The first major novel of Trinidad development was Sam Selvon's *A Brighter Sun* (1952), a new departure in form as well as subject. Selvon's opening panorama of Trinidad in 1939, using a calypso perspective, gives equal status to national and to incidental private life. The outbreak of World War Two, a man riding the streets of Port-of-Spain on a bicycle with a bottle of rum on his head, and heavy September rains, have equal emphasis, and the marriage of the sixteen-year-old Tiger in a West Trinidad Asian village is an event 'bigger even than the war'.[14] The marriage has been arranged by the two families, and Tiger views the ceremony with incomprehension. Shortly afterwards he takes his girl bride, Urmilla, to live in Barataria, a new suburb of Port of Spain, and Tiger's personality, and modern, urbanised Trinidad, come of age together. The new nation is multi-racial. Tiger's neighbours are the African Joe and Rita, the shop-keepers Tall Boy and Otto are Chinese, a community looking to the 'brighter sun' of the future. The assertive lifestyle of the negro Rita helps Urmilla resist her Hindu subservience to her husband. Tiger works for the Americans building an airbase on the island, his name indicating aggressive ambition. A dinner with his GI employers as guests is a comedy of crossed intentions, the Americans looking for Indian culture ('I expected hula hula girls in grass skirts') and Tiger showing off his acquired Western culture ('My humble abode is not a massive structure'). But it turns to tragedy when they leave and Tiger, drunk, vents his pent-up frustration by kicking Urmilla in the stomach, killing his unborn child. Selvon's first ambition was to be a philosopher, and the novel repeatedly questions the meaning of manhood, of books, and of life itself. For Tiger, the answer lies in the land, and the 'brighter sun' of the title refers in part to its creative power. Sookdeo, an old Indian gardener, usually drunk, plants his crops by moonlight and enjoys an instinctive rapport with growing things, in contrast to the Americans, who clear the gardens with bulldozers to make a road. Sookdeo hides his savings under his mango tree, and when the Americans bulldoze it, he dies, heart-broken.

With the ending of the war, 'too much Yankee man leave Trinidad girl with child and go away. Hooliganism soared, and people kept off the streets at night'.[15] But Tiger moves on. He builds a house of his own. He has learnt to write, and sends a short story to the *Trinidad Guardian*. He feels the tightening draw of the land. 'Now is a good time to plant corn,' he muttered, gazing up at the sky. Yet for all its 'peasant' nostalgia, Tiger, like the Trinidad society he inhabits, is now urbanised. The sequel, *Turn Again Tiger* (1958), reverses the story. Tiger goes back to work under his father in the country. But the emancipated Tiger cannot endure the indignity of plantation life. Sugar is still run by the postcolonial system, and the manager is a white man called Robinson, a Crusoe to Tiger's Friday. Tiger becomes his houseboy, expressing his pent-up humiliation and desire by making violent love with Robinson's wife. He works out the natural cycle of the year, then is ready to return to Barataria and the pregnant Urmilla.

Fiction in the 1960s continued to reflect the changes taking place in Trinidad society. The title of Ian McDonald's *The Humming-bird Tree* (1969) refers to a cassia seen by the 'white' young narrator, Alan Holmes, by a mountain stream in a bright, 'immortal morning', where 'the humming-birds came to suck in the sweet-blossom bells of gold'.[16] The tree is symbolic of the island, whose national bird is the humming-bird, and like 'a high, green-sailed ship freighted with ingots and gold coin', it reflects its history. The 'lovely bracelets' of light the birds weave link it with Jaillin, the Indian servant girl in the Holmes family, and the racial and sexual innocence Alan enjoys in his relationship with her and Kaiser, her elder brother. As Gordon Rohlehr notes, in this Eden the serpent is 'the Caribbean history of race and caste prejudice'.[17] Alan's father is an estate manager at a time of rioting on the island, and his courtesy to his workers belies impregnable class and colour prejudice. Jaillin's passion for Alan is as tactful as Alan's snobbish treatment of her is insensitive. Yet when, in an innocent episode, the father finds the pair nightbathing and summarily dismisses them both from his service, Alan sinks into his privileged white status with relief, betraying more than Jaillin's self-offering. Jaillin 'was at the heart of all the crises which one by one moulded me. When I first met her I was a child, the last time I was with her childhood suddenly came to an end'.[18]

Alan's fractured sense of identity may be compared with that of Francis in Michael Anthony's *The Year in San Fernando* (1965), which Kenneth Ramchand has seen as the first Trinidadian novel 'committed to involving

us in the feel of a peculiarly open state of consciousness'.[19] Anthony wrote
out of a childhood in a working-class area of Mayaro, beginning life in an
iron foundry. A domestic crisis, not a desire to be a writer, brought him
to England where he found an outlet and encouragement in the BBC's
Caribbean Voices, then edited by Naipaul.[20] *The Year in San Fernando*, based
on Anthony's own experience, tells the story of a twelve-year-old boy
coming from the country to the bustling sea-port as houseboy to the
formidable Mrs Chandles, and, his mother hopes, to 'take in education' at
the local school. The novel follows the natural plot of the year's cycle,
unobtrusively reflected in the plants the twelve-year-old Francis has to
tend, and the boy's own growth in self-confidence away from his mother
and family under what is at first the suspicious and grudging eye of his
employer.

Anthony, the narrator, remains invisible. It is from fragmentary conversations overheard by Francis that the reader can piece together the sub-
plot that Mrs Chandles has two sons, the Forestry Officer and the engaging
Edwin. Mr Chandles is in bad odour with his mother for his sexual
exploits, and Edwin is waiting in the wings hoping for the family property
on her death. The story succeeds through an extreme simplicity of style,
by which the everyday becomes illuminated, as in Twain's *Huckleberry
Finn*, by a knowing innocence. Mrs Chandles, lonely and vulnerable herself, underfeeds Francis and does not buy him his promised new clothes.
Sensing this, the mother comes to visit and, instead of complaining,
cannily charms Mrs Chandles, by giving her a brooch. When she has left,
Francis meets Mrs Chandles in her night grown, and seeing the brooch,
he involuntarily smiles.

> Mrs Chandles thought I was smiling with her. She looked
> strangely pleased. Her smile had big pleats on her cheeks
> and under the chin and the flabby skin round her eyes were
> now a thousand tiny folds. Her gums showed pink. I could
> see the sockets and her eyes shone out like two jumbie-
> beads. It was strange, because she looked spooky somehow,
> and yet she looked so sincere, I believed in her. We smiled
> broadly.[21]

Francis's tentative movement through estrangement to a moment of shared
warmth is perfectly conveyed by the slightly awkward prose. The pivotal
word is 'sincere': as with Huck, Francis's one criterion is authenticity. By
the end of the year, Francis has mastered his duties of shopping and water-
ing the plants. He is doing well in school. But Mrs Chandles is dying, and
the year in San Fernando is coming to an end. On the bus back he is no
longer the confused, homesick boy of his journey down; he has grown
up. In the more polished but less convincing sequel, *Green Days by the*

River (1967), the adolescent Shellie is shaken out of his flirtation with two girls into adult responsibility when the father of one of them sets drug-crazed dogs on him, and he agrees to marry his daughter.

Although Trinidad literature was emerging, Anthony, like Selvon and most West Indian novelists of the 1960s, wrote from exile in Britain. The emigration had left Trinidad intellectuals isolated. Derek Walcott, speaking to a gathering in the University of the West Indies at St Augustine, declared:

> As a poet in the West Indies I find my position more and more idiosyncratic. I have no wish to be a public person, but there are so few of us left to practise poetry, and even fewer who have elected to stay behind, these unhappy few are always called upon to make pronouncements.[22]

Eric M. Roach, whose remarkable verse first appeared in 1938 under the name of 'Merton Maloney', was also among those who stayed in the Caribbean, challenging writers like George Lamming to return: 'O man, your roots are tapped into this soil,/ Your song is water wizard from these rocks'.[23] Roach did not experiment with Trinidad Creole, and his strongest literary influence was that of W.B. Yeats. Yet his passion for the land, the peasants, and their African heritage, gave his verse a strongly Caribbean authenticity. He wrote without sentiment of the 'barefoot, earthy men':

> They are my very bone
> Whose rugged strength compels
> The stone-song in my blood
> Whose simple speech dictates
> Rough rhythms to my head.[24]

Roach was still writing strongly in the 1960s. Staying in the Caribbean, he wrote with hope for West Indian 'Poets and painters, thinkers, strugglers' who endeavour 'to write the future with fire splendour'.[25] In his most celebrated poem, Roach identified the warring identities within West Indian societies as an archipelago which the hope of Federation will attempt to weld together:

> . . . I am the shanty town,
> Banana, sugarcane and cotton man;
> Economies are soldered with my sweat
> Here, everywhere; in hate's dominion;
> In Congo, Kenya, in free, unfree America.
>
> 'I am the Archipelago'[26]

But the Federation failed. In April, 1974, Roach, a fighter refusing defeat, took poison and swam out to die in Quinam Bay, a tragic union with the Caribbean that had been his life and his despair.

Roach was being succeeded by a group of writers who were too young to share his optimism for the Federation and who took a tougher, flexible approach to the first years of Independence. Born in Trinidad in 1944, Wayne Brown read English at the University of the West Indies at Mona, where he became associated with the Jamaican poets Morris, Scott and McNeill. His poetry is, however, distinctive, with a small islander's sense of the sea, and a lyrical gift, which he shares with Derek Walcott, of giving archetypal resonance to sensuous experience. This talent is exemplified in his poem 'Noah' in *On the Coast* (1972), which perfectly transmutes the Biblical fable of Noah's crammed, redemptive voyage, into a parable of poetic despair and recreation. Wayne Brown's experience of a life divided between Jamaica, Trinidad and Europe extends the range of his collection *Voyages* (1989), and a prose chiaroscuro, charting the borders of recollection and imagination, *The Child of the Sea* (1989).

If Wayne Brown kept to a formal literary mode, Trinidad culture as a whole became increasingly shaped by its popular arts. This is even true of work critical of this movement. Victor Questel[27] ironically exposed the realities behind the clichés of calypso culture. His poem 'This Island Mopsy', looked behind the flaunting sexual attitudes of a calypsonian, 'The Mighty Bomber', and revealed a battered woman. Marion Jones's novel *Pan Beat* (1973) came from a feminist perspective, describing the breakup of a steel band formed by a middle-class sixth form, a process of betrayal that imaged the failure of Trinidad society as a whole. Performance poetry took its place beside the annual flood of calypsoes. Paul Keens-Douglas, with his eye for the bizarre in the commonplace, raised the 'tall story' into an art form. Some of his work, which however requires to be seen and heard, was printed in such collections as *Tell Me Again* (1979) and *Twice Upon a Time* (1989). The performance arts shaped printed fiction in creative ways as will be noticed later in the discussion of a Caribbean aesthetic. Carnival provides Lawrence Scott with the organising motif for his richly inventive historical epic, *Witchbroom* (1992). With a calypsonian's combination of irony, fantasy and dramatic panache, the narrator Lavren (Lawrence?) Monagas, at once Latin and Anglo-Saxon, male and female, weaves a colourful, grotesque, carnival of Caribbean history from Columbus to the present. Maria Omowale Maxwell has combined a framework of musical performance with 'magical realism' in *Chopstix in Mauby* (1996). But, supremely, it was Earl Lovelace who made Trinidad popular culture the basis for a distinctive form of writing, and his work will be given a chapter on its own.

Notes

1. Lowenthal, *West Indian Communities*, p. 78.

2. C.L.R. James, 'Discovering Literature in Trinidad: the Nineteen-thirties', *Savacou* 2 (September 1970), pp. 54–5.

3. C.L.R. James, ibid., p. 60.

4. [Albert Gomes attrib.], 'A West Indian Literature', *The Beacon* II, 12 (June 1933). Reprinted in *From Trinidad*, edited by Reinhard W. Sander (London, 1978), p. 31.

5. Albert Gomes, 'Back to "Banana Bottom"', *The Beacon* III, 3 (October 1933), reprinted in *From Trinidad* (London, 1978), pp. 33–5.

6. See Anna Grimshaw (ed.), *The C.L.R. James Reader* (Oxford: Blackwell, 1992); Hennessey, *Intellectuals*, vol. 1, chs. 6–8.

7. See below, p. 113.

8. C.L.R. James, 'Triumph', *Trinidad* I, 1 (Christmas 1949), reprinted in *From Trinidad*, p. 86.

9. C.L.R. James, ibid., reprinted in *From Trinidad*, pp. 93–4.

10. Reinhard W. Sander, 'Ralph de Boissière', in *Fifty Caribbean Writers*, edited by Daryl Cumber Dance (New York, 1986), p. 152.

11. Gordon Rohlehr, *Calypso and Society in Pre-Independence Trinidad* (Tunapuna, Trinidad, 1990), pp. 125–212.

12. Eric Williams, 'Foreword' to Errol Hill, *The Ping-Pong* (Kingston, 1955), p. 6.

13. Judy S.J. Stone, *Studies in West Indian Literature: Theatre* (London, 1994), pp. 36–7.

14. Samuel Selvon, *A Brighter Sun* ([1952] London, 1971), p. 4.

15. Ibid., p. 201.

16. Ian McDonald, *The Humming-bird Tree* ([1969] London, 1974), prologue.

17. Ibid, p. vi.

18. Ibid., p. 19.

19. Kenneth Ramchand, *The West Indian Novel*, p. 218.

20. Michael Anthony, 'Growing up with Writing: a Particular Experience', *Savacou* no. 2 (September 1970), pp. 64–5.

21. Ibid., p. 92.

22. Derek Walcott, 'The Figure of Crusoe' (1965), *Critical Perspectives on Derek Walcott*, edited by Robert Hamner (Washington DC, 1993), p. 33.

23. 'Letter to Lamming' [1952], reprinted in E.M. Roach, *The Flowering Rock* (Leeds, 1992), p. 82.

24. 'Men', ibid., p. 83.

25. 'Poets and Painters' (1950), ibid., p. 70.

26. Ibid., p. 128.

27. Victor D. Questel and Anson Gonzalez, *Score* (Port-of-Spain, 1972); *Caribbean Verse*, edited by Burnett, pp. 345–7.

Chapter 6

British Guiana/Guyana

The brown sea laps over the coastal mudflats of Guyana, and across the sea dikes, the flat paddy fields and irrigation canals stretch westward. Green villages intercut the reflecting patchwork of flooded rice fields. Here, in the narrow coastal strip, and in the white towns of Georgetown and New Amsterdam, most Guyanese people live. Further inland lies eighty-three thousand square miles of mainly uninhabited jungle, pierced by great black rivers, and shadowed by escarpments plumed with waterfalls – one of them, Kaietur, is nearly five times the height of Niagara. As John Hearne has written, 'This is one of the great primary landscapes of the world, and it can crush the mind like sleep'.[1] It has also shaped some of the most remarkable West Indian literature in English. Placed on the South American mainland south of the Caribbean Sea, Guyana's geography, history and racial composition set it apart from the West Indian islands. The Dutch established a colony on the Essequibo in 1616, only two years after the founding of Manhattan, making it the first non-Spanish region in the area to be settled by Europeans. Life on the remote riverine plantations possessed a claustrophobic intensity later evoked in Mittelholzer's *Kaywana* novels, and the Berbice slave rebellion led by Cuffy in 1763 was the most highly organised and bloody insurrection in Caribbean history after that in Haiti. Frequent skirmishes between colonial forces further bloodied a violent history.

Peace came in 1831 when the Dutch-governed provinces of Demerara, Berbice and Essequibo came together as British Guiana. But social change continued apace. After the abolition of slavery, between 1838 and 1917 some 238,000 East Indian indentured labourers were imported to work the fertile land, besides large numbers of Chinese and Madeiran Portuguese. Although indenture contracts lasted between two and ten years, most workers stayed, settling alongside Africans, Europeans, and an indeterminate number of aboriginal Indians, creating an extraordinary racial mix. Economically, the country was controlled by one expatriate company. The recruitment of single Asian males, the break-up of families, and the creation of racially segregated communities helped to lay the basis for the bloody racial riots of the 1970s. Guyana's racial diversity and fertile terrain offered massive potential for achievement. But after independence, under the oppressive Forbes Burnham government, the country became one of the poorest of the ex-British territories.

The cultural potential was also great. The centres of New Amsterdam and Georgetown had created the earliest significant literary culture in the British West Indies, and the writing collected in N.E. Cameron's *Guyanese Poetry 1831–1931* (1931) is superior in quality and range to the exotica of J.E.C. McFarlane's Jamaican anthology, *Voices from Summerland* (1929). Cameron's anthology included the work of Guiana's leading Victorian poet, Egbert Martin ('Leo'). He fervently supported the British Empire, and at the Queen's Jubilee in 1887 won a London newpaper's prize for the best additional stanzas to the national anthem. 'Leo's' verse, while sharing the limitations of its time, is unaffected, and his narrative poem 'Ruth', reprinted by Cameron, is genuinely touching, a simple narrative of a young peasant couple defeated by poverty and the need for the man to emigrate.[2] A contemporary of Leo, Michael McTurk, was a remarkable Liverpool-born sugar planter on the Essequibo who later became a surveyor in the interior, living among the Amerindian community. His experiments in phonetic Creole verse, published under the pen-name 'Quow' in the *Argosy*, a Georgetown newspaper, were collected in *Essays and Fables in the Vernacular* (Georgetown, 1899).[3] They have rough vigour and immediacy, and the distinction of being the first recorded literary attempts at writing in West Indian Creole.

In the European popular imagination, British Guiana meant jungle adventure, and Conan Doyle placed *The Lost World* (1912) in its interior. The first known novel of a Guianese working life was A.E. Rodway's *In Guyana Wilds* (1899), the story of a clerk from Glasgow who enters the dissolute life of Georgetown. Adventure soon breaks in, as he is taken by a half-Amerindian girl into the jungle interior of Roraima, where they are stalked by Kanaima, the ghostly destroyer of Indian legend. In spite of a conventional ending, the discovery of Elizabethan gold, Rodway evidently knew Guiana, and authentically evoked its atmosphere. More ambitious was the curious novel by A.R.F. Webber, *Those that be in Bondage* published locally in 1917. Born on Tobago in 1880, and largely self-taught, Webber emigrated to British Guiana when aged nineteen, and became a leading journalist, trades union leader, and politician. His historical romance chronicles two generations of the Walton family in Guyana, Tobago and Trinidad between 1890 and 1913, recording a battle between the corrupting effects of the plantation system and private spiritual regeneration. Written, as Wilson Harris has noted, 'as a Sunday painter takes time off to paint at the weekends',[4] this is a curiously mixed work; it is Gothic in being linked by the mysterious wanderer St Aldwyn, and powerfully realistic in passages such as the burning of Georgetown Cathedral. Webber's work can be put alongside that of Eric Walrond, born in

Georgetown in 1896, a Radical journalist who moved to New York in 1913, where he became associated with both Marcus Garvey and Claude McKay. The ten short stories collected in *A Tropic Death* (1926) create with stark power a kaleidoscope of peoples on the Caribbean islands and Panama, united under a death-bringing environment. Hunger kills the marl-eating child Beryl in 'Drought'; in 'The Yellow One', the young mother La Madurita dies in a brawl inflamed by racial tension, on a crowded inter-island boat. 'The Vampire Bat' tells how Bellon Prout, an overseer, rescues what appears to be an abandoned Negro baby, and in the morning is discovered with his blood sucked dry. Perhaps stunned by the violence of his own imagination, after these stories Walrond wrote nothing else of significance.

Green Mansions (1904), by the Argentine-born naturalist W.H. Hudson,[5] is very different. It is the first novel to treat the Guyanese interior as a place of changed consciousness, where imagery and language shift to accommodate new dimensions of reality. Abel Guevez de Angensola, the narrator, is a Venezuelan prospecting for gold in the Guyanese heartlands. The search for 'the glittering yellow dust' fails, but sitting wearily by the river his eyes are drawn to a distant vista, dominated by the mountain Ytaioa. As he watches the darkening scene he experiences a strange peace. He 'felt purified and had a strange sense and apprehension of a secret innocence and spirituality in nature'.[6] Exploring this world, which is forbidden by the Indians, he finds himself in a 'wild paradise' of rain forest. Hudson wrote with a naturalist's eye.

> Here Nature is unapproachable with her green, airy canopy,
> a sun-impregnated cloud – cloud above cloud; and though
> the highest may be unreached by the eye, the beams yet
> filter through, illumining the wide spaces beneath –
> chamber succeeded by chamber, each with its own special
> lights and shadows.[7]

There in the half-light, her colours blending with those of the forest, he meets the mysterious bird-woman, Rima, 'a girl-form, reclining on the moss among the ferns and herbage, near the roots of a small tree'.[8] Rima is the pure embodiment of nature, and Hudson relates her love affair with Abel with delicacy. Hudson's attitude to the Indians, however, is ambivalent, and their savagery can be both life-enhancing and cruel. They believe Rima is a witch, and while Abel is away, burn her alive in her tree haunt. The novel became a best-seller in England, and in 1925 when a bird park was built in Hyde Park, Jacob Epstein sculpted a statue of Rima for it.

A darker tone is struck in *Shadows Move Among Them* (1951) by Edgar Mittelholzer. For Mittelholzer, the Guyanese interior created altered psychic states. The young Gregory Hawke, depressed after his wife's death, travels

a hundred miles up the Berbice river to Berkelhoorst, a Utopian settlement founded by his uncle, the Reverend Gerald Harmston. Berkelhoorst
is free from European inhibitions, particularly those of sex. 'We believe
that natural urges must of necessity be normal and healthy or they wouldn't
be natural, so why should we stifle them and turn ourselves into warped,
unwholesome personalities'?[9] Mabel, Harmston's daughter, asks Gregory.
There is also freedom of imagination, and fantasy is encouraged. 'We
believe in our ghosts and things, but in the same spirit as we'd believe in
the actors in their roles on the stage. We deliberately frighten ourselves
because it gives us a thrill'.[10] But although Gregory's emotions are liberated,
the borders between sanity and nightmare are fragile and shifting. 'There
were always ghouls, but you had to see that they only circled and not
settled'.[11] Emotional freedom involves sadism, and recidivists are eliminated,
their deaths recorded as 'snake-bite'. The novel is prophetic of Jonestown,
the sinister commune James Warren Jones formed in north-west Guyana
in 1977, a topic later revisited in Shiva Naipaul's journalistic investigation
Black on White (1980) and Wilson Harris's novel *Jonestown* (1996).
Mittelholzer's *My Bones and my Flute* (1951) moved deeper into Guianese
history. In a crumbling manuscript the protagonist reads the account of a
Dutch planter murdered with his family in Cuffy's 1763 slave revolt, and
incurs the planter's death curse, becoming haunted by a spectral bone
flute. With a party he follows the flute music into the dense jungle,
drawn towards the old plantation site.

> Time seemed a myth, a meaningless symbol. We lurched
> on, driven by an incomprehensible compulsion. We had
> no will in the matter. Our mouths opened and shut as we
> attempted to yell at each other, but there was no sound.
> Evanescent twigs and leaves and branches brushed past us,
> grey and unsubstantial; furry softness charged into our
> rushing bodies without injury or pain.[12]

The frightening climax evokes a history of violence that can only be
exorcised by confrontation. It is a resonant symbol of Mittelholzer's own
mentality, disturbed by his ancestral past.

In Jan Carew's *Black Midas* (1958), the jungle becomes an exotic Eden.
Aaron Smart (called 'Shark' because of his small white teeth, shark grin
and devouring ambition) is a black orphan in the remote coastal village of
Mahaica, 'a bowl axed out of swamps and forests on a river bank'.[13] The
village is a place of order, of 'the secret rhythms which reach from the
earth, out of which the village child is born'.[14] Shark's feelings, however,
are ambivalent. 'Mahaica was my prison, but I was safe in it'. The old oral
culture is passing, and when his guardian teaches him to read, he becomes
divided from it.

On one hand, the language of books had chalked itself on
the slate of my mind and, on the other, the sun was in my
blood, the swamp and river, my mother, the amber sea, the
savannahs, the memory of surf and wind closer to me than
the smell of my sweat.[15]

Shark leaves the village to search for gold and diamonds in the interior,
undeterred by learning that his own father had been betrayed to death by
drowning in a dangerous seam by the greed of the white overseer. In his
own unscrupulous quest, Shark betrays the two women who offer him
love and security, the innocent Indra and the warm-hearted prostitute,
Belle. Having gained and lost a fortune, Shark is reminded of a story told
by Brother C. of the election of three successive village headmen. The
first climbed a sacred mountain and returned with a flower, the second
found a diamond. The third climbed highest and filled his hand with a
white substance that glittered. When he opened his hand, it was empty, for
the snow had melted. Nevertheless, says the elder, he was the wisest, for
'the best of God's gift had to be something no eye can see'.[16] This does
not save Shark, who dies like his father, trapped in a mine filling with
water.

   While Hudson, Mittelholzer and Carew wrote on Guiana for the
international reading public, in the colony itself, writers were confronting local social and racial issues. While he was a scholar at Cambridge,
Norman E. Cameron, later the editor of the anthology *Guianese Poetry*
noticed above, had become passionately concerned with African history,
and on his return to British Guiana he wrote his epic drama *Balthasar*
(staged in 1931), focused on the third (Ethiopian) wise man at the Nativity.
In a succession of dramas, too wordy to be good theatre, but ground-
breaking in content, Cameron celebrated the cultures of Africa and the
Middle East for a colony whose horizons previously had been bounded
by Europe. Cameron's work was taken further by A.J. Seymour.[17] Seymour,
a prolific author who published fifteen collections of verse in forty years,
remained indebted to the style of late Victorian and Georgian literary
models. Yet his vision of a Guianese history rooted in its aboriginal
cultures and landscapes opened new territories for the imagination, and
irradiate his long poems 'The Legend of Kaietur', 'For Christopher
Columbus', 'Amalivaca' and 'Over Guyana, Clouds':

A cinema of rapid figures
Thrown by wood-torches on the trees,
Impassive faces with passion forcing through,
Then the hard treks, and the long full canoes
Rustling down the river-night.[18]

Like Collymore in Barbados, Seymour's great achievement was to encourage local talent. But where Collymore was studiously non-political, Seymour saw the socio-political role of the Caribbean artist as central. *Kyk-over-Al*, which he edited from 1945 to 1961, was named after the ruined Dutch fort that overlooks the Essequibo, Mazaruni and Cayuni rivers: *Kyk* surveyed Caribbean culture as a whole.[19] Its articles and reviews included articles on 'The Novels of the West Indies', 'The Artist in Society' and 'A Survey of West Indian Literature'.[20] It published creative writing from across the Caribbean, including translations from the French and, in 1952 and 1958, important anthologies of West Indian poetry.

The creative writing in *Kyk* was uneven, but Seymour's contributors included two outstanding talents, Martin Carter and Wilson Harris. Carter, like Mais and de Boissière in the 1930s, had rejected privileges of middle-class life in favour of popular Radicalism. His parents had encouraged his passion for reading and philosophy, but secondary education in Queen's College, Georgetown, left him alienated and restless. A succession of jobs in situations from an iron foundry to the prison inspectorate strengthened sympathy for the working classes, and detestation of British colonial rule. His first published verse in *The Hill of Fire Grows Red* (1951) eschewed tropical landscapes for politics. In 1950 Cheddi Jagan had founded the People's Progressive Party, a Radical movement that united both African and Indian communities, and in the first Guyanese elections held with universal suffrage, it swept to victory. Jagan's socialist programme, however, alarmed the British, and within five months they suspended his government. In the riots that followed, Carter was arrested and jailed. He was to write

> This is the dark time, my love.
> It is the season of oppression, dark metal, and tears.
> It is the festival of guns, the carnival of misery.
> Everywhere the faces of men are strained and anxious.[21]

The experience reshaped Carter's consciousness and poetic method.

> Now to absorb and be absorbed again
> and in such fashion marry to the world
>
> Sky blue, grass green, glittering noon.
> Dust white, bones naked, – beautiful world!
> No mark, no madness like this sanity.[22]

It was the baptism of his political imagination. 'So I was born again, stubborn and fierce/screaming in a slum'.[23] If his verse at times was trapped in political gesture, it could also achieve a definitive simplicity: 'is the university of hunger the wide waste';[24] 'not hands/like mine/these carib altars knew';[25] 'I come from the nigger yard of yesterday'.[26] His poems became part of the history of his time, recited at political meetings, the crowd repeating the lines in unison.[27] His best verse transcends any specific political context.

> The slave staggers and falls
> his face is on the earth
> his drum is silent
> silent like night
> hollow like boat
> between the tides of sorrow.
>
> In the dark floor
> in the cold dark earth
> time plants the seeds of anger.[28]

Carter survived the ensuing years of racial division and internal oppression, serving in Forbes Burnham's government until 1971, when he retired to write and lecture. His later collections, *Poems of Succession* (1977) and *Poems of Affinity* (1980), reflected acceptance and fulfilment rather than protest, but the creative flair remained:

> Orbiting, the sun itself has a sun
> as the moon an earth, a man a mind.
> And life is not a matter of a mother only.
> It is also a question of the probability of the spirit,
> strength of the web of the ever weaving weaver
> I know not how to speak of, caught as I am
> in the great dark of the bright connection of words.[29]

A different shift in consciousness lies at the heart of Wilson Harris's writing. His reviews in *Kyk-over-Al* argued for revolutionary forms of West Indian writing, and his struggle with 'the immediate tool of the words' emerged in hauntingly original visions of the Guyanese interior.

> The living jungle is too full of voices
> not to be aware of collectivity
> and too swift with unseen wings
> to capture certainty.
>
> Branches against the sky tender to heaven the beauty
> of the world: the store-house of heaven
> breaks walls to drop tall streams.

Green islands
and bright leaves lift their blossom of sunrise
And the setting sun wears a wild rose like blood.[30]

The Lost Steps [*Los pasos perdidos*] by the Cuban writer Alejo Carpentier
appeared in 1953. The first-person narrator is a Latin-American music
academic who went into voluntary exile in New York after the war.
Stultified by its urban culture, he makes a geographical and metaphysical
journey up the Orinoco and into primitive time, searching for his own
racial 'lost steps', and those of mankind itself. Among the primitive tribes
he recovers primal human consciousness. 'And when from seeing I turned
to looking, strange lights sprang up and everything took on meaning'.[31]
He returns to civilisation with a transformed perception of reality. There
are significant parallels between *The Lost Steps* and Wilson Harris's *Palace
of the Peacock* (1960), although Carpentier's symphonic, wide-ranging work
begins from a surrealist and intellectual tradition, while Harris's rises
overwhelmingly from his encounter with the jungle, however complex
its development. In an early passage the narrator finds himself alone.

> A brittle moss and carpet appeared underfoot, and dry pond
> and stream whose course and reflection and image had been
> stamped for ever like the breathless outline of a dream
> skeleton in the earth. The trees rose around me into
> upward flying limbs when I screwed my eyes to stare from
> underneath above. At last I lifted my head into a normal
> position. The heavy undergrowth had lightened. The forest
> rustled and rippled with a sigh and ubiquitous step. I
> stopped dead where I was, frightened for no reason
> whatsoever. The step near me stopped and stood still.[32]

The narrator is standing on the forest floor, but also on the 'living skeleton' of past rivers: his awareness of self evokes the terrifying awareness of
other presences, for he is taking part in a ghostly journey, the reenactment
of an earlier expedition in which all had drowned.

The story begins when Donne, an early explorer and tyrannical coloniser, is shot by Mariella, the Amerindian serving-girl he had beaten and
abused. The name 'Donne' conjures up the poet and divine John Donne,
contemporary with the first exploration of Guiana. Harris quotes lines
from Donne's 'Hymn to God my God, in my Sickness', which identifies
the body as a map, life as a journey, and the paradox that as

> In all flat maps (and I am one) are one,
>   So death doth touch the resurrection.

                                                        (ll. 14–15)

Harris's story, too, explores the voyage through death to life. The historical John Donne had two identities, the carnal poet of *Songs and Sonnets*, and the spiritual divine of *Holy Sonnets*. Harris's Donne too is divided between the materialist and idealistic aspects of Europe's encounter with the New World, and is conceived of as two 'characters', the expedition leader seeing through a 'dead seeing material eye', and the narrator with a 'living closed spiritual eye'.[33] As the narrator 'pored over the map of the sun my brother had given me', he finds himself precipitated into his terrifying journey. The expedition into the inner self involves different racial identities both in the individual (Harris himself is of mixed blood) and in the Guyanese nation. Donne's crew includes the Indian (Vigilance), African (Carroll and Jennings), Portuguese/Afro-Scot (Cameron), German/Arawak (Schomburgh) and British (Donne/Dreamer and Wishrop). The identities are both ethnic and psychological. Vigilance steers the boat with the spiritual insight of Indian mysticism; Carroll represents the African genius for music and rhythm, plying his paddle 'like violin', while Jennings, the engineer, powers the boat with African endurance. However diverse, they are also intimately related. 'The whole crew was one spiritual family living and dying together'.[34]

Donne's death from the bullet of Mariella terminates the first, violent stage of colonialism, and initiates a search for redemption. 'Mariella' is now conceived as being a mission station in the interior. As the expedition progresses, the two 'visions' begin to merge. The narrator in a nightmare realises Donne's need for 'the devil of resistance and incredulity' to resist the 'flaw of a universal creation' in a fallen world, while Donne the leader softens, determined not to be 'involved in my own devil's schemes any more'.[35] Yet they remain unable to accept life in its full reality.

> 'Put it how you like', I cried, 'it's fear of acknowledging
> the true substance of life. Yes, fear I tell you, the fear that
> breeds bitterness in our mouth, the haunting sense of fear
> that poisons us and hangs us and murders us'.[36]

This 'true substance' takes shape in the form of an Arawak woman who emerges from the jungle to be their guide. Her timeless face is beyond opposition and conflict, the divisions of race and culture. 'An unearthly pointlessness was her true manner, an all-inclusive manner that still contrived to be − as a duck sheds water from its wings − the negation of every threat of conquest and of fear . . .'[37] Confronting the ultimate reality the crew find themselves fighting a terrifying rapid, in which the Arawak woman and the waterfall become one. 'Her crumpled bosom and river grew agitated with desire, bottling and shaking every fear and inhibition and outcry'.[38] Carroll, the youngest of the crew, tries to stand up, and is drowned.

In the violence of the second half of the novel, one by one the crew die, merging into the expanding consciousness of personal and national identity. This transformation is signalled through the narrative style, which shifts from stark objectivity into surrealist poetic prose. The horizontal voyage through time changes to the vertical climb up a huge waterfall, into eternity: 'Time had no meaning'.[39] In the 'holy room' of living rock we find Mariella, now with aspects of Mary the mother of God, radiant amid surging images of creation. Donne passes the ultimate stage of self-knowledge and self-abnegation. 'It was the unflinching clarity with which he looked into himself and saw that all his life he had loved no one but himself'.[40] He goes blind and sees; he loses himself and discovers identity. In John Donne's poem, redemption was expressed as harmony –

> Since I am coming to that holy room
> Where, with Thy choir of saints for evermore
> I shall be made thy music.[41]

Harris's Donne, too, becomes one with 'the inner music and voice of the peacock I suddenly encountered and echoed and sang as I had never heard myself sing before'.[42]

Harris draws on an eclectic range of sources, only a few of which have been mentioned here. The epigrams to the four books refer to the poets Yeats, Donne, and Hopkins; Michael Gilkes relates the work to the processes of medieval alchemy,[43] and Harris himself has drawn attention to the parallel with Rimbaud's dream poem 'Bateau Ivre' ['The Drunken Boat'].[44] More recently Harris has linked the narrative to the Carib ritual where, the mourners 'ate a ritual morsel and fashioned the bone that supported that morsel into a magical flute'. The music of the flute becomes a 'transubstantiation complex' which simultaneously embodies the tragedy of death and the beauty of life, 'the impulse to re-trace one's steps over lost ground, to visualise a womb of recovery'.[45] The intuitive web of the Caribbean past becomes woven into the woof of Harris's narrative.

Earlier, in 1972, the Guyanese scholar, musician and writer Michael Gilkes had been commissioned to write the play *Couvade* for the first Caribbean Festival of Arts, which was held in Guyana. In the Amerindian/Carib ritual of the title, the father painfully shares in the birth of his child, a subject Wilson Harris had recently explored in *The Sleepers of Roraima* (1970). Gilkes dramatises the 'Couvade' of Lionel, a contemporary painter whose work pivots between the tribal and modern, and as Pat his wife gives birth to a child of mixed ancestry, the bloodstained robe of Lionel's initiation becomes his work of art, a painting of the many races of Guyana. Using music and dance and vision, Gilkes evokes the perspectives of Amerindian and African shamanism, popular preaching, and political oratory, ending with a prayer for the 'Couvade' of the birth of the Guyanese nation – 'Sleep, Couvade, and dream our dream'.[46] Harris's pervasive influence has been all the more creative in focusing on ways of seeing, not ways of writing. It can be traced in the distinctively individual poetry of Mark McWatt, published in *Interiors* (1988) and *The Language of El Dorado* (1994), and Ian McDonald, whose *Essequibo* appeared in 1992. In both, a haunting awareness of the Caribbean interior modulates the artist's explorations of inner space, and his ancestral intuitions.

A very different sensibility emerges in the work of another Guyanese novelist, Roy Heath. Heath's eye for detail vividly evokes middle-class life in Georgetown, trapped in a limbo between jungle and ocean. His characters hover on the edge of psychic disintegration under pressures often only suggested. In his first novel, *A Man Come Home* (1974), Foster Bird becomes unaccountably rich, disappearing for long periods. In the final catastrophe the reason eerily emerges: he has been possessed by the love of a 'Fair Maid', the Guyanese vampire. For Galton Flood, in *The Murderer* (1978), the vampire is within, the invisible presence of his dominating mother that draws him, with the logic of paranoia, to separate from, and then coldly murder, his wife Gemma. An extraordinary novel that fuses misty riverine landscapes and bleak tenements with Galton's internal wasteland, it stands as Heath's finest achievement. His 'Georgetown trilogy', *From the Heat of the Day* (1981), *One Generation* (1981) and *Genetha* (1981), details the claustrophobic Armstrong family relationships that invisibly framed Galton's retributive act, a world in which women are the sensitive victims or, like Mrs Singh in the later *The Shadow Bride* (1988), the dark oppressor. *Kwaku* (1982) stands apart from Heath's novels of psychosocial realism, a sequence of fantastic tales united by its eponymous trickster hero, a character he developed in *The Ministry of Hope* (1997).

A more positive vision emerges in the work of two women writers, both of whom reflect the turmoil surrounding the achievement of Guyanese independence and its aftermath. Grace Nichols's *Whole of a Morning Sky* (1986) is a radiant first novel, partly autobiographical, in which passages of poetic evocation are interwoven with the experiences of the Walcott family as they move from a country village to Georgetown city in the 1960s, a time of strikes, racial riots and the struggle for independence. In *Timepiece* (1986), Janice Shinebourne draws on her childhood experiences as a Guyanese Indo-Chinese. It is a more consciously political work, in which plantation life is contrasted with the challenges facing the young Sandra Yansen as a cub reporter in Georgetown. Shinebourne herself has a journalist's eye for idiosyncrasies of behaviour and an ear for local speech, gifts that also enliven *The Last Plantation* (1988), set in the New Dam community in the 1950s. Here the twelve-year-old June Lehall, half Indian and half Chinese, wins a scholarship to a local high school, where crisis within the sugar industry and the intrusion of British troops are implicated in racial conflict, and the rival claims of Hinduism and Christianity.

Two outstanding younger Guyanese writers, Fred D'Aguiar and David Dabydeen, grew up largely in England, and their writing, which will be discussed below, reflects life between two cultures. New ground was broken by Pauline Melville's fine first novel, *The Ventriloquist's Tale* (1997). In turns funny, hallucinatory, erotic and speculative, Melville's conjuring prose explores the life of three generations of Wapisiani Indians. She evokes multiple perspectives and voices. In the background resonate the records of past visitors into the interior. One is Evelyn Waugh, who wrote a dismissive travelogue *Ninety-two Days* (1934) and an episode in *A Handful of Dust* (1934) out of his experience. Another is Claude Lévi-Strauss, who deconstructed Indian myth into the social science of tribal relations. The ultimate narrator or 'ventriloquist' is revealed as Macunaima, the Amerindian hunter and revenge figure, who uses mimicry to lure his prey. He stalks the non-Amerindian reader, adapting the mask of realism because this 'is what is required nowadays', with the aim of 'revenge or tribute. Take your pick'.[47]

The unifying image of the book is incest, the ultimate intimacy and taboo, linked to the eclipse of the sun, which in Wapisiana legend is caused by the illicit coupling of the sun and moon. In the jungle interior, the incestuous passion of the Amerindian siblings Beatrice and Danny brings about the recovery of their tribal identity. It also brings their eclipse, as their love is relentlessly destroyed by the pursuit of Father Daniel, the voice of colonial morality. Their intimacy is paralleled by the passionate love affair between Rosa, an Anglo-Jewish scholar and another 'ventriloquial voice' in the book, and Chofoye, who has mixed Wapisiani and European blood. This relationship, too, transgresses cultural taboos, and also ends in personal darkness but social enlightenment. In the end the logic of Eurocentric realism, encoded in written language, fails. Chofy's son Bla-bla, working for contractors, is killed in an accident, a failure of communication with his American employers. Father Daniel goes insane, and his meticulously kept diaries are burnt. The end foregrounds Indian intuition. The Wapisiani girl Marietta dreams of 'eggs everywhere'. 'Fertility and growth', interprets her Aunt Wilfreda. But Marietta cautions, 'Or maybe I was just thinking of eggs'.[48] The ventriloquist's vision, like Marietta's, remains open.

Notes

1. John Hearne, 'The Fugitive in the Forest', in *The Islands in Between*, edited by Louis James (London, 1968), p. 141.

2. See Norman E. Cameron, *Guianese Poetry* ([1931]; reprinted Nedeln/ Lichtenstein, 1970), pp. 44–58.

3. Reprinted in Paula Burnett, *Caribbean Verse*, pp. 13–15, 374–5.

4. Wilson Harris, 'Afterword', in A.R.F. Webber, *Those that be in Bondage*, with an introduction by Selwyn R. Cudjoe ([1917] Wellesley, 1988), p. 237.

5. See Michael Gilkes, *The West Indian Novel* (Boston, 1981), pp. 132–8.

6. W.H. Hudson, *Green Mansions* ([1904] London, 1957), p. 32.

7. Ibid., pp. 41–2.

8. Ibid., pp. 65–6.

9. Edgar Mittelholzer, *Shadows Move Among Them* ([1951] London, 1961), p. 201.

10. Ibid., p. 182.

11. Ibid., p. 254.

12. Edgar Mittelholzer, *My Bones and my Flute* ([1955] London, 1974), p. 168.

13. Jan Carew, *Black Midas* (London, 1958), p. 9.

14. Ibid., p. 165.

15. Ibid., p. 42.

16. Ibid., p. 213.

17. *AJS at 70*, edited by Ian McDonald (Georgetown, Guyana, 1968).

18. A.J. Seymour, 'Over Guiana, Clouds' (Georgetown Guyana, 1944), reprinted in *Caribbean Voices*, edited by John Figueroa, vol. 1 (London, 1966), p. 42.

19. l.e. brathwaite [Edward Kamau Brathwaite], 'Kyk-over-Al and the Radicals', *New World* (Guyana Independence Issue, 1966), p. 55.

20. Ibid., pp. 55–63.

21. *Selected Poems* (Georgetown, Guyana, 1989), p. 59.

22. 'No Madness like this Sanity', *Selected Poems* (Georgetown, Guyana, Demerara Publishers, 1989), p. 25.

23. 'I come from the Nigger Yard', ibid., p. 62.

24. Ibid., p. 45.

25. Ibid., p. 52.

26. Ibid., p. 61.

27. Peter Trevis, 'Interview with Martin Carter', reprinted in *Hinterland*, p. 68.

28. 'The Death of a Slave' (excerpt), ibid., p. 50.

29. Martin Carter, 'The Great Dark', from *Songs of Succession* (1977), reprinted in *Selected Poems* (Georgetown, Guyana, 1989), p. 115.

30. 'Amazon', Wilson Harris, *From Eternity to Season* ([1954] London, 1978), p. 15.

31. Ibid., p. 209.

32. Wilson Harris, *The Palace of the Peacock* (London, 1960), pp. 27–8.

33. Ibid., p. 14.

34. Ibid., p. 40.

35. Ibid., p. 57.

36. Ibid., p. 59.

37. Ibid., p. 74.

38. Ibid., p. 73.

39. Ibid., p. 133.

40. Ibid., p. 140.

41. John Donne, 'Hymn to God my God, in my Sickness', ll. 1–3.

42. Wilson Harris, 'The Enigma of Values', *New Letters* 40, 1 (1973), pp. 146–8; *Palace*, p. 152.

43. Michael Gilkes, *Wilson Harris and the Caribbean Novel* (London, 1973); see also Hena Maes-Jelinek, *The Naked Design* (Aarhus, 1976).

44. '. . . another window upon the Universe, another drunken boat . . .', Wilson Harris, *Tradition, the Writer and Society* (London, 1967), p. 35.

45. Wilson Harris, 'The Enigma of Values', *New Letters* 40, 1 (October 1973), pp. 146–8.

46. Michael Gilkes, *Couvade. A Dream-play of Guyana* (London, 1974), p. 65.

47. Pauline Melville, *The Ventriloquist's Tale* (London, 1997), p. 9. I am indebted to Paula Burnett for part of this reading.

48. Ibid., p. 352.

Chapter 7
'Brit'n'

What Lamming called the 'phenomenon' of West Indian literature began, not with the work of de Lisser, McKay and C.L.R. James, but after the Second World War. It was created not in the Caribbean, but in London. For West Indians educated under colonialism, the exile of slavery had been succeeded more subtly by the alienation of West Indians from their home ground in the Caribbean. In Lamming's Barbados 'something called culture, all of it, in the form of words, came from outside: Dickens, Jane Austen, Kipling and that sacred gang'.[1] For Shiva Naipaul, growing up in Trinidad,

> Port-of-Spain was a ghost city. Real places were cold places and this city with its narrow, choked streets and crowded pavements smothered by an unbearable heat of steaming in the aftermath of a heavy downpour, could not be taken seriously. . . . To use the Platonic analogy, we lived in a cave and could only follow the dim play of the shadows thrown on its walls by the bright sun shining outside; a sun we could see for ourselves when we grew up and 'went away' from the island.[2]

A literary invasion of Britain was led by Edgar Mittelholzer, who arrived in England in 1948 with the text of a novel, *A Morning at the Office*, in his suitcase. He felt himself 'a general at the head of an army, and the objectives were clearly defined . . . Final victory would be represented by the acceptance of a novel by a publisher'.[3] In 1950, it was published by Hogarth Press, a propitious work with which to open a West Indian literary movement, for in a *tour de force* portraying a microcosm of Trinidadian society with its diversity, tensions and creative potential in five hours traffic in the Office of Essential Products Ltd, Mittelholzer identified the issues of cultural displacement and racial identity that were to be central to the explosion of West Indian writing that was to follow.

Between 1950 and 1970 over 125,000 workers were recruited from the Caribbean by a Britain in need of cheap labour. As George Lamming

noted, the immigrants gained a new self-awareness, as those from individual islands found themselves for the first time categorised as 'West
Indian'.[4] In 1950 George Lamming and Samuel Selvon arrived at Tilbury
on the same ship, forming the nucleus of what was to become a literary
movement. In *The Emigrants* (1954), Lamming titled his fictional ship the
'Golden Image', ironically reversing Europe's seventeenth-century quest
for El Dorado. But on arrival, those on the boat train express a coda of
bewilderment:

> When we get outta this smoke,
>   When we get outta this smoke, w'at happen next?
> More smoke.[5]

The image of blurred vision, as Sandra Paquet notes,[6] reflects a mental
paralysis, and the confusion of the crowded 'middle passage' of the voyage
is repeated in the immigrants' fragmented experience of London, much of
which is set in spaces below ground, in a darkened hairdresser's, or a
cellar club. Encounters with the English further alienate the immigrants.
Black males are objects of sexual curiosity, and Collis, a writer and Lamming's fictional alter ego, is patronised by a 'liberal' middle-class English
couple. The novel ends in a riot at a night club in which the West
Indian proprietor decamps, leaving an African to take responsibility for
the chaos. Collis 'returned to the window and watched the night slip by
between the light and the trees',[7] poised between despair and desire.
Simon Gikandi has argued persuasively that the state of exile takes the
colonised out of the 'twilight zone of colonial culture' to recover their
lost consciousness of self, and recreate a new psychic and social identity.[8]
Lamming's fiction, however, was to explore his own insight that 'to be
colonial is to be in a state of exile'[9] with increasing pessimism. Caliban's
words, cited in the title of his novel, *Water with Berries* (1972), from *The
Tempest*, draw the reader to see Teeton as a West Indian Caliban living in
Hampstead in thrall to the Prospero of his white landlady, a love–hate
relationship he can only escape by murdering her and burning her body.
Another immigrant, the actor Roger, playing a corpse on stage, comes
alive and rapes the heroine, who is called Miranda. The novel ends in
escalating violence, conflict precipitating into the void of an unknown
future. Lamming's *Emigrants* was the first of a series of novels exploring
West Indian alienation in Britain. Andrew Salkey's uprooted black protagonists in *Escape to an Autumn Pavement* (1960) and *The Adventures of
Catullus Kelly* (1969) are young middle-class males who seek fulfilment
largely in sex, but sex is itself trapped in stereotypes of race and gender. In
Escape Johnny Sobert, unhappy in heterosexual relationships, is drawn to
his homosexual friend Dick, but held back by his black macho self-image.
Alienation became global. The protagonists of Salkey's *The Late Emancipation*

of Jerry Stover (1968) and *Come Home Malcolm Heartland* (1976) are lost 'immigrants' back home in Jamaica, as is the young sociologist Alex, in Orlando Patterson's novel *An Absence of Ruins* (1967).

Sam Selvon gave the immigrant experience a quite different voice, one coming from outside any 'literary' tradition. His parents in Trinidad could not afford his further education, and he was to declare 'I never consciously made the decision to be a writer. It kind of worked out because about the best thing I was good at at school was writing essays'.[10] He consistently refused to take part in any West Indian 'literary movements', and his fictional persona in *Moses Ascending* was to declare 'I know of Accles and Pollock, but not of Lamming and Salkey'. When he turned experimentally from standard English to the Trinidad idiom while writing *The Lonely Londoners*, he found that 'it worked, and suddenly you know it was like sailing along . . .'.

The novel begins

> One grim winter evening, when it had a kind of unrealness
> about London, with a fog sleeping restlessly over the city
> and the lights showing in the blur as if it is not London at
> all but some strange place on another planet, Moses Aloetta
> hop on a number 46 bus at the corner of Chepstow Road
> and Westbourne Grove to go to Waterloo to meet a fellar
> who was coming from Trinidad on the boat-train.[11]

London fog has been used by writers from Dickens to T.S. Eliot, but Selvon transforms the perspective. The intimacy of boarding 'a number 46 bus at the corner of Chepstow Road' is in tension with the strangeness of 'a fog sleeping restlessly over the city . . . as if it is not London at all', and further distanced by the language 'it had a kind of unrealness about London.' The reader is aware of the familiar, reshaped by a Caribbean sensibility and idiom. Selvon's emigrants come to 'old Brit'n', but see it anew. Marble Arch, Virginia Water, Paddington become places to 'lime' [idle], to hustle pussy [chase girls], to cook rice and peas huddled over basement gas fires, or just 'watch the big life'. Individual origins are irrelevant: Jamaicans, Barbadians, Trinidadians, and even Africans are distinguished not by provenance, but by personality. The social structures are Caribbean, and a West Indian village appears in London city. The matriarchal Tanty Bessy sets up credit scores in the local shops, West Indian style, and insists that shop-keepers wrap up the bread. Ostensibly this society is male-centred, but the men are characteristically insecure, at once part of a community and isolated within it. In this vulnerable context, names take on a mock-heroic status. The reluctant leader of these lost tribes is called Moses. Henry Oliver arrives in London armed with only three pounds and a toothbrush, and Moses christens him the heroic Galahad. A blue-black Barbadian is called Five (five past midnight). Expectations are reversed. Galahad sweats in winter and shivers in summer. London altern-ates between decay and glamour. 'The houses round here old and grey and weatherbeaten, the walls cracking like the last days of Pompeii'.[12] Yet London is the centre of the imaginative universe. 'Always, from the first time [Galahad] went there to see Eros and the lights, that circus have a magnet for him, that circus represent life, that circus is the beginning and the ending of the world'.[13]

Against all probability, Lamming and Selvon found themselves in the centre of a literary movement. To quote Lamming again:

> This historical fact is that the 'emergence' of a dozen or so novelists in the British Caribbean with some fifty books to their credit or disgrace, and all published between 1948 and 1958, is in the nature of a phenomenon. There has been no comparable event in culture anywhere in the British Commonwealth during the same period.[14]

The 'movement' at the time was the cumulation of chance meetings in the bed-sitters, bars, barber shops and other meeting points of the im-migrant's metropolis. There were introductions and recommendations to editors and literary agents. There were poems and short stories written to pay the gas meter and the rent. A key resource was the BBC programme which had grown out of Una Marson's 1938 programme, 'Calling the West Indies'. In 1946 it became *Caribbean Voices*, a half-hour programme beamed on Sunday afternoons to the West Indies, edited by Henry Swanzy, whose previous work in West Africa gave him an interest in non-British writing. The programme provided money for struggling authors, and an incentive to write. Swanzy and, from 1954, V.S. Naipaul also gave free editorial advice. Although there was some editing, *Caribbean Voices* was *spoken*, and by West Indians, breaking down the barrier between print and the popular oral tradition at a time when writers were beginning to challenge the colonial linguistic models. It linked the Caribbean with its emigrants, and forged a common identity among the islands themselves. Visiting Barbados, the Jamaican John Figueroa was greeted familiarly by an islander who 'knew' him from his voice, broadcast from London. The programme became a club through which West Indian writers came to recognise each other, and share the common typing room reserved by the BBC for freelance writers. It helped launch the careers of V.S. Naipaul, Edgar Mittelholzer, Samuel Selvon, George Lamming, Michael Anthony and Andrew Salkey, forming a nucleus for the West Indian literary 'phenomenon' that followed. Andrew Salkey's work as freelance writer and reporter was also central. Salkey, who had come to London in 1952 as a student at University College, made it his professional interest to discover and keep track of West Indian writers, whether in London or the Caribbean. A tireless organiser, his great gift for friendship made his Moscow Road flat a meeting point for the constant flux of immigrant talent. A brilliant editor, he assembled and introduced new work through his pioneering anthologies, *West Indian Stories* (1960), *Stories from the Caribbean* (1965) and *Breaklight: An Anthology of Caribbean Poetry* (1971).

The 1960s began with three important works, each of which is considered elsewhere in this book. Wilson Harris's *Palace of the Peacock* (1960) opened up new vistas for Caribbean fiction, a visionary exploration of the Guyanese hinterland, its history and identity. Harris's influence on West Indian literature was a submerged one, his work too 'difficult' to attract a popular readership, yet it challenged writers to reject Eurocentric forms and concepts for a new Caribbean aesthetic. V.S. Naipaul's *A House for Mr Biswas* (1961) massively validated Trinidadian common life as the subject for serious fiction. In 1962, Derek Walcott's *In a Green Night* demonstrated that West Indian poetry could encompass both European and Caribbean traditions, without being confined by either.

Meanwhile, West Indian writing was setting down roots in Britain. A redoubtable pioneer had been Beryl Gilroy, who arrived in London from Guyana in 1951, trained as a child psychotherapist, and became the first black headmistress of a London primary school, a remarkable career recorded in her autobiographical *Black Teacher* (1976). Her short stories for children, and later her adult novels, such as *Boy-Sandwich* (1989), both reflect and contribute to the shaping of a multi-cultural consciousness in Britain. James Berry arrived in London in 1947, and his verse, from *Fractured Circles* (1979) through to *Chain of Days* (1985), records simultaneous immersion in the immigrant experience, and a recovery, in exile, of his Afro-Jamaican inheritance. Starting as a writer-in-residence in a London comprehensive school in 1977, and editing the major collections of West Indian-British verse, *Blue-foot Traveller* (1976) and *News for Babylon* (1984), Berry played a significant role in establishing a cultural bridgehead for the Caribbean in London. Archie Markham from Montserrat moved to Britain in 1956. His first love, theatre, brings a multi-vocal quality to his writing which relates the Caribbean to the international scene, including Continental Europe, Northern Ireland, and Papua New Guinea, where he has taught. A tireless editor and publicist, with a body of lively verse selected in *Human Rites* (1984), Markham reflects a centrifugal dynamic in Caribbean writing. Notable among a growing body of 'Black British' writers was the Guyanese poet John Agard, who declared that 'mugging de Queen's English/is the story of my life . . .'[15]

There was, equally, a centripetal impulse. In 1965 Edward (now Kamau) Brathwaite began research at the University of Sussex, fired with enthusiasm for a Caribbean cultural movement, but he found little common purpose in the expatriate community. He turned to Andrew Salkey, with his energy and encyclopaedic knowledge of the West Indian writers, and John la Rose, a Trinidadian with Marxist trades union experience. La Rose, with Sarah White, had just set up an independent West Indian publishing firm in London, New Beacon Books, and had himself published a volume of engagé poems, *Foundations* (1966). He shared with Salkey an interest in the French and Spanish, as well as the British, Caribbean. At a meeting in Salkey's flat in late 1966, the Caribbean Artists Movement, or 'CAM', came into existence. During the next two decades the Movement held over fifty meetings[16] in private homes and in the West Indian Student Centre in London, culminating in two major conferences at the University of Kent, Canterbury, in 1977 and 1978. CAM circulated a *Newsletter*, and from 1970 to 1989, an important occasional periodical, *Savacou*. The historian Elsa Goveia in a landmark paper, 'The Social Framework',[17] called for a new vision of the Caribbean. The Movement set out to create a holistic, Caribbean-based perspective on its cultures, including literature, social history, the performing and visual arts, folk-lore, education and publishing.

The arguments of Frantz Fanon's *The Wretched of the Earth* (1962) were much in the air. Fanon, a Martinican whose experience of race and colonialism in the French Caribbean had been brought sharply into focus by the Algerian civil war, demanded that the colonised intellectual tear himself with violence from Western culture, 'painful and difficult though it may be', and shake his people out of lethargy by creating a 'fighting literature, a national literature'.[18] 'In this work', wrote one CAM member, Orlando Patterson, 'Fanon has pointed the way to the creation of the new man. Let us follow in his footsteps'.[19] The revolutionary atmosphere was intensified by political unrest in the Caribbean itself, and Black Rights movements in the United States. Martin Luther King visited London in 1964, Stokely Carmichael (now Kwame Ture) in 1967; both events had a direct impact on CAM discussions of Afro-Caribbean black identity.[20] There was no place for private feelings, and after heated sessions in the London West Indian Student Centre, CAM speakers could be found soothing their wounded egos with Red Stripe beers, or something stronger, in the smoke-filled bar.

CAM brought to prominence the views of the artists Aubrey Williams, Ronald Moody and Jerry Craig; the writers C.L.R. James, Wilson Harris and Michael Anthony, and the critics Gordon Rohlehr and Kenneth Ramchand. It had an impact both in England and abroad, with the Brathwaites continuing to campaign for the CAM agenda when they returned to Jamaica in 1972. The achievement of the Movement has been finely researched by Anne Walmsley in *The Caribbean Artists Movement: 1966–1972* (1992). Yet as noticed above, other cultural movements were developing in the Caribbean itself. The first Carifesta was held in Guyana in 1972, a massive arts festival that brought together over a thousand delegates from across the Caribbean, including Brazil, Venezuela, Colombia and Mexico. Carifesta shared CAM's ideals, and featured prominent CAM members, including Kamau Brathwaite. But it had been conceived, independently, at the Caribbean Writers' and Artists' Convention held in Guyana in early 1966. In retrospect, important as CAM was, it was but one strand in a worldwide awakening of Caribbean culture.

Notes

1. George Lamming, *Pleasures* (London, 1960), p. 27.

2. Shiva Naipaul, 'The Writer Without a Society', in Anna Rutherford (ed.), *Commonwealth* (Aarhus, 1971), p. 115.

3. Edgar Mittelholzer, *A Swarthy Boy* (London, 1963), p. 147.

4. George Lamming, *Pleasures* (London, 1960), p. 214.

5. Ibid., p. 124.

6. Sandra Pouchet Paquet, *The Novels of George Lamming* (London, 1982), p. 35.

7. George Lamming, *The Emigrants* (London, 1954), p. 271.

8. Simon Gikandi, *Writing in Limbo. Modernism and Caribbean Literature* (1992), p. 13, and passim.

9. George Lamming, *Pleasures* (London, 1960), p. 229.

10. Daryl Cumber Dance, *New World Adams* (Leeds, 1992), p. 232.

11. Samuel Selvon, *The Lonely Londoners* ([1956] London, 1972), p. 7.

12. Ibid., p. 57.

13. Ibid., p. 74.

14. George Lamming, *Pleasures* (London, 1960), p. 29.

15. John Agard, 'Listen Mr Oxford don', *Mangoes and Bullets* (London, 1985), p. 44.

16. Anne Walmsley, *The Caribbean Artists Movement 1966–1972* (London, 1992), pp. 323–7.

17. *Savacou* 2 (2 September 1970), pp. 7–15.

18. Frantz Fanon, *The Damned* [*Les damnées de la terre*], translated by Constance Farrington (Paris, 1973), p. 176.

19. Orlando Patterson, 'Frantz Fanon: my Hope and Hero', *New World*, Guyana Independence Issue, (1966), p. 95.

20. Anne Walmsley, *The Caribbean Artists Movement* (1992), pp. 27–8; 90–1.

Part III
Towards a Caribbean Aesthetic

Every dialect is a way of thinking . . .

Frantz Fanon[1]

A return of our writers to a sense of responsibility to West Indian society will be reflected I think in a sense of style: in a greater and more careful understanding of what the novel form means.

Kamau Brathwaite[2]

Both Anglophone and Hispanophone Caribbean writers have followed Carpentier by asserting that the New World possesses an original aesthetic virtually embedded in its social and natural landscapes, a magical reality unavailable to the European artist or writer. Not the writer's style, but the historical scene that his or her writing reveals, provides the magic.

David Mikics[3]

Alongside creative writing in the Caribbean, an aesthetic debate has developed. Three main lines of inquiry may be discerned: the impact of the area's geography, its history and its language. Each of these will be considered in turn.

Chapter 8
Place

Like the other 'new literatures in English' of Africa, Australia, Canada or North America, West Indian writing is rooted in the place of its conceiving. Wilson Harris has written that the West Indian artist 'lives in a comparatively bare world – mountains, jungles, rivers – where the monumental architecture of the old world is the exception rather than the rule',[4] and from the logbooks of the earliest explorers to the recent poetry and fiction, Caribbean literature has recorded elemental encounters with sea, island, or primal forest. Writers have increasingly found that these encounters with a new world required new forms of expression. Early West Indian writers took their models from the English Romantics and Victorians, from Yeats or Edward Thomas. But by the 1960s poems like 'We who do not know the snow' by the St Vincentian Daniel Williams,[5] or the Jamaican H.D. Carberry's 'Nature', were consciously attempting to shape their form to Caribbean landscapes and seasons:

> We have neither Summer nor Winter
> Neither Autumn nor Spring.
>
> We have instead the days
> When gold sun shines on the lush green canefields –
> Magnificently.[6]

Lloyd Brown has demonstrated how West Indian poets from Carl Rattray to Wordsworth McAndrew developed 'John Crow' (the West Indian vulture) as a vernacular image, expressive of the harsh Caribbean landscape, and the paradox of black 'ugliness' and power in its peoples.[7] As a child in St Lucia in the 1930s, Derek Walcott had contemplated 'as through the glass of some provincial gallery . . . the stuffed dark nightingale of Keats'[8] so loved by his father. But his own early volume, *Selected Poems* (1964), included a 'Tropical Bestiary',[9] the 'Ibis', 'Octopus', 'Lizard', 'Man o' War Bird', 'Whale' and 'Tarpon'. The sea-crab's

> cunning, halting, awkward grace
> Is the syntactical envy of my hand;

Obliquity burrowing to surface
From hot, plain sand.
Those who require vision, complexity,
Will tire of its distressing
Limits: sea, sand, scorching sky.
Keep to your ground, though constellations race,
The horizon burn, the wave coil, hissing
Salt sting the eye.[10]

Other poets addressed sensibilities attuned to drought, to tropical light and colour.

Daylight like yellow cassia flowers
Daylight like clean water
Daylight like green cacti
Daylight like sea sparkling with white horses
Daylight like sunstrained blue sky
Daylight like tropic hills
Daylight like a sacrament in my hands.
Amen.

George Campbell, 'Litany'[11]

Writers distinguished the range of Caribbean topography. A.L. Hendrik's elegant verse explored the edges of silence in the Jamaican highlands;[12] Frank Collymore described the sounds, sight and scents of the sea permeating his Barbadian experience:

Like all who live on small islands
I must always be remembering the sea,
Being always cognizant of her presence; viewing
Her through apertures in the foliage; hearing,
When the wind is from the south, her music, and smelling
The warm rankness of her . . .

'Hymn to the Sea'[13]

Peculiarly, West Indian landscapes were both alien and familiar. Uprooted slaves found themselves still in a tropical world, eating yams and drinking coconut milk. British travellers encountered islands imaginatively mapped in the wilderness of *Robinson Crusoe*. There appeared to be little evidence of past civilisations. The region is in fact stubbled with relics, but a history of European rapacity conspired with the tropical climate to green over these ruins, both literally and metaphorically, draining their historical significance and absorbing them into the cyclical flux of tropical rain, drought and hurricane. Derek Walcott has written of 'an absence of ruins':

If art is where the greatest ruins are
Our art is in the ruins we became
You will not find in these green, desert places,
One stone that found us worthy of the name . . .[14]

The real West Indian history was written not in its stones, but in African palm trees or Indian banana groves, in the living seeds brought from other worlds in the holds of privateers, in the cabinets of amateur botanists, and in the guts of slaves. The naming of Caribbean places began as acts of colonial possession. But Old World names given by Europeans 'in nostalgia or irony' shimmered into the Caribbean landscape, and were changed. Derek Walcott wrote of two Trinidad villages named after Spanish towns:

[The immigrants'] memories turned acid
but the names held,
Valencia glows
with the lanterns of oranges,
Mayaro's
charred candelabra of cocoa.[15]

Liberated by his creative imagination, the young Walcott felt the intoxication of being another Adam, recreating the world through language:

We were blest with a virginal, unpainted world
with Adam's task of giving things their names . . .[16]

Yet the image of Adam's world was itself imported from another culture: to reinterpret it, writing had to be a constant effort of self-abnegation, a purification of style.

I seek,
As climate seeks its style, to write
Verse crisp as sand, clear as sunlight,
Cold as the curled wave, ordinary
As a tumbler of island water . . .[17]

As will be seen below,[18] Walcott was to change his figure for the poet from Adam and the marooned Crusoe, looking to find ways of apprehending the landscape that lie beneath those of the English classics. He turned to Homer's *Odyssey*, which predated the shaping of a European literary tradition. Homer embodied an ancient Mediterranean culture based on exploration and commerce. Its maps marked not conquest but quest, offering the writer an alternative aesthetic to the coloniser's, one based on voyaging and spiritual encounter.

Southwards in continental Guiana, Wilson Harris also found that his encounter with the jungles of the interior affected his art.

> I had penetrated 150 miles. It seemed as if one had
> travelled thousands and thousands of miles, and in fact had
> travelled to another world, as it were, because one was
> suddenly aware of the fantastic density of place. One was
> aware of one's incapacity to describe it, as if the tools of
> language one possessed were inadequate.[19]

His writing was to be a continuous search for an alchemy of language through which to communicate what he experienced.

> Untangled the trees mount to the sky
> and the silence is filled with a different wave like sound
> that alters dimension. The cool cave of ship
> is suddenly beached with sun
> is drowned in a fluid ecstasy that devours and is devoured
>   in turn
> external yet profound.
>
> The voyage between two worlds
> is fraught with this grandeur and this anonymity.[20]

Behind the intense coloration lay a nature drained by heat and drought, flooded by hurricane, cataclysmic with earthquake and volcano. It was not the sun of a European or North American poet. Harris wrote:

> I have lived for long periods in savannahs so much exposed
> to heat and fire, that the sun becomes an adversary – one
> of two antagonistic principles – night and day – and only
> an association of these two principles provides
> release. . . . The sun is indeed a great reality in the West
> Indian world in a more terrible sense than the poet realises
> when he exclaims:
>   Sun's in my blood.[21]

Harris became aware not only of natural presences but of other ancestors of the forests, 'the Amerindian/Arawak . . . in the long march into the twentieth century out of the Pre-Columbian mists of time'. It is an intuition luminously explored in visual art by his friend and compatriot, Aubrey Williams, who before his untimely death in 1990 fused landscape and the cultural inheritance of the past in his extraordinary paintings, some of which are reproduced in *Guyana Dreaming* (1990).[22] There are

few more moving witnesses to the interpenetration of words and image
than the shared Guyanese world of Williams's speaking art and Harris's
visionary writing.

Landscape and peoples became fused in other ways, in Caribbean writing. Rural writing in Jamaica was dominated by the human experience
of the mountains: in Roger Mais's haunting lines, 'All men come to the
hills/Finally . . .'[23] The island labourer's rhythmic toil and love of the
earth is vibrantly evoked in Evan Jones's 'Song of the Banana Man':

> 'I leave m'yard early-mornin time
> An set m'foot to de mountain climb,
> I ben' m' back to de hot-sun toil,
> An' m' cutlass rings on de stony soil,
> Ploughin' an weedin', diggin an plantin
> Till Massa Sun drop back o John Crow mountain,
> Den home again in cool evenin time,
> Perhaps whistling dis likkle rhyme,
>
> (*Sung*) Praise God an m' big right han
> I will live an die a banana man'.[24]

In Trinidad, Eric Roach explored in stabbing verse a harsher vision of
constricted toil on an often barren island.

> Prisoners of history
> Our skin and circumstance
> We have small room to dance;
> A thin shard of land
> Defiant of the sea
> Defines our destiny.
>   'Caribbean Calypso'[25]

For Roach, Trinidad is a 'flowering rock' out of which the poor wrest a
hard and uncertain living, where 'hearts break not, though they are ever
broken'.

> Oh, from gaunt rock
> As white as sanctity
> The lily blooms:
> Essence of darkness is
> Too pure for fragrance,
> The stilled stone,
> The still voice of the skeleton.[26]

Roach can be taken as culminating the progression from early Caribbean writing of landscape, heavily influenced by Keats and Wordsworth, to a vision baptised into the Caribbean experience of a tropical environment. European images may persist, yet they have now become exotic; metaphysical rather than natural. Thus in Roach's 'Hawk Heart', man's lot is symbolised as a leafless tree, a motif taken from European winter. But it is transformed by a Caribbean experience of heat, drought and hurricane:

> Oh, may the sun burn open cages
> Of my being, heal my halt hope.
> Hawk my desire past horizoning islands
> To cry world over wisdom's words,
> A tempest to the spirit, beating
> Rank darkness back, a fire to crack
> Man's winterfall of fear,
> And recall pentecostal spring.[27]

Notes

1. Frantz Fanon, *Black Skin, White Masks* ([1952] London, 1986), p. 25.

2. Kamau Brathwaite, 'Roots' [1963], reprinted in *Roots* (Ann Arbor, 1993), p. 54.

3. David Mikics, 'Derek Walcott and Alejo Carpentier', in *Magic Realism: Theory, History, Community*, edited by Lois Parkinson and Wendy B. Faris (Durham, North Carolina, 1995), p. 373.

4. Wilson Harris, *Tradition, the Writer and Society* (London, 1967), p. 13.

5. *Caribbean Voices*, selected by John Figueroa (London, 1966) vol. I, p. 29.

6. Ibid., p. 25.

7. Lloyd W. Brown, *The Emergence of Modern West Indian Poetry 1940–1960*, 2nd edition (London, 1984), pp. 70–5.

8. Derek Walcott, *Another Life*, p. 41.

9. *Selected Poems* (New York, 1964), pp. 63–66.

10. Ibid., p. 65.

11. George Campbell, *First Poems* (London, 1945), p. 14.

12. A.L. Hendriks, *On this Mountain* (London, 1965).

13. *Caribbean Voices*, vol. II, p. 84.

14. Derek Walcott, 'The Royal Palms', *The London Magazine* 1, 11 (February 1962), pp. 12–13.

15. Derek Walcott, 'Names', in *Sea Grapes* (London, 1976), pp. 40–2.

16. Derek Walcott, *Another Life*, p. 145.

17. 'Islands', Derek Walcott, *In a Green Night* (London, 1962), p. 77.

18. See below, pp. 181–3.

19. Wilson Harris, 'A Talk on the Subjective Imagination', *New Letters* 40, 1 (Fall, 1973), p. 38.

20. Wilson Harris, 'Behring Straits', *Eternity to Season*, revised edition ([1954] London, 1978), p. 13.

21. Wilson Harris, *Tradition*, p. 10.

22. *Guyana Dreaming. The Art of Aubrey Williams*, compiled by Anne Walmsley (Sydney, 1990).

23. 'All men come to the hills', reprinted in *Caribbean Voices*, vol. I, p. 98.

24. From *Focus* (Kingston, Jamaica, 1956), edited by Edna Manley, pp. 160–71. Much anthologised. Later versions indicate more strongly the Jamaican enunciation.

25. E.M. Roach, *The Flowering Rock* (Leeds, 1992), p. 155.

26. Ibid., p. 65.

27. Ibid., p. 121.

Chapter 9

Ideas

Until the 1930s, most Caribbean political and social theory developed outside the English-speaking area.[1] In the Spanish Caribbean, the first Dominican universities had been founded in San Domingo as early as 1528 and in Cuba in 1728. The Anglophone Caribbean had to wait until 1949 for the opening of a University College of the West Indies in Jamaica. The early Spanish universities were extensions of the metropolis, but by the beginning of the twentieth century José Marti (1853–95) had established the basis for a Radical intellectual tradition in Cuba, and Hispanic South American independence movements were shaping a pan-Caribbean ideology, *Mundonovismo*. However, if the British area remained in the main intellectually isolated, it could not be totally impervious to debates taking place in the Caribbean region as a whole, even if 'the unity' was, in Kamau Brathwaite's phrase, 'submarine'.[2] These were, in the opening decades of the century, largely focused on race, for in spite of the ethnic mixture of the region, the abolition of slavery had left a 'white' hierarchy of power largely intact, and the great 'black' majority disenfranchised. From the late 1920s the *Poesia negra* ('Black Poetry') movement in Cuba was led by Nicolás Guillén. Guillén's anti-imperialism was directed in particular against the United States, and was racial but not racist. To Guillén, it was obvious that the essential culture of Cuba and the Caribbean was African-based, but it was there to be shared by all ethnic groups. His sensual, vital poems drew on Afro-Cuban 'son' [folk-dance] rhythms, language and folk-lore, part of a popular culture that was, he argued, at once both 'black' and 'mestaje' [mixed blood].[3] Guillén, who later took a leading role in Castro's intellectual revolution, was elected Cuba's *poet nacional* in 1961, but he had been a pan-Caribbean force from the 1930s.

In Haiti, direct American control of the country between 1914 and 1934 provoked a fierce conflict between a Radical intellectual élite and the conservative establishment complicit with US interests. The Radicals, who produced the journal *La revue indigène* (1927–8), looked to the peasant poor with their Creole language, African-based rhythms and Vodun religion for the 'authentic' Caribbean.[4] They were led by Jean-Price

Mars, whose *La Vocation d'Élite* (1919) and *Ainsi Parla l'Oncle* (translated as *Thus Spoke the Uncle* in 1928) became central documents for the movement. They rejected the endemic violence that characterised the lives of the poor and, in general, their raw practice of vodoun, but were profoundly drawn to their vibrant, African-orientated lifestyle and spiritual consciousness.[5] The movement's conversion of Haitian folk values into a Radical political perspective can be seen in Jacques Roumain's novel, *Gouverneurs de la Roseé* (*Masters of the Dew*) (1944),[6] where Manuel, a Haitian cane-cutter, returns from Cuba to his drought-stricken and socially divided village. Challenging the villagers' despair, he uses Marxist insights and practical skills to regenerate the soul of the peasant community. The book's power lies not in the parable, but in the art of its telling. Written in modified French with Creole elements, Roumain transforms an account of poverty and reconstruction in a Haitian village into a poetic vision of humanity recovered.

While Haiti was exploring its black folk culture, French Guadeloupe and Martinique were being drawn closer to Europe, and in 1946 both became Overseas Departments of France. In St-John Perse (born Alexis St-Leger Leger), Guadeloupe had produced the first major poet to emerge from the French Caribbean. Perse was a white Creole who emigrated to France when only twelve, but the island had shaped his sensibility, and his radiant recreation of his childhood in *Eloges* (written 1907–8) was the first work of many to revision the West Indies through a child's eye. The cantos of his epic *Anabase* ([1924], English translation by T.S. Eliot, 1930), dramatise a fresco of heroic characters moving across a giant desert backcloth.[7] If the scene is suggestive of the Middle East, the sensibility is West Indian, evoking the great sweep and confusion of the history of the region. Its landscapes anticipate the opening of Kamau Brathwaite's landmark poem, *Rights of Passage* (1967). Derek Walcott found that Perse's work liberated his imagination from the provincial colonialism of the St Lucian culture. For him, Perse 'conducts us from the mythology of the past to the present without a tremor of adjustment'. His hero 'moves through the ruins of great civiizations with all his worldly goods by caravan or pack mule, the poet carrying entire cultures on his head, bitter, perhaps, but unencumbered'.[8] It opened epic perspectives on Caribbean culture that later fed into his own long poem *Omeros* (1990).

The Francophone Caribbean concept that made the most immediate impact on the British West Indies was, however, that of négritude, a concept initiated by Aimé Césaire and by his fellow-Radical French Guyanese poet Léon Damas, author of *Pigments* (1932). Césaire's *Cahier d'un Retour au Pays Natal* (*Notebook of a Return to my Native Land*) (1939, extensively revised 1956), was provoked by French assimilation policy in Martinique. His reverie begins in despair at the vision of a devasted Caribbean, diseased with poverty and colonialism:

At the brink of dawn budding with frail creeks, the hungry
West Indies, the West Indies pockpitted with smallpox, the
West Indies blown up by alcohol, stranded in the mud of
this bay, in the dust of this town sordidly stranded.[9]

His thoughts turn to Paris where, seeing a tall, ungainly 'Nigger shrouded
in a threadbare jacket . . . COMICAL AND UGLY',[10] he is filled with
disgust. But horror becomes revelation as he realises that in rejecting this
'Nègre', he abnegates his own race. As he accepts his own black identity,
he experiences a mounting ecstasy of self-assertion. Turning the European
white/black dichotomy against itself, he sees the white world as a worn-
out machine, sterile and void of meaning.

Listen to the white world
horribly weary from its immense effort
its refractory joints cracking under the hard stars
its stiffness of blue steel piercing mystic flesh . . .[11]

Denied wealth and political power by the whites, however, the black
man recovers his humanity. His négritude [black identity]

reaches deep down into the red flesh of the soil
it reaches deep into the blazing flesh of the sky
it pierces opaque prostration with its straight patience.

Eia for the royal Kailcedrate! [a giant African tree
    transplanted to Martinique]
Eia for those who have never invented anything
For those who have never explored anything
for those who have never subdued anything

those who open themselves up, enraptured, to the essence
    of things . . .[12]

Césaire was associated with the French surrealists.[13] Yet both the tech-
niques and the imagination of his extraordinary poem remain essentially
Caribbean. It evokes the violence of hurricane and earthquake, the intensity of tropical colour and heat. The language is skewed from standard
usage by its ferment of Martinican Creole with Metropolitan French.
'For all the complexity of its surrealism,' wrote Walcott, 'it sounds, at
least to a listener familiar with French patois, like a poem written tonally
in Creole',[14] and the whole has the rhythmic thrust of black jazz.
    Césaire's impact was greater in Africa than in the Caribbean itself. In
Martinique, one writer outside its influence[15] was Joseph Zobel. Zobel's

moving novel *La Rue Cases-Nègres* (1950, translated as *Black Shack Alley* in 1988), is a semi-autobiographical account of a talented black boy growing up in a Martinican village in the first decades of the century that focuses more on the social and educational repression of the French colonial system than on blackness. Césaire's concept of négritude was also questioned by the Martinique-born Frantz Fanon in *Peau noir, masques blancs* (*Black Skin, White Masks*) (1952). As a black intellectual, Fanon was horrified by the way the French philosopher Jean-Paul Sartre, in 'Orphée Noir [Black Orpheus]', his influential preface to Senghor's *Anthologie de la nouvelle poésie nègre et malagache* (1948), had turned Césaire's ideas into an anti-racist racism, in which black identity was defined only by its opposition to the white.[16] For by this definition, 'the black man has no ontological resistance in the eyes of the white man'.[17] Césaire himself finally rose beyond this false dichotomy by asserting his individuality. Fanon, too, sought to 'reject the two terms [of racial identity] which are equally unacceptable, and, through one human being, reach out to the universal'.[18]

Homi Bhabha has pointed out[19] that Fanon's solution cannot evade the necessity for the colonised to confront the 'Other'. Yet by separating the 'mask' of racial metaphor from the 'skin' of individual identity, Fanon identified the problem facing opponents of racism in a multi-racial society like the Caribbean – that by opposing one racial stereotype, they could become trapped in its opposite. *Peau noir* was only translated into English in 1967, but was available in French to alert observers such as Lamming, who published *In the Castle of my Skin* the year after Fanon's work had appeared. In 1956 George Lamming joined Césaire as a speaker at the First International Congress of Black Writers and Artists in Paris. In his address, 'The Negro Writer and his World',[20] he acknowledged that a black identity can effectively bring together writers from Africa, America and the Caribbean. But in an argument that echoes Fanon, Lamming noted that 'the term Negro . . . represents at one shot a fact and fallacy'. 'Negro' was not used as an ethnic term to denote the African peoples, but means only 'a man who the Other regards as a Negro'. This poses the writer with a dilemma. He has 'a real and primary responsibility to himself', where such concepts have no meaning. Yet he also has a duty to those 'who are moved by the power of his speech, his judgement and his good faith', in a world where the 'fallacy' of the Negro is a 'fact'.

In 1961, Fanon's *The Damned* (*The Wretched of the Earth*) called for a 'combat literature' that 'moulds the national consciousness, giving it form and contours and flinging open before it new and boundless horizons'.[21] Again, Fanon and Lamming were thinking on parallel lines. A year earlier, in *The Pleasures of Exile* (1960), Lamming had championed imaginative literature through which the colonised who had been 'slowly and ultimately separated from the original ground where the coloniser found him',[22] could rediscover an identity.

> The novelist was the first to relate the West Indian
> experience from the inside. He was the first to chart the
> West Indian memory as far back as he could go. It is to the
> West Indian novelist − who had no existence twenty years
> ago − that the anthropologist and all other treatises about
> West Indians have to turn.[23]

Creative literature revealed a West Indian sensibility that was 'essentially peasant', for its writers of whatever class are linked with the land 'that once claimed their ancestors like trees'.[24]

> For the first time the West Indian peasant became other
> than a cheap source of labour, fear, involved in riot and
> carnival. It is the West Indian novel that has restored the
> West Indian peasant to his true and original status of
> personality.[25]

Lamming's focus on the Caribbean peasant linked with earlier debates initiated in the early 1930s by members of the 'Beacon' group[26] in Trinidad. They included C.L.R. James, whose seminal work on the Haitian revolution, *Black Jacobins*, appeared after his emigration to Britain in 1938, having found no place for a black man in Trinidad politics. Like Lamming and Fanon, James saw that the central problem facing the Caribbean was not race itself, but racial history as perpetuated by Europe. While European colonial writers like Froude had taken Haiti as proof that black men were by definition unable to govern, on the contrary, James asserted that 'West Indians first became aware of themselves in the Haitian Revolution'.[27] He demonstrated that Toussaint L'Ouverture and the Haitian peasants were not the brutal savages of European history, but champions of Rousseau's revolutionary vision that all men are born free, an ideal that Europe had betrayed. Instead of a history in which white masters educated decadent races, James showed free black men enslaved and brutalised by Europe to produce a luxury product, sugar. James's passionate and meticulously researched thesis revolutionised self-awareness in the Caribbean at a time when its future leaders, like Eric Williams in Trinidad, sought an intellectual base on which to build an alternative political economy. Williams developed James's insights in *The Negro and the Caribbean* (1940) and *Capitalism and Slavery* (1943), studies which underpinned the victorious Trinidadian People's National Party's programme in 1955.

James's holistic politics were informed by his enthusiasm for West Indian popular culture and, above all, cricket. Not only is *Beyond a Boundary* (1963) arguably the best book ever written on the game, it relates sport to the wider sphere of Caribbean history and politics. For James, the humanist arts from sculpture to cricket formed a continuous spectrum, and it was no accident that Greek culture produced both Sophocles and the Olympic games. In a later article he claimed that 'we will learn the answer to Tolstoy's question, "What is Art?" only when we learn to integrate our vision of [Clyde] Walcott on the back foot through the covers with the outstretched arm of the Olympic Apollo'.[28] The brilliance of James's political strategy was to use classical civilisation and British gamesmanship, basic tenets of Imperialist culture, to subvert the authenticity of the colonial process itself.[29]

In the 1960s, the political future of postcolonial Caribbean society was an issue hotly debated on the University of the West Indies campuses, which now included sites in Jamaica, Trinidad, Barbados and Guyana. If the Department of English Literature at first conservatively followed the London University syllabus, this was taught alongside Caribbean-based programmes in History, French, Spanish, Linguistics and Education. This created a holistic basis for debate, and the first significant poet to emerge from its academic circle came not from English, but History. Edward [now Kamau] Brathwaite was a Barbadian who had come to Jamaica from Ghana, where he had worked for eight years as an education officer, and, like Lamming, he had become aware of 'the Black Rock of Africa'[30] in the Caribbean. He was to write:

> Slowly, slowly, ever so slowly, I came to a sense of
> identification of myself with these [African] people, my
> living diviners . . . The problem now was how to relate this
> new awareness to the existing, inherited non-African
> consciousness of educated West Indian society.[31]

In *The Development of Creole Society in Jamaica, 1770–1820* (1971), and in the locally published *Contrary Omens* (1974), he addressed the problem of an authentic Caribbean identity, distinguishing between the 'White Creoles of the English and French West Indies', who had separated themselves from the true task of West Indian Creolisation, and the 'subordinate but spiritually vital culture of the African slaves' whose task was to begin a process of spiritual repossession.[32] He urged that the future of Caribbean culture 'lies with the folk, and that by folk we mean not in-culturated, static groups, giving little; but a people who, from the centre of an oppressive system have been able to survive, adapt, create . . .'.[33]

Creolisation was also being debated in the Francophone Caribbean. Edouard Glissant, born on Martinique, studied law and anthropology in Paris, and established his Radical credentials as co-founder, with Paul Niger, of the Front Antillo-Guyanese pour l'Independance. His novel *Le Lézarde* (1958; translated as *The Ripening*, 1985) won the prestigious Prix Renaudot, and brought him international fame. This haunting poetic work evolves around the Lézarde River, integral to the rich island landscape of

Martinique as it flows towards the sea, and through the narrative the river also becomes symbolically interfused with the lives of eight Radical activists as they progress towards political enlightenment. In his subsequent novels, poems, plays and essays,[34] Glissant developed the concept of 'Antillanté', a holistic experience which embraces the 'folk' experience together with all other elements of the Caribbean reality, held in a profoundly realised instant of the present. For Glissant, the search for intellectual 'clarity' in Western thought is a destructive obsession which denatures the culture that it analyses: the Caribbean intellectual must search for the dense substance of Caribbean experience, its *opacity*. The search for 'origins' is based on an illusion, since the past can never be recovered. If Western philosophy looks for the 'racine', or single root, the Antillean must explore the 'rhizome', multiple spreading filaments of simultaneous being.

Glissant's work was read by Derek Walcott, who prefaced his autobiographical *Another Life* with a quotation from *Le Lézarde*.

> One day when I finally fasten my hands upon its wrinkled stem and pull with irresistible power, when my memories are quiet and strong, and I can finally translate them into words, then I shall perceive the unique and essential quality of this place. The innumerable petty miseries, the manifold beauties eclipsed by the painful necessities of combat and birth, these will be no more than the network of down-growing branches of a banyan tree, winding about the sea.[35]

Walcott, too, questioned the concept of racial continuity, and the use of the past to unlock the West Indian present. 'But who in the New World', he asked, 'does not have a horror of the past, whether his ancestor was torturer or victim? Who, in the depth of conscience, is not silently screaming for pardon or for revenge?'[36] Preoccupation with the slave past brought self-destructive Narcissism. 'In the New World servitude to the muse of history has produced a literature of recrimination and despair, a literature of revenge written by the descendants of slaves or a literature of remorse written by the descendants of masters.' Instead, 'the truly tough aesthetic of the New World neither explains nor forgives history. It refuses to recognise it as a creative or culpable force'.[37]

The debate had moved from race to history, from history to the problem of consciousness. In 1943 the Cuban writer Alejo Carpentier had visited Haiti, and found the experience shattered his Westernised sense of logical 'reality', placing in its place *le réalisme merveilleux* [magical realism].[38]

> I found myself in daily contact with something that could be defined as the marvellous real. I was in a land where thousands of men, anxious for freedom, believed in

Macandal's [a slave rebel leader] lycanthropic powers to the
extent that their collective faith produced a miracle on the
day of his execution. . . . I breathed in the atmosphere
created by Henri Christophe, a monarch of incredible zeal,
much more surprising than all of the cruel kings invented
by the surrealists . . . I found the marvellous at every turn.[39]

For Carpentier, this awareness broke through the confining structures of
European rationalism, offering a pan-American vision. His novel, *The
Kingdom of this World* (1949), experiences the Haitian revolution through
the 'magical' awareness of a slave groom Ti Noel, to whom the world is
controlled by the power of vodoun embodied in the rebel slave leader,
Macandal. Haiti was becoming the epicentre of a seismic shift in Caribbean consciousness. In 1956 the Haitian novelist Jacques Stéphen Alexis,
speaking with Lamming at the Congress of Black Artists and Writers, again
invoked 'magical realism', arguing that, for the Haitian people, dream, the
fantastic and magic formed the basis of their 'reality'. Barbara Webb has
described how:

> For Alexis, the marvellous in Haitian art is a dynamic, all-
> embracing realism linked to myth, symbol, and even the
> sacred, that goes beyond preestablished notions of harmony,
> beauty and logic. Yet it is firmly rooted in the everyday
> realities of the Haitian people, since at the centre of its
> violent profusion of contradictory forms 'man bursts forth,
> working towards his destiny and happiness'.[40]

In 1956 George Lamming, too, visited Haiti and witnessed the 'Ceremony of the Souls', finding that the ritual of re-establishing spiritual
contact with the dead profoundly shifted his awareness of the Caribbean
reality. Its importance will be considered later.

Wilson Harris was also concerned with the problem of Caribbean
consciousness, although he focused not on Haiti, but Guyana. As early as
1951 he had written in the Guyanese 'little magazine', *Kyk-over-Al*,[41] that
while Europe remained locked in materialism and moribund tradition,
the emptiness of Caribbean basin offered a profound potential for regeneration: 'the very bareness of the West Indian world reveals the necessity
to examine closely the starting point of human societies.' West Indian
man, free from a false individualism, can remain in harmony with 'all the
levels of his life', at one with 'the rhythms within the welter of his
existence'.[42] Harris set about reversing what Benedict Anderson has called
the destructive imposition of a European 'apprehension of time' on colonised cultures.[43] As Anderson demonstrates, the rigidity of its chronology,
reinforced by printing and a materialist logic of cause and effect, shattered

the dimensions of folk memory, fable and spiritual intuition possessed by traditional societies. With breathtaking assurance, Wilson Harris replaced the European world view with his own personal vision, one rooted in his experience of the open spaces of Guyana, and in the consciousness and practices of its autochthonous cultures.

His 1970 Edgar Mittelholzer lectures, *History, Fable and Myth in the Guianas*,[44] explored the relationship between belief, ritual, and artistic form. In *Vodun* possession, the shaman's dance dissolves the Western division between history and imagination, between the imagined, the mythical and the collective consiousness. In the ritual, the dancer becomes 'the dramatic agent of the subconscious', bringing into being a new creative reality as 'the life from within and the life from without overlap'. The backwards-leaning Limbo dance was, it was believed, developed as the slaves' only exercise in their cramped galleries. It is seen by Harris as an image of the African, bunched 'like a spider' to creep through a 'gateway of the gods', moving from the dismemberment of the slave experience into 'a psychic reassembly' of personal and religious identity in the New World.[45] Elsewhere Harris examines other New World manifestations of psychic reality, such as the magical icons, zemi, of Arawak shamanistic practice, whose distortion of natural forms disclose their inner energies,[46] and, supremely, Tumatumari petrographs mysteriously appearing in the Guyanese interior, linking rock, language and the human hand. From a base in past cultures, Harris's fiction and critical essays break into a creative future, to 'look afresh with somewhat shattered yet curiously liberated eyes at the living museum of creation . . .'.[47]

Harris was one of the first to identify two central figures in the West Indian aesthetic debate. In *The Palace of the Peacock*, Anancy the Spider is the symbol of human resilience and creativity. The crew 'swarmed like upright spiders'[48] as they commenced their expedition towards recovered selfhood. Later, 'the boat still crawled, driven by the naked spider of spirit'.[49] Wishrop, the self-destructive/recreative representative of desire, is in particular identified with Anancy, and after his second death becomes 'a spidery skeleton crawling into the sky'.[50] As Helen Tiffin has demonstrated,[51] Anancy has recurred throughout West Indian literature, a 'complex metaphor for both the Caribbean historical experience and the Caribbean psyche as product of this experience'. For Kamau Brathwaite, Anancy is the voice of the African identity, 'and the potentially rebellious reconstitutive and creative power of the African heritage in the Caribbean'.[52] The 'Anancy principle' animates Derek Walcott's ground-breaking folk play, *Ti-Jean and his Brothers* (1958), where the youngest of three sons survives by outwitting 'Papa Bois' who is both Devil and Planter boss, taming his goat by castrating it, counting his sugar canes by firing them, and escaping from his house by burning it down.[53] Anancy's resilience is foregrounded with wit and oral agility in Andrew Salkey's political parables, collected in *Anancy's Score* (1973), *One* (1985) and *Anancy, Traveller* (1992): Peter Nazareth also sees the Spider Man behind a web of misdirections operating in Salkey's 'realistic' fiction.[54] Salkey's fables may be compared with James Berry's lively collection of tall folk-tales, *Anancy Spiderman* (1988). Anancy the Spider Man is a ubiquitous presence in Caribbean writing.

A survivor in a destructive element, Anancy has also been seen as 'par excellence the metaphor of the artist in the postcolonial world' who must write against the grain of Western tradition.[55] Joyce Jonas, in *Anancy in the Great House* (1990), takes the 'Great House' ideology as 'a colonial worldview of binary oppositions: black/white, exploiter/exploited, First World/Third World' and so forth. In this, 'Anancy represents the suppressed *energeia* of such a formulation – a deconstructive energy that finds expression through the artist'.[56] Using insights from anthropology and psycholinguistics, Jonas analyses novels by George Lamming and Wilson Harris to demonstrate how these authors explore liminal spaces between structures of colonialist meaning. Thus Fola, in *Season of Adventure*, through the spiritual experience of the *tonelle*, prises open her past knowledge of herself and discovers her hidden identity.

Anancy is a 'shape-shifter', and Pauline Melville's story collection of that name[57] brilliantly demonstrates the imaginative potential of cross-cultural transformation in creative writing. Her story, 'The Conversion of Millicent Vernon', cross-cuts the Christian perspective of Millie's mother with Millie's own magical, Africa-oriented consciousness, both set within a town haunted by the polyphony of its history.

> In this place the ghosts walked openly and brazenly in the streets. The blue eyes of a Dutch planter looked inquiringly out of the black face of the local midwife; the wrists of an Indian indentured labourer who had died a hundred years earlier were the same wrists that twisted brown paper round the peanuts Millie bought at the stall. . . . Jumbie [ghost] people. That is the best way of describing the population of New Amsterdam, capital of Berbice county. Jumbie people.[58]

Melville's 'shape-shifting' vision is not confined to the Caribbean: it moves trickily between different areas and social groups of Britain and the Caribbean. It is witty, dramatic, constantly inventive, seeing myth within the everyday and intuitive depths in the comic absurd.

Anancy as 'shape-shifter' has affinities with West Indian Carnival. The classic definition of the Carnivalesque is in *Rabelais and his World* by the Russian formalist Bakhtin.[59] For Bakhtin, Carnival is simultaneously mockery and life-affirming, a demotic celebration undermining established authority. But arguably Caribbean Carnival goes beyond the subversion out of which it rose; it has become autonomous, a culture's genesis of meaning out of mimicry and the fragments of other cultures. Having lost its religious context, it is democratic and carnal; it is spontaneous and complete within its experiential moment. By custom, costumes are destroyed each year with the end of Carnival.[60] Wilson Harris's fascination with Carnival, as Hena Maes-Jelinek has pointed out, is again with its creativity, but whereas Anancy is the shape-shifting individual, Carnival subverts historical and social reality itself. Again, it features in Harris's *Palace of the Peacock*. At a crucial moment, Donne's crew, disorientated in the jungle and facing the terror of their second death, find 'vision and idea mingled into a sensitive carnival . . .'.[61] In later work Harris has defined Masquerade as the creative process by which the masked individual reaches the reality beyond delusion, as costume and dance become 'extensions of an absent body into which present humanity descends'.

> Save that the absent body, in this context, is ceaselessly
> unfinished, ceaselessly veiling and unveiling itself, ceaselessly
> alive to proportions of intuitive conscience.[62]

In an interview with Stephen Slemon, Harris identified Carnival as a figure for the postcolonial predicament itself, for 'it did seem to me that in the twentieth century, which is so implicated in colonialism, "Carnival" was the best system of values one could evolve. The carnival frame goes on but allows different content to play through'.[63]

Originally often identified with Jamaica and Trinidad, 'Anancy' and 'Carnival' are part of the life of the peoples that have developed as central tropes in the creative writing and the critical concepts of the Caribbean. Yet as aesthetic principles they are impossible to categorise. This itself reflects the essentially subversive quality of Caribbean culture, typified in the shape-shifting of Caribbean folk-lore and folk-tale, in the ever-changing form of Jonkonnu processions, and in the patterned disorder of massed masquerades. At its centre it is as fluid as the human imagination, yet held together by an articulate energy: as in Benítez-Rojo's terms, 'the rhythm, the beat of the chaos of the islands'.[64]

Notes

1. See *Intellectuals in the Twentieth-century Caribbean* (London, 1992), vol. II, edited by Alistair Hennessy.

2. Edward Brathwaite, *Contrary Omens* (Kingston, Jamaica, 1974), p. 64. See also Bridget Jones, '"The unity is submarine": aspects of a pan-Caribbean

consciousness in the work of Kamau Brathwaite', in *The Art of Kamau Brathwaite* (Bridgend, 1995), edited by Stewart Brown, pp. 86–100.

3. 'Nicholas Guillén, "National identity" and "Mestaje"', reprinted in *Carifesta Forum* (Jamaica, 1976), pp. 35–40; see also Antonio Benítez-Rojo, *The Repeating Island*, ch. 3.

4. Naomi M. Garret, *The Renaissance of Haitian Poetry* (Paris, 1963).

5. See Michael Dash, *Literature and Ideology in Haiti* (London, 1981).

6. Jacques Roumain, *Masters of the Dew*, translated by Langston Hughes and Mercer Cook, with an introduction by J. Michael Dash (Oxford, 1978).

7. Roger Little, *Saint-John Perse* (London, 1973), p. 20.

8. Derek Walcott, 'The Muse of History', in *Is Massa Day Dead?*, edited by Orde Coombs (New York, 1974), p. 3.

9. Aimé Césaire, *Notebook of a Return to my Native Land* (*Cahier d'un retour au pays natal*), translated by Mireille Rosello with Annie Pritchard ([1939] Newcastle-upon-Tyne, 1995), p. 73.

10. Aimé Césaire, *Notebook*, p. 109.

11. Ibid., p. 115.

12. Ibid., p. 115.

13. See *Refusal of the Shadow. Surrealism and the Caribbean*, edited by Michael Richardson (London, 1996).

14. Derek Walcott, 'The Muse of History', in *Is Massa Day Dead?*, edited by Orde Coombs (Garden City, N.Y., 1974), p. 13.

15. Joseph Zobel, *Black Shack Alley*, translated by Keith Q. Warner (Colorado Springs, 1980), p. xix.

16. Frantz Fanon, *Black Skin, White Masks* ([1952] London, 1986), p. 133.

17. Ibid., p. 110.

18. Ibid., p. 197.

19. 'Foreword', ibid., pp. xix–xxv.

20. George Lamming, 'The Negro Writer in his World' [1956], in *Conversations with George Lamming*, edited by Richard Drayton and Andaiye (London, 1992), pp. 36–45.

21. Frantz Fanon, *The Damned* ([1961] Paris, 1963), translated by Constance Farrington, p. 193.

22. *Pleasures*, p. 157.

23. Ibid., p. 38.

24. Ibid., p. 45.

25. Ibid., p. 39.

26. Alistair Hennessy, *Intellectuals in the Twentieth-Century Caribbean* (London, 1992), vol. I, pp. 115–78.

27. C.L.R. James, *The Black Jacobins* ([1938] Vintage edition, New York: Random House, 1963), p. 391.

28. C.L.R. James, 'What is Art?' [1963] in *The C.L.R. James Reader* (Oxford, 1992), edited by Anna Grimshaw, p. 326.

29. See Gikandi, *Writing in Limbo*, pp. 42–56.

30. The phrase from E.M. Roach's poem 'Fighters' gave Lamming the title for his essay, 'Black Rock of Africa', *African Forum*, I, 4 (1966), pp. 32–52.

31. Kamau Brathwaite, 'Timehri', *Savacou* (September 1970), p. 38.

32. Edward Kamau Brathwaite, *Contrary Omens* (Jamaica, 1974), pp. 38, 62.

33. Ibid., p. 64.

34. The most easily accessible English selection is *Caribbean Discourse*, translated by Michael Dash (Charlottesville, 1989).

35. Derek Walcott, *Another Life*, p. [vi].

36. Derek Walcott, 'The Muse of History', in *Is Massa Day Dead?* (Garden City, New York, 1974), p. 4.

37. Derek Walcott, 'The Muse of History', revised version, in *Critics on Caribbean Literature* (London, 1978), p. 39.

38. The term 'Magical Realism' was first coined in 1924 by the German art critic Franz Roh to characterise post-Expressionism.

39. Alejo Carpentier, 'On the Marvellous Real in America', preface to *El reino de este mundo* (1949), reprinted in *Magical Realism*, edited by Louis Parkinson Zamora and Wendy B. Faris (Durham and London, 1995), pp. 75–88.

40. Barbara Webb, *Myth and History in Caribbean Fiction* (Westport, Conn., 1990), p. 14.

41. Wilson Harris, 'Art and Criticism' [1951], reprinted in *Tradition, the Writer and Society*, pp. 7–8, 12.

42. Wilson Harris, 'The Question of Form and Realism' [1952], reprinted in *Tradition*, pp. 14, 16.

43. Benedict Anderson, *Imagined Communities* ([1983], revised edition, London, 1991), pp. 22–36.

44. Wilson Harris, *History, Fable and Myth in the Caribbean and the Guianas* (Georgetown, Guyana, 1970), revised and reprinted in Harris, *Explorations* (Mandelstrup, 1981), pp. 20–42; and further updated by Calaloux Publications (Wellesley, MA, 1995).

45. *History, Fable and Myth* (Wellesley, MA., 1995), pp. 18–25.

46. Wilson Harris, 'Metaphor and Myth', in *Myth and Metaphor: CRNLE Essays and Monographs* (Adelaide, 1982), p. 7.

47. Wilson Harris, *The Womb of Space: the Cross-cultural Imagination* (Westport, Conn., 1983), p. xvii.

48. Wilson Harris, *Palace of the Peacock*, p. 22.

49. Ibid., p. 102.

50. Ibid., p. 103.

51. Helen Tiffin, 'The Metaphor of Anancy in Caribbean Literature', in *Myth and Metaphor* (Adelaide, 1982), pp. 15–52.

52. Ibid., p. 23.

53. Derek Walcott, *Dream on Monkey Mountain and other Plays* (London, 1972), pp. 81–166.

54. Peter Nazareth, *In the Trickster Tradition: the Novels of Andrew Salkey, Francis Ebjer and Ishmael Reid* (London, 1994).

55. Ibid., p. 47.

56. Joyce Jonas, *Anancy in the Great House. Ways of Reading West Indian Fiction* (New York, 1990), p. 2.

57. Pauline Melville, *Shape-Shifter* (London, 1990).

58. Ibid., p. 28.

59. Mikhail Bakhtin, *Rabelais and his World*, translated by Helen Iswolsky (Bloomington, 1984), p. 40. On the laughter of Carnival, see pp. 10–12.

60. Derek Walcott, 'The Caribbean, Culture or Mimicry?', in *Critical Perspectives on Derek Walcott*, pp. 55–6.

61. Cited by Hena Maes-Jelinek in 'Carnival and Creativity in Wilson Harris's fiction', in *The Literate Imagination: Essays on the Novels of Wilson Harris*, edited by Michael Gilkes (London, 1989), p. 45.

62. Wilson Harris, 'Carnival Theatre: a Personal View', in *Masquerading*, Arts Council of Great Britain (London, 1986), p. 41.

63. Stephen Slemon, 'Interview with Wilson Harris', *Ariel* 19, 3 (July 1988), p. 54.

64. Benítez-Rojo, *The Repeating Island*, p. 29.

Chapter 10
Language

As Frantz Fanon argued in *Black Skins, White Masks*, language was the central issue in establishing a Caribbean identity. As a psychologist, Fanon found the imposition of an alien language to be a key factor in breakdown and psychosis among his colonised patients. The language of imperialism had a particular impact on the Caribbean. In the colonised countries of Africa there had been a conflict between the indigenous and imposed European languages, but the Antillean had no such choice. To advance socially, the 'black' people were required to speak a language which simultaneously devalued them, in which 'Negro' signified the physical and brutish, and 'white' the moral and intellectual. The creation of Creole out of the language of the coloniser therefore offered not so much an alternative language as 'a new way of being', for 'every dialect is a way of thinking'.[1] As Kamau Brathwaite noted, 'it was in language that the slave was perhaps most successfully imprisoned by his master, and it was in his (mis-)use of it that he perhaps most effectively rebelled'.[2] Creole forms began to emerge by the end of the eighteenth century, enabling slaves from different tribes to communicate with each other in forms that varied from that of their masters. 'White' children learnt this Creole from their nurses and, as the language of childhood, it infiltrated West Indian society as a whole.

In 1774 Edward Long in Jamaica complained that the speech of white Creoles was corrupted by 'the incessant intercourse from their birth with Negroe Domestics, whose drawling, dissonant gibberish they insensibly adopt, and with it no small tincture of their awkward carriage and vulgar manners'.[3] But as the Trinidad schoolmaster J.J. Thomas demonstrated as early as 1869 in *The Theory and Practice of Creole Grammar*, the 'gibberish' should be seen not as a corruption of English, but the evolution of distinct languages, with their own grammar, syntax and vocabulary. Creole forms vary across the Caribbean, where even today a Trinidadian may find it hard to understand demotic Jamaican. Moreover, regional forms themselves shift in register according to the context. 'Standard English', in linguistics the 'acrolect', shows respect and respectability; the modified form or 'mesolect' is used in a familiar group, graduating into the 'basilect'. To take an example used by David Lawton, a Jamaican may say to a

European, 'it is my father's car'; to an acquaintance, 'it is mi faadaz kyaar', and to an intimate, 'di kyaar a fi me faada'.[4] (The intonation cannot be reproduced in print.) All versions would be 'Jamaican speech'.

In the first decades of the century, the Jamaican Claude McKay pioneered the literary use of Creole. His 'A Midnight Woman to the Bobby', published in *Constab Ballads* (1912),[5] is one of a series of verse monologues in the Jamaican idiom. It dramatises a black policeman's attempt to arrest a prostitute, and his receiving a torrent of abuse in return. The verve and wit of 'cursing' spices the 'midnight woman's' tirade.

> No palm me up, you dutty brute,
> You' jam mout· mash like ripe bread-fruit
> You fas'n now but wait lee ya,
> I'll see you grunt under de law.

> ['Don't feel me over, you dirty brute, your protruding lips
> burst open like a ripe bread-fruit; you are grabbing me
> now, eh, but wait a little and I will see you grunt when
> the law sits down on *you*.']

But it is not just the content that insults: the 'midnight woman' should use a standard form addressing the policeman's authority, and she doesn't. Her reference to 'bread-fruit' points up his country origins. Under his uniform he is nothing but a black peasant, and his boots cover a countryman's infested feet – 'An chigger nyam you' tumpa toe,/ Til nit fill i' like herring roe' [a burrowing chigoe flea eats your stumpy toe/ until it swells with maggots like the roe of a herring]. She, on the other hand, is a city girl 'born right way in 'panish [Spanish] Town'. The Constab's authority is not his own, but a uniform given by the white man, and only lent him. She delivers a final thrust. The judge knows the Constab well enough not to trust his word against hers.

> Say wa'? – 'res [arrest] me? – you go to hell!
> You t'ink Judge don't know unno [you] well?
> You t'ink him gwin' go sentance me
> Widout a soul fe witness i'?

The unpretentious piece is quite complex in its effect. It creates a little theatre, with conflicting protagonists. Most importantly, the dramatic form turns the reader from an observer into a participant in a fragment of Jamaican life.

As here, the shifting codes of Creole provide the writer with a sensitive indicator of the speaker's identity and context. In a passage that I have taken at random from de Lisser's first novel, *Jane's Career* (1912), Jane's employer, Mrs Mason, attempts to assert a middle-class authority, scolding Jane for breaking a plate, using a modified acrolect:

> 'An' what were y'u looking at?'
> 'Noten.'
> 'Well, if you were looking at nothing, you couldn't 'ave
>   been doing you' work properly, Jane.'
> 'I doan't mean dat, ma'am.'

Cynthia, Mrs Mason's niece, looks in from the bedroom, half-dressed for church, and the ensuing informality drops Mrs Mason's register several points into the mesolect:

> 'What's it but this gurl again,' Mrs Mason answered. 'She
> mash me plate an put it back on me dinner-wagon. Don't
> you see she getting bad already before she been here two
> days?'[6]

Such variations in speech offered a major resource for the West Indian writer. Evelyn O'Callaghan has demonstrated how, in the novel that heralded the postwar explosion of West Indian literature, Edgar Mittelholzer's *A Morning at the Office* (1950), 'the language register is used as a formal device to highlight the grading process that is an intrinsic part of that novel's world'.[7] Each character's status is precisely placed by language, from the black cleaner, Mary ('Ah so worried Ah ain' eat nutting for de morning') to the formal English of Mr Waley, the white boss ('The first interruption. When did you predict it would come, Mrs Hinckson?').[8] Social uncertainty is reflected in a wavering register. The East Indian Jagabir, insecure in his authority, constantly shifts his spoken idiom, using 'Ent you is keep de broom in de lunch-room?' to the cleaner, Mary, but awkwardly attempting a standard form when speaking to a superior: 'But, miss, Ah tell you you must always ask me if you in doubt about any figure I write down'.[9]

Creole registers offered rich resources for literary development. Derek Walcott's sonnet sequence *Tales of the Islands*, first published in 1958, is an often cited example.[10] 'Chapter VI' begins in a modified Creole:

> Poopa, [daddy] da' was a fête! I mean it had
> Free rum free whisky and some fellars beating
> Pan from one of dem band in Trinidad . . .

Then the idiom abruptly changes. A 'black Oxbridge chap, one of them Oxbridge guys', quotes 'Shelley' [sic], 'Each/ Generation has its *angst* but we has none', too drunk to realise that two 'tests' [white men] are making love to his wife up the beach. The confusion of the linguistic codes indicates incomprehension both in the cuckolded would-be intellectual, but also in the bland observer who ends the sonnet in 'standard' English, dismissing the dark underside of Caribbean 'bacchanal' [noisy fun]:

> And it was round this part once that the heart
> Of a young child was torn from it alive
> By two practitioners of native art,
> But that was long before this jump and jive.[11]

Dennis Scott's 'Uncle Time' appeared in the *Focus* annual of 1960. The poem used the popular tradition of Anancy the Spider Man, and the rhythms and idiom of Jamaican folk speech, to explore the experience of ageing and death. Using the term 'Uncle', which in Caribbean folk usage shows respect for any old male person, Scott builds an image of Death as physical and quietly intimate ("im voice is sof' as bamboo leaf') – yet terrifyingly alien. The style gives the poem the immediacy of folk-tale:

> Watch how 'im spin web roun' yu house, an' creep
> inside; an' when 'im touch yu, weep. . . .[12]

'Literary' usage, however, left the social prejudice against West Indian English largely intact. In 1966 this began to change when Louise Bennett's *Jamaica Labrish* [gossip], was published by Sangsters, a local Kingston Bookstore with an important introduction by Rex Nettleford of the University Extramural Department. Bennett's verse came directly from Jamaican streets and markets. The following year the first number of the *Jamaica Journal* featured a seminal essay on Bennett by Mervyn Morris.[13] Morris praised her sanity and generosity of spirit, but also her literary skill. Bennett herself had claimed in 'Bans a [plenty of] Killing' that to kill off dialect would involve the murder of Chaucer, Shakespeare and Burns,[14] and Morris demonstrated that Bennett's work possessed the craft and complexity of writers accepted in the literary 'canon'. If Creole poetry could be taken seriously, however, this should not be interpreted as 'solemnly'. Bennett told Dennis Scott 'I believe in laughter', claiming that laughter was essential to Jamaican 'dialect'. This was not because it was trivial; on the contrary, laughter reflected black people's ability to forgive and to endure, a sense of humour which enabled them to survive the hardships of their history.[15] Often this humour is honed on the struggle for existence, and in 'Roas' Turkey', where Miss Marie's lone pet bird has been killed, the speaker's sympathy competes with her anticipation of a feast which poor Marie is too distressed to eat.[16]

A brilliant raconteur and scholar, Louise Bennett preserved the disappearing Jamaican folk-tales, proverbs and dramatic idiom.[17] She also created a popular tradition in the present.[18] Much of her early work appeared in the Kingston newspaper, *The Gleaner,* and was journalism mediated though the canny intelligence of a market woman, 'Miss Lou', whose irony and common sense satirised middle-class pretentions. It also, as Lloyd Brown[19] has noted, served to 'immerse her audience in the experience of the folk themselves'. And while she wrote on contemporary events and social conditions, she recorded how these were perceived by the Jamaican people. Her verse remains imbedded in the oral traditions out of which it came. Although she also uses puns, word-play and literary references, in print the nuances of timing, gesture, verbal emphasis and often her irony, are lost. Thus in her cautious celebration of Jamaican 'Independance', her metaphor for political maturity, typically grounded in the physical, is effective: 'Jamaica start grow beard, ah hope/ We chin can stan' de strain'.[20] But the reader misses Bennett's ironic emphasis on the final syllable of 'indepen*dance*'. Bennett's Jamaicans have independence in themselves alone. In 'Back to Africa' Miss Lou wonders if their African ancestry makes Jamaicans want to return to Africa, what their English, Jewish, French or American blood will do. In 'Jamaica Oman' she casts a caustic glance at imported Western 'Woman's Lib':

> An long before Oman Lib bruk out
> Over foreign lan
> Jamaica female wasa work
>
> Her liberated plan![21]

The work of McKay and Louise Bennett formed the basis for the development of the Creole monologue. The form is based both on performance and the craft of written words, in gesture and the energy of verbal rhythms. Many of its most effective practitioners, including Binta Breeze, Merle Collins and Valerie Bloom, have been women. In subject the genre ranges from street altercation to intimations of the supernatural in Wordsworth McAndrew's dramatic confrontation with a Guyanese vampire woman in 'Ole Higue' (evil spirit):

> Ball o' fire, raise up high.
> Raise till you touch de sky.
> Land pon' top somebody roof.
> Tr'ipse in through de keyhold – poof!
>
> Open you ol' higue eye.[22]

Lloyd Brown has noted how Bennett's verse 'involves the searching analysis of the specific function of language as oral technique in her characters' lives',[23] and poems like Amryl Johnson's 'Granny in de Market Place'[24] immerse the audience in the process of everyday survival, with language a weapon, a reconciler, an assertion of identity. It dramatises situations which allow the reader/listener to identify with the everyday resilience in particular of the Caribbean poor. Arguably it is a Caribbean form in the way the novel or the 'literary' poem is not. Ian McDonald is most widely known outside the Caribbean for *The Humming-bird Tree*. But his verse monologues 'Jaffo the Calypsonian' or 'Ysif Ali, Charcoal Seller' are what West Indians are more likely to know.

The vitality of this popular idiom is reflected in the achievement of the Trinidadian Samuel Selvon. V.S. Reid's *New Day* (1949) was written in a modified literary form of Jamaican speech, distanced from everyday speech: Jeremy Taylor has written of Selvon's *The Lonely Londoners* (1956), the first novel written throughout in the fully demotic form, that 'this was the first time in West Indian literature that a writer had managed to put Caribbean speech, with all its intricacies and subtle rhythms, onto the page not as a curiosity, not as something exotic, but natural as sunlight. Caribbean language suddenly found a narrative voice of its own'.[25] Selvon, who consistently distanced himself from all literary movements, wrote by instinct. He had an infallible ear for the rhythms of popular speech. His stories are shaped from within, directed by the dynamics of dramatic anecdotes that Selvon himself called an 'episode' or 'ballad'. Selvon's best long narratives, such as *The Lonely Londoners*, are essentially a linked succession of 'episodes'. Central to his effect is what Derek Walcott has called 'reflective laughter',[26] a comedy inseparable from underlying pathos: when Selvon consciously attempts either solemnity, or hilarity, he falters. An example of this balance is his short story 'Brackley and the Bed',[27] which neatly reverses the stereotype of the sexually rampant West Indian. Desperation drives the sleep–starved Brackley to marry his girl–friend Tina in order to share the room's one bed. But he finds that marriage has trapped him into an extended family, and he is banished back to the floor, Tina sleeping with 'Tanty', who has been summoned from Jamaica. It is murder to dissect Selvon's spontaneous style. Yet the effect is precise and subtle. Kenneth Ramchand has shown how a single passage in *A Brighter Sun* uses shifting registers to mediate between the awareness of the narrator and that of the autodidactic 'peasant' protagonist, Tiger. Within this, language shifts within Tiger's consciousness between the idiom of his village background and the awkward 'literary' English of his attempts at reading.[28]

A major influence on Selvon's work has been the calypso. Gordon Rohlehr has pointed out that 'the breathless prose and quicksilver fluidity' relates to the 'same tradition and style of rhetoric which produced calypsonians like the legendary Spoiler, Wonder, Panther, Melody, Lion . . . all figures of the forties'.[29] Selvon's debt to both the form and the imaginative worlds of Trinidad calypso can be seen in one of his most reprinted and revised short stories, 'Calypsonian'.[30] The plot is that 'Razor Blade' is down on his luck. The opening phrase 'it had a time when things was really *brown* in Trinidad' [my emphasis] is racially pointed, and the name 'Razor Blade' (his only given identity) sounds jaunty but thin, with a mean edge. Blade has no money, is deep in debt, and the calypso season, his one chance of making money, is six months away. It is raining, and as he takes off his leaking shoes his calypsonian's bravura tempts him to 'bounce' [steal] a pair off a cobbler's shop-front table. Pliers of panic go 'clip clip' in his stomach, but it was so easy that he follows this up by ordering a huge Chinese meal: he eats it, and leaves without paying. A darker note intrudes as the tired waitress begins to weep, for she will now lose her meagre wages. But the Blade is already on his way, laughing, buoyed up by Barbados rum, rice and chicken. He writes himself into a calypso, and discusses it with the circle in the tailor's shop:

> It have a time in this colony
> When everybody have money excepting me
> I can't get a work no matter how I try
> It looks as if good times pass me by.[31]

The Carnival King of his imagination, he 'bounce' an orange from a drowsing streetvendor out of sheer high spirits. The ending, without faltering in its idiom, shifts suddenly from objective comedy into interior nightmare:

> He look back and he see three fellars chasing him. And is
> just as if he can't feel nothing at all, as if he not running, as
> if he standing up in one spot. The only thing is the pliers
> going clip clip, and he gasping oh God, oh god.[32]

Selvon's successful use of the calypso idiom to find syntax and rhythm appropriate to Caribbean speech has implications for Caribbean writing as a whole, as Gordon Rohlehr pointed out in a 1970 address to a CAM audience:

> What I am thinking of here is not merely an attempt to
> reproduce the vernacular, but to appropriate the *metrical*
> forms of calypso for use in poetry. I feel that just as the
> calypsonian is able to use speech rhythms in his songs, the
> poet, working from the opposite direction, may be able to
> use calypso rhythms in his verse *and still preserve* the sense of
> being true to the speaking voice.[33]

Calypso is now established as a literary sub-genre, the subject for studies such as Keith Warner's *The Trinidad Calypso* (1982), and Rohlehr's own monumental *Calypso and Society in Pre-Independence Trinidad* (1990).

If Trinidad writing took from the calypso, in Jamaica a rich vein of writing was emerging from the music industry, in lyrics to mento, reggae and blue beat hits written by such artistes as Bob Marley, Peter Tosh and Bunny Wailer. In 1979 Oku Onuora (Orlando Wong) experimented with reading against the rhythm of the base line in a reggae song with the melody left out, calling it 'Dub Poetry, a term which had been used in the term "dub-lyricist" by the Jamaican Linton Kwesi Johnson in 1976'.[34] Its pulsing beat made 'dub poetry' the voice of black youth in cities from Kingston, Jamaica, to London and New York, with poets including Oku himself, Michael Smith and Mutabaruka.[35] Linton Kwesi Johnson, who came to Brixton from Jamaica in 1963 at the age of eleven, has recorded, 'I don't know how or why it happened, but from the moment I began to write in the Jamaican language music entered the poetry. There was always the beat, or a bass line, going on at the back of my head with the words'.[36] In packed public performances, Johnson spoke his verse against a background of reggae, mento, and blue beat music. *Dread Beat and Blood* (1975) was made into a best-selling disc by Virgin Records in 1978. But the balance between poetry writing and performance remained. Mervyn Morris has recorded the care with which a performance poet like Michael Smith worked at getting the right transcription of his spoken words,[37] and in 1985 Johnson paused his public appearances because 'I've realised that over the last few years my poetry has suffered as a consequence'.[38] Dub and performance verse is genuinely of the people, its omnivorous sensibility devouring the whole gamut of popular concerns from sex to the environment. Its robust expression of political and social views has led to sporadic banning in the Caribbean, and its leading poets, including Michael Smith, Brian Meeks, Oki Onuora, Mutabaruka and Abdul Malik, as Gordon Rohlehr noted, live (or lived) dangerous and sometimes cruelly shortened lives.[39]

Caribbean poetry has also been linked to jazz. In early 1967 Edward [Kamau] Brathwaite read a paper to the CAM meeting, considering this as 'a possible alternative to the European cultural tradition that has been imposed on us'.[40] At the time, the concept was being much discussed among black writers in the United States. Marshall Stearns in *The Story of Jazz* (1956) and LeRoi Jones in *Black Music* (1963) had related jazz forms to the history of the black peoples, and Ralph Ellison had used the Fats Waller composition 'Black and Blue' as a central motif in his 'jazz' novel, *The Invisible Man* (1953). Nearer to home, the young Jamaican Lindsay Barrett (later, Eseoghene) had in 1966 claimed jazz as the link between the Caribbean and Africa in his poetic reverie, *The State of Black Desire*. But if Brathwaite shared North American interest in jazz as the expression of the black psyche, as a West Indian he distinctively emphasised its ability to absorb and modify fragmented cultures. The genre

> in fact, started as a brilliant amalgam of late 19th century New Orleans musical culture: the French quadrille, the tanto tinge, Catholic liturgical harmonies, brass band and military music, boat songs, shanties, sankies, traditional Euro-American fiddle tunes, all superimposed on African rhythms and the Afro-American slave blues musical scale.[41]

Its sensibility remained essentially Negro, a creation of the black experience, but it was inclusive and open-ended. It was a communal performance, improvised by the group working together, yet it was also individual, for the solo playing expressed the 'cry from the heart of the hurt man, the lonely one'.[42] It was rooted in physical rhythms.

> The alternative tradition is belly-centred: in the beat, the drum, the apparent bawdy. This region, as opposed to the Romantic/Victorian virtues of the 'head', is the centre of Sparrow's art [the Mighty Sparrow, Trinidad calypsonian]; is the source of Louise Bennett's vitality; is the blood-beat of the ska and jazz.[43]

As Paule Marshall, a fellow-Barbadian living in the United States, recognised, jazz as a musical medium is a partial form for cultural expression:

> While non-literary forms . . . music, dance, paint and the like can transmit something of the emotional tone of our lives both past and present, they cannot really communicate that content which must be interpreted in words.[44]

Brathwaite, too, argued that 'words, then, are the notes of this new New Orleans music'.[45] He turned his attention in particular to the novel, where West Indians were making their most distinctive mark. Wilson Harris in *Tradition, the Writer and Society* (1967) had rejected what he saw as the closed form of the classical European novel, which restricted character within formal structure. Brathwaite envisaged a West Indian novel as open as the improvised solo of the jazz solo, directed only by the inner impulse of the imagination and by interaction with the audience.

Brathwaite's analysis of West Indian novels to show their 'jazz' content was strained. However, a month after delivering his CAM paper, Brathwaite electrified his audience in the Jeanetta Cochrane Theatre, London, with his reading of the first part of his *Arrivants* trilogy, *Rights of Passage*. Brathwaite's long poem powerfully illustrated his ideas, and his presentation framed and affected its content. Using his voice as a jazz solo, he created 'bridges of sound'[46] between the present Caribbean and an invoked African past. His speech rhythms unified a wide range of West Indian idioms – Barbadian chatter in a village shop, a Jamaican Rastafarian in his shanty, West Indian emigrants – locating them in a transcendent sweep of time and place. Like Louise Bennett's *Jamaica Labrish* and Selvon's *Lonely Londoners*, Brathwaite's *Rights* significantly shifted the use of Caribbean language within West Indian literature as a whole towards the demotic vernacular.

With his *History of the Voice* (1984), Brathwaite introduced the now widely used term 'Nation Language' for West Indian speech. He defined this as 'influenced very strongly by the African model, the African aspect of our New World/Caribbean heritage', and based, above all, 'on oral tradition'.[47] It was rooted in the rhythms of work songs, dance and popular religious ritual, and reflected in contemporary calypso, jazz and reggae/dub. Brathwaite's emphasis on context was particularly useful. The Caribbean popular arts emerged out of the workplace, religious meetings, and folk celebration, and bear the mark of their origins. *Voice-print* (1989), an anthology of Caribbean oral literature edited by Stewart Brown, Mervyn Morris and Gordon Rohlehr, abandons conventional categories and substitutes 'Dreadtalk, Dub, Sermon, Prophesight and Prophesay', or 'Tracings, Curses and other Warnings'. One important category has been the religious. Gordon Rohlehr has analysed an early example of 'jazz' writing, 'Shaker Funeral' (1950) by the musician and poet Elsworth (Shake) Keane, to demonstrate how the paradigm of per-formed ritual reconstructs the poem's sense. By evoking the experience of a Shaker ceremony, Keane 'combines the symbolic and dramatic mode, preserving balance between sight and sound and establishing an interrela-tionship between rhythm or vibration and image, which combine in unique ways to illuminate idea'.[48] Religious rituals provide the sub-text for a significant body of Caribbean writing, a subject considered below.[49]

A particularly strong religious influence has been the Rastafarian move-ment. In a special issue of the CAM periodical *Savacou* (1970/1) devoted to West Indian writing, Brathwaite had scandalised conservative West Indian critics by including the work of two Rastafarians, Ras Dizzy and Bongo Jerry (Robin Small). They placed the street style of preacher rhetoric alongside the measured tones of Derek Walcott and A.L. Hendriks:

> for the white world must come to blood bath
> and blood bath is as far as the white world can reach; so
>   when MABRAK [a Rastafarian prophet]
> start skywriting
> LET BABYLON BURN
> JEZEBEL MOURN
> LET WEAK HEART CHURN

BLACK HOUSE STAND: for somewhere under
  ITYOPIA [Ethiopia] rainbow,
AFRICA WAITING FOR I.[50]

Brathwaite's selection was attacked by Eric Roach as sponsoring 'clap-trap', and championed with equal vigour by Gordon Rohlehr. The issues were complex.[51] West Indian English was by now accepted as a valid literary medium: in question was the rhetorical use of urban demotic forms in poems such as Ras Dizzy's, quoted above. This focused part of a wider debate. In Jamaica the Rastafarian Movement was creating a vividly independent lifestyle in opposition not only to the cultural models of Europe and America, but also to those of the West Indian establishment. Its 'soul language' grew out of African usages and the rhythmic prose of the St James's Bible. The Rastafarian ethos was strongly communal, and even its grammar of speech was based on the belief that 'binary opposi-tions are overcome in the process of identity with the other sufferers in the society'.[52] The Rastafarian use of the first person pronoun originates, it is said, in a misunderstanding of the numeral in the title, 'Haile Selassie I', but it has developed to assert the simultaneous dignity of both the self and community. Thus a Rasta will not address a fellow believer as 'you', but as 'I and I'.

Brathwaite's publication of the Rastafarian poets can be seen as pro-phetic in more senses than one. Rastafarian beliefs have had a creative impact on West Indian writing. One example is the work of Dennis Scott who in 1984 spoke of being 'intrigued, fascinated and excited by the kind of strategies – linguistic strategies – that (Rastafarians) have used to define themselves in the world'. He believed 'this strategy is particularly interest-ing to me and useful for my own work sometimes'.[53] This led to such experiments as 'Guard-ring' (talisman), where which surface meanings are syntactically dissolved into a visionary dimension:

> I singing so loud, down to de moon
> going shake, I crying out,
> Chris' yu hear!
> An de moonshine wetting my face up
> like oil of plenty.[54]

More recently, Marlene Nourbese Philip has written that her reformula-tion of 'i-magination' and 'i-mage', 'draws on the Rastafarian practice of privileging the "I" in many words'.[55] Laurence Breiner has noted that at one time 'nation language' could refer to 'oral practice with visions of traditional, usually African, society'.[56] The creative development of 'nation language' has continued both within and outside this context. Glissant has argued that the slave's Creole speech was an act of refusal against the prison of the master's tongue, and writing in the Caribbean must continue to embody the creative tension between the oral vernacular tradition and its literary development.[57] Marlene Nourbese Philip has declared:

> To say that the experience can only be expressed in standard English (if there is any such thing) or only in the Caribbean demotic (there *is* such a thing) is, in fact, to limit the experience for the African artist working in the Caribbean demotic. It is in the *continuum of expression* from standard to Caribbean English that the veracity of the experience lies.[58]

David Dabydeen has taken this further, protesting that by 'using Creole in a social-realist manner' the writer loses 'a sense of its psychic energy and disturbing quality'.[59] In the poems of *Slave Song*, which won the Commonwealth Poetry Prize for 1984, he set out deliberately to exploit the inner resources of Creole from a literary angle, including critical apparatus, glossary and notes. Such an academic approach is controversial, and must be set against the directly demotic writing of an author like Selvon. The debate is an on-going one, for it arises out of the creative nature of Caribbean language, which looks forward not back. In Grace Nichols's often quoted lines:

> I have crossed an ocean
> I have lost my tongue
> from the root of the old
> one
> a new one has sprung[60]

Notes

1. Frantz Fanon, 'The Negro and Language', *Black Skin, White Masks*, translated by Charles Lam Markham ([1952] London, 1986), pp. 17–14.

2. Kamau Brathwaite, *Folk Culture of the Slaves in Jamaica* (London, 1971), p. 31.

3. Edward Long, *The History of Jamaica*, 3 vols (London, 1774), p. 278.

4. David Lawton, 'Language Attitude, Discreteness, and Code-Shifting in Jamaican Creole', *English World-Wide* 1, 2 (1980), pp. 211–26.

5. Claude McKay, *Songs of Jamaica* (Kingston, 1912), pp. 74–6; reprinted in Stewart Brown, Mervyn Morris and Gordon Rohlehr (eds), *Voiceprint* (Harlow, 1989), pp. 222–3.

6. H.G. de Lisser, *Jane's Career* ([1914] London, 1971), pp. 44–5.

7. Evelyn O'Callaghan, 'Selected Creole Sociolinguistic Patterns in the West Indian Novel', in *Critical Issues in West Indian Literature*, edited by Erika Sollish Smilowitz and Robert Charles Knowles (Parkersburg, IA, 1984), p. 129.

8. Edgar Mittelholzer, *A Morning at the Office* ([1950] London, 1974), pp. 71, 86.

9. Ibid., pp. 72, 91.

10. *Bim* 7 (Jan.-June 1958), p. 26; shortened version, *In a Green Night* (London, 1962), pp. 26–30.

11. Derek Walcott, *In a Green Night* (London, 1962), p. 28.

12. Dennis Scott, *Uncle Time* (Pittsburg, 1973), p. 32.

13. Mervyn Morris, 'On Reading Louise Bennett, Seriously', *Jamaica Journal* 1, 1 (December 1967), pp. 69–74.

14. Louise Bennett, *Selected Poems*, pp. 4–5.

15. Louise Bennett interviewed by Dennis Scott, 'Bennett on Bennett', *Caribbean Quarterly* 14, 1 & 2 (March 1968).

16. Louise Bennett, *Labrish*, pp. 199–200.

17. See, e.g., Louise Bennett, *Anancy and Miss Lou* (Kingston, Jamaica, 1979).

18. Lloyd Brown, *West Indian Poetry*, 2nd edition (London, 1984), pp. 106–17; Mervyn Morris, 'Introduction' to Bennett, *Selected Poems* (Kingston, Jamaica, 1982); 'Louise Bennett', in Daryl Cumber Dance (ed.), *Fifty Caribbean Writers* (Westport, Conn., 1986). I am much indebted to these.

19. Lloyd Brown, *West Indian Poetry*, 2nd edition (London, 1984), pp. 106–17.

20. Louise Bennett, *Selected Poems*, pp. 117–19.

21. Ibid., pp. 21–3.

22. Reprinted in *Voiceprint*, edited by Stewart Brown, Mervyn Morris and Gordon Rohlehr (Harlow, 1989), pp. 261–2.

23. Lloyd Brown, *West Indian Poetry*, p. 110.

24. Ibid., pp. 30–2.

25. Jeremy Taylor, 'Play it again, Sam', *BWee [BWIA] Caribbean Beat* (Autumn 1994), p. 34.

26. Derek Walcott, 'The Action is Panicky' [1963], reprinted in *Critical Perspectives on Samuel Selvon*, edited by Susheila Nasta (Washington D.C., 1988), p. 126.

27. Samuel Selvon, 'Brackley and the Bed', in *Ways of Sunlight* (London, 1957), pp.151–5.

28. Kenneth Ramchand, *An Introduction to the Study of West Indian Literature* (Sunbury-on-Thames, 1976), pp. 62–4.

29. Gordon Rohlehr, 'The Folk in Caribbean Literature' [1972], in *Critical Perspectives*, p. 39.

30. 'Calypsonian', first published in *Bim* 5, 17 (1952), pp. 40–7. Modified with a London setting as 'Calypso in London', *Ways of Sunlight*, pp. 125–31.

31. Samuel Selvon, *Foreday Morning* (London, 1989), edited by Kenneth Ramchand and Susheila Nasta, p. 147.

32. Samuel Selvon, 'Calypsonian' [1952], reprinted in *Foreday Morning*, p. 154.

33. Gordon Rohlehr, 'Sparrow and the Language of Calypso', *Savacou* 2 (September 1970), p. 99.

34. Mervyn Morris, 'A Note on Dub Poetry', *Wasafiri* 26 (Autumn 1997), p. 66.

35. See Christian Hebekost, *Verbal Riddim: The Politics and Aesthetics of Afro-Caribbean Dub Poetry* (Amsterdam/Atlanta, 1993).

36. Mervyn Morris, 'Interview with Linton Kwesi Johnson', reprinted in *Hinterland*, p. 253.

37. Michael Smith, *It a Come*, edited by Mervyn Morris (London, 1986), pp. 9–13.

38. Mervyn Morris, *Hinterland*, p. 260.

39. Gordon Rohlehr, introduction to *Voiceprint*, pp. 10–11.

40. 'Jazz and the West Indian Novel', *Bim* 44 (1967), pp. 275–84; 45 (1967), pp. 39–51; 46 (1968), pp. 115–16; reprinted in Kamau Brathwaite, *Roots*, pp. 55–110.

41. Kamau Brathwaite, *Roots*, p. 56.

42. Ibid., p. 56.

43. Ibid., p. 74.

44. Paule Marshall, 'Shaping the world of my art', *New Letters* 40, 1 (Autumn 1973), pp. 107–8.

45. Ibid., p. 63.

46. Brathwaite uses the phrase in *Islands* (London, 1969), p. 3. Reference courtesy of Dr Carolyn Cooper.

47. Edward Kamau Brathwaite, *History of the Voice* (London, 1984), p. 13.

48. E.M. Keane, 'Shaker Funeral', *L'Oubli* (Bridgetown, Barbados, 1950), quoted by Gordon Rohlehr in 'The Problem of the Problem of Form', *The Shape of that Hurt* (San Juan, Trinidad, 1992), pp. 16–20.

49. See pp. 138–47.

50. Bongo Jerry, 'Mabrak', *Savacou* 3/4 (Dec. 1970/March 1971), p. 16.

51. The issues are well summarised by Laurence E. Breiner in 'How to behave on paper: the *Savacou* debate', *Journal of West Indian Literature* 6, 1, pp. 1–9.

52. Leonard E. Barrett, Sr, *The Rastafarians*, rev. edn ([1977] Boston, Mass., 1988), p. 144.

53. Mervyn Morris, 'Interview with Dennis Scott', in *Hinterland,* p. 138, and 'Introduction' to Scott, *Uncle Time*, pp. xx–xxi.

54. Dennis Scott, *Dreadwalk* (London, 1982), p. 45.

55. Marlene Nourbese Philip, *She Tries her Tongue, Her Silence Softly Breaks* (Charlottetown, Canada, 1989), p. 12.

56. Laurence E. Breiner, 'How to Behave', p. 4.

57. Edouard Glissant, *Le discours antillais* (Paris, 1981), p. 282.

58. Marlene Nourbese Philip, *She Tries her Tongue*, p. 18.

59. 'David Dabydeen: Coolie Odyssey', in *Frontiers of Caribbean Literature in English*, edited by Frank Birbalsingh (London, 1996), p. 172.

60. Grace Nichols, *i is a long-memoried woman* (London, 1983), p. 80.

Part IV
Groundation

Ground.ing(s)/ groundation(s)/ groundsing (Bdos). *The act of talking together, sincerely and for as long as necessary, with or among socially deprived peoples in their own neighbourhood or dwelling-places, many sitting relaxed on the ground (hence the term).*

Dictionary of Caribbean English Usage[1]

Achille saw the same dances

that the mitred warriors did with their bamboo stick
as they scuttered around him, lifting, dipping their lances
like divining rods turning the earth to music,

the same chac-chac and ra-ra, the drumming the same,
and the chant of the seed-eyed prophet to the same
response from the blurring ankles. The same, the same.

Derek Walcott[2]

The experience of slavery created an amnesia in Caribbean consciousness: the implications of the area's history were too appalling, and too complex, to be easily faced by Caribbean writers. Yet only when the division left in their society began to be explored could there be a communal 'grounding'. This section explores ways by which West Indian writers have renegotiated the area's historical and ethnic roots.

Chapter 11
African (Re)possession

'Thank God nobody in Barbados was ever a slave', Lamming's schoolboy mused, without conscious irony, in *In the Castle of my Skin*. 'It didn't sound cruel. It was simply unreal'.[3] Derek Walcott, too, identified 'a deep amnesiac blow' that sealed off the inheritors of the Middle Passage from 'a life we never found,/ customs and gods that are not born again'.[4] When Edgar Mittelholzer published the first sustained imaginative exploration of plantation society, the 'Kaywana trilogy', Denis Williams declared that the novels 'had to be written . . . not only for clothing the bare bones of history with the vestments of creative imagination, but also for proposing this unique problem of our relationship with the ancestors'.[5] *Children of Kaywana* (1952), *The Harrowing of Hubertus* (1954) and *Kaywana Blood* (1958) may well be the most popular West Indian novels ever published, although they have received little attention from literary historians. The first volume sold out four reprints of the first edition in three years, went through at least seven subsequent editions, and was translated into six European languages. The violence of the subject affects the artistic control, and there is little room for rounded characters in the intense tropical Gothic world that Mittelholzer creates. Yet the novels were a meticulously researched project in which he explored his own ancestry back to Herr C. Mittelholzer, Manager of the de Vreede plantations on the Essequibo at the time of the bloody 1763 slave rebellion.[6] They deserve respect both as opening up Caribbean history, and as Mittelholzer's own psychic self-exploration.

Children of Kaywana opens in 1616, a year before Raleigh's El Dorado expedition, and follows the fortunes of the van Groenwegel family, plantation owners on the Essequibo and Corentyne rivers, from the mating of an Indian of mixed blood Kaywana with a young Dutch planter. It proceeds through a history bloodied by skirmishes between Spanish, French, Dutch and British, and savagely repressed slave unrest, to Cuffy's bloody slave rebellion of 1763–4. Kaywana was a Nietzschean believer in superior force. 'I know human beings', she says, 'they only respect you when you show them you are strong'.[7] The van Groenwegel family establishes itself on a belief in 'Groenwegel blood. Fire-blood. The van Groenwegels never run'. Respect and even loyalty depend on cruelty. 'Stop punishing [slaves] and they fancy you have ceased to love them. That is the mentality of the slave'.[8] Kaywana's granddaughter, Hendrickje van Groenwegel, rules her slaves with sadistic cruelty, aided by her favourite slave and paramour, the Obeah man Bengara. She thinks nothing of burying an ageing slave alive in quicklime, and is tyrannical over her own children. Even those repelled by her cruelty are attracted to her power, and at the age of ninety she still dominates the van Groenwegels. Yet the family will to power turns to nihilistic despair. Her gentle grandson Jacques, tortured by the rebel slaves, thinks 'Grandmother is right. Life is a brutal, haphazard game'.[9] But he dies recklessly fighting the rebels not out of heroism: human bestiality has destroyed his wish to live.

Van Groenwegel blood has been tainted, and miscegenation casts an hereditary doom over the family saga. When Laurens van Groenwegel marries a slave girl his brother exclaims, 'I shall never be reconciled to this slave-blood which Laurens has seen fit to introduce into our family. Never, Rol. Never'.[10] The subsequent novels unravel the horrific heritage of slavery. The family come to believe that Hendrickje is afflicted with insanity. The violent ethic of the slave system is outmoded as Guyana moves towards emancipation. In *The Harrowing of Hubertus* the 'harrowing' is Hubertus's moral dilemma, caught between his affection for his wife and his passion for his cousin, Faustina. It would never have occurred to Hendrickje that this could be a problem. Guyanese society, too, is changing. The British administration takes over from the Dutch, bringing a new legal order. In *Kaywana Blood* (1958), which takes the family saga towards the present, Hendrickje's documents, discovered in a canister, inspire the young Dirk van Groenwegel, who to some extent is Mittelholzer's *alter ego*, to recover Hendrickje's ethos, with disastrous results. He is horrified to find that he himself has black blood. He changes his name to Patrick, and is researching the van Groenwegel history when the family documents are consumed in the Georgetown Library fire of 1913. As the novel closes in 1953, the ageing Patrick hears a Radical speech by one Georgie Boodoo. 'Confounded fool', Patrick mutters. 'Thank God he is no relative of mine'.[11] A Michael Boodoo was in the Radical People's Progressive Party, elected when Guyana gained independence in 1945.

Mittelholzer's work opened up the slave past to West Indian writers. Yet his vision was one of terrifying violence. Andrew Salkey explored the theme with elegant control in *A Quality of Violence* (1959). The novel is set in the Morant Bay area of rural Jamaica during the drought of 1900. As their suffering intensifies, the villagers turn to the rituals of Pocomania. The community is divided between the cultists and Parkin, a 'brown' intellectual who rejects the Pocomania as ignorant superstition. Bill Carr found that 'the book offers little in the way of character. The protagonists are, rather, disparate points of view, conflicting figures in a pattern whose design is the form of the book'.[12] Yet the heart of the novel is not logic, but the power of ritual, going back to Africa. As the cult leader, Mother Johnson, tells a villager:

> Me and you and the rest-a-people in St Thomas all belong
> to the days that pass by when slavery was with the land.
> Everybody is a part of the climate-a-Africa and the feelings
> in the heart of Africa is feelings that beating there, far
> down.[13]

In this past the sufferings of slavery and those of the drought-parched Jamaican peasants come together, and both demand sacrifice. Salkey comments that 'drought first began on Calvary'.[14] In a competitive frenzy of pain, both Dada Johnson and his deputy flog themselves to death on the cross of the 'Big X', and Dada's wife, Mother Johnson, assumes authority. Parkin has narrowly escaped death at the hands of three ganja-crazed 'addicts', and the villagers turn against Ma Johnson. But suffering brings her, too, back her power. 'Kill me, you stinking, dirty Judas people, you kill me!' she screams as she awaits the stones of the crowd. And 'then, for the first time that night, she relaxed, and waited'.[15]

Violence has been a crux in Caribbean radical thought since the debates over whether to kill French militia and settlers divided the leaders of the Haitian rebellion.[16] Frantz Fanon's *The Damned* (1961) rooted the issue in the Caribbean psyche, seeing violence as essential to the process by which the colonised peoples eradicated the subservient attitudes deep within their identity. 'The native discovers reality and transforms it into the pattern of his customs, into the pattern of violence and his plan for freedom'.[17] These issues were foregrounded in the years 1952 to 1960 by the Kenyan Mau Mau emergency. The Jamaican V.S. Reid's novel *The Leopard* (1953) enthusiastically championed the Mau Mau cause. The Kikuyu warrior Nebu embodied the vitality of the African veldt, a paradise degraded by monstrous settlers like Gibson, and by the British soldiers who, like leopards, prey on the wounded and weak. Gibson's wife sees Nebu dancing naked in the rain, and their shared passion creates the crippled child Toto. Gibson murders his wife at childbirth in a jealous rage, and sets out with Toto to stalk Nebu, now a Mau Mau warrior. Nebu kills Gibson, and though wounded by him, sets out to take his treacherous son to safety in Nairobi, a noble act terminated by the bullet of a British soldier. If Reid celebrates the Mau Mau, he creates an ambivalent image of the West Indian in Toto, the crippled grey child of both Africa and Europe. The theme of mixed ancestry was taken up by Derek Walcott in his poem 'A Far Cry from Africa' (1956), where 'guerrilla' war becomes the 'gorilla' wrestling with the (Nietzschean) 'superman'. Walcott asks:

I, who am poisoned by the blood of both
Where shall I turn, divided to the vein?
I who have cursed
The drunken officer of British rule, how choose
Between this Africa and the English tongue I love?
Betray them both, or give back what they give?
How can I face such slaughter and be cool?
How can I turn from Africa and live?[18]

Denis Williams's *Other Leopards* (1963) is based on personal experience of emigration from Guyana, and is set in a vividly drawn mid-Saharan country 'between Europe and Africa', culturally the West Indian situation.

Ochre. Semi-scrub. Not desert, not sown. Different colour
on the atlas (look it up, you'll see); different from the
empty blowing spaces of the true Sahara. To the north,
though, a few hundred miles outside the cities – outside
Kutam, for instance – you do get blowing spaces: bellied
sand, violent hills, volcanic plains, black chasms like the
tired creations of a god gone crazy.[19]

At one level, the novel is neatly schematised. The Guyanese main protagonist, Froad (a 'fraud, without identity') has an African name, Lobo, and a European one, Lionel. He is tórn between the sensual Eve, an African, and Catherine, a taut, self-controlled girl from Wales. Lobo works as a draftsman for Hughie King who wishes to claim Meroetic tomb carvings for European archaeology, while the Muslims of the newly independent state want Froad to prove that the country's origins are Arabic. For Hughie, 'opposition is the fundamental attitude of being for *homo sapiens*; . . . therefore, to encounter all experience in struggle is really the tragic state – the state of human being'. But Froad retorts, 'Balls! Why can't a man – equipped *as he is* – be happy? That's what I want to know'.[20] Eve and Catherine are also tormented by confusions of identity; Eve passes successively from a Christian father to a Muslim husband, to the indeterminate Froad/Lobo. But it is Froad's identity crisis that lies at the centre of the novel. Froad hopes for an act of cultural 'repossession' at the carved tomb of Queen Amanishakete, a monument preserving 'the ancient creativity of this Negro kingdom, *ergo*, of my race'. But the vision brings horror. She is Walcott's 'muse of history',[21] the tyranny of outward form. 'She was Queen and destroyer. She knew hate and law. No trace of love and care. She was a spreading desert'.[22] In an act of despair, he stabs Hughie in the throat and hides up a tree, his skin covered with mud. The ending is ambivalent. Is a light in the sky his pursuers, or a hopeful dawn? Does Froad disintegrate into madness, or is his clay 'egg-shell' a symbol of rebirth?

Besides Denis Williams, a significant number of West Indian intellectuals visited West Africa after the war, including George Lamming, Lindsay Barrett (now Eseoghene), Edward (now Kamau) Brathwaite, Jan Carew, Neville Dawes, C.L.R. James. Some, like Eseoghene, stayed, though not all visits to Africa were happy, as some found themselves strangers separated from African traditions by centuries of New World experience. The Guyanese O.R. Dathorne's *The Scholar Man* (1964), based on his own experiences of teaching in Nigeria, was a hilarious account of a young West Indian academic attempting to bring intellectual enlightenment to his ancestral homeland. But it was a return not to Africa, but to Haiti, that was significantly to shift attitudes to the Caribbean past. In 1956, visiting Haiti to write an article for *Holiday* magazine, Lamming watched an enactment of the vodoun Ceremony of the Souls[23] in which the Hougan [priest] summons up the spirits out of their purgatory of water, so that the living may ask their forgiveness, and the dead be released into eternity. Lamming had recently been to West Africa; now he was present as the ancestors of the villagers rose through the *vèvè*-patterned[24] earth of the Haitian *tonelle* [vodoun temple]. Both the ceremony itself, and its symbolism of returning to the ancestors for cleansing and redemption, deeply affected Lamming's awareness of the West Indian predicament.

Lamming vividly recreated the scene in the second chapter of his novel *Season of Adventure* (1970), which is set on the imaginary island of San Christobal. Fola has been brought to the tonelle out of curiosity by her history lecturer:

> . . . she felt the hands pushing her forward now; first a jerk which soon tailed off into the play of fingers moving down her back. Gently after each jerk, the hands were moving her forward like a pawn; forward to the forbidden circle of maize; forward, forward to the *ververs* that would burst her toes.
>
> Fire of spirits in her eyes, and no longer a child as she watched the shadows strangled by her wish for hair blazing from the summit of the bamboo pole! She trampled upon the circle of maize, exploding shapes like toys under her feet, dancing the dust away. For the gods were descending to the call of voices: 'Come! Come! in O! In O spirit of water come! Come'![25]

The moment of possession catapults her into the troubled questioning of her own identity, and she breaks with her adoptive parents. The illegitimate daughter of Agnes, wife of Piggott the island Commissioner of Police, she is ignorant as to her real father. She turns to the self-taught artist Chiki, who promises to paint a portrait of her father, but the Protean image only reflects her racial confusion. Her search leads her to the world of the Forest Reserve where the villagers, under their leader Powell, still retain their ancestral rituals, and a spiritual identity embodied in Gort's drumming. Personal and communal crises come together when Piggott is murdered, and the police destroy Gort's drum. Unable to overcome prejudice, Powell viciously repels Fola's attempt to claim kinship with the black cause. The novel, however, ends with revolution, and Fola finds a place in the social reconstruction of the island, projected into a new identity by the 'backward glance' of her first experience in the tonelle.

When Lamming visited Haiti, Edward (now Kamau) Brathwaite was in his second year as Education Officer for the Ministry of Education in Ghana, savouring the heady mood of the country's newly acquired independence. Living there until 1962, he wrote, 'I came to connect my history with theirs, the bridge of my mind now linking Atlantic and ancestor, homeland and heartland',[26] and on return to Barbados, felt that 'African culture not only crossed the Atlantic, it crossed, survived, and creatively adapted itself to its new environment'.[27] Out of this experience, Brathwaite wrote his *Rights of Passage* (1967), *Masks* (1968) and *Islands* (1969), collected as *The Arrivants* (1973). Brathwaite has written that the exiled Caribbean culture 'was focused on a religious core which survived and flourished under slavery',[28] and the motif of religious possession is the heart of his seminal trilogy. The poet 'sings, shouts, groans and dreams',[29] a *griot* caught up in his vision.

In *Rights of Passage*, the 'ancient histories' of the Caribbean remain fragmented. The old slave Uncle Tom puts down spiritual roots in new earth, creating the negro spiritual out of his exile, but his children mock his acceptance as weakness.[30] The ganja-inspired Jamaican Rastafarian of 'Wings of a Dove'[31] in his vermin-ridden 'down-/ town shanty-town' Kingston kitchen, dreams of apocalypse, yet remains trapped in the poverty of his Dungle room. In 'Dust',[32] a group of Barbadian women gossip in the village shop. In this brilliantly orchestrated development of 'nation language', Brathwaite seamlessly transforms everyday speech into the controlled rhythms of vision:

> Bolinjay,
> spinach, wither-face cabbage,
> muh Caroline Lee an' the Six Weeks too;
> greens swibble up and the little blue
> leafs o' de Red Rock slips gettin' dry
> dry dry.[33]

Gordon Rohlehr[34] has pointed out that the section echoes both a popular 1937 Shanto song, 'West Indian Weed Woman', by the Guyanese singer Bill Rogers, and the 'Red Rock' section of T.S. Eliot's *The Waste Land*

(1922). The villagers' lament for their drought-stricken vegetables opens into a universal vision of desolation. They talk of drought, sickness, debts, and the catastrophic eruption of Mount Pelee on Martinique that, in 1902, turned night into day with the death of thirty thousand inhabitants. The 'dust' of the title opens up to encompass the volcanic ash, Caribbean drought, and the 'dust to dust' of the human body, ending in a haunting cry, 'Why is that? What it mean'?[35]

The mysteries and intuitions of *Rights of Passage* lead on to *Masks*, the central book of the trilogy, set in Africa. The implied spiritual possession of the first part is now foregrounded, as he consecrates his craft as a talking drum to be inspired by the African gods:

> the dumb
> blind drum
> where Odomankoma speaks[36]

In his vision he traverses vast tracts of space and time, recording the fourth-century migration of the African peoples from the kingdom of Kush on the upper Nile, travelling across the Sahara to found the kingdoms to the West. Brathwaite compresses history, and at times distorts it,[37] to create a swirling drama of movement centred around the dark, still waters of Lake Chad. In the third section, as the tribes cross the Volta river into the forests, they meet the *omowale* (visiting stranger, the poet) moving northwards across the Bosompra river to Kumasi. Kumasi was the centre of the Ashanti kingdom from the late seventeenth to early nineteenth century, the centre of the Asante Confederation, an ambiguous emblem of African splendour, controlling the flow of gold, ivory, kola and slaves. When, at the end of the seventeenth century, Osei Tutu and Akomfo Anokye sought to unite the nation around the ceremonial Golden Stool as a symbol of the nation's soul, the kingdoms disintegrated; the greed for gold was the flaw at the heart of the great African civilisations, as it was for the Jews worshipping the Golden Calf in the wilderness, and Europe locked into the slave trade. The seer has penetrated the cycle of destruction within all civilisations. Anokye, priest of the Golden Stool, speaks:

> And when the cycle is ripe
> I, giver of life to my people,
> crack open the skull, skill
>
> of shell, care-
> fully carved craft
> of bones, and I kills.[38]

Yet out of death comes rebirth. A black Orpheus, the poet descends into the darkness borne on the music of the African peoples, and now invokes the Divine Drummer for the rhythms to take him up towards morning. The closing lines echo the beginning, 'Let us succeed . . .', only now it is also a personal quest, 'Let *me* succeed . . .' [my emphasis].[39]

In the third part of the trilogy, *Islands*, the poet returns to the Caribbean, reinterpreting the experience of *Rights* in the light of his understanding. Uncle Tom refuses to answer force with force knowing that 'cruelty breeds/ a litter of bright/ evils';[40] while the village women of 'Dust' plan to burn the plantation, recognising their oppressor,[41] and 'Leopard' demands the liberation of caged energies in the Caribbean so that hunter and hurt can be 'by this fatal lunge made whole'.[42] The central sections of *Islands* explore immanent religious presences in Caribbean life. In 'Rites' a village shoemaker talks of cricket played by boys on the beach, and the discussion involves a test match at the (Bridgetown) Oval, revealing the fragility of the modern Caribbean 'rite' when a momentary failure can bring universal collapse. Disregarded individuals channel repressed spiritual forces. The poet's carpenter Uncle, put out of work by cheap imports, carves in his 'darkened Sunday shop', his hands guided by Ogun, Yoruba god of iron-work and war, crafting an 'emerging woodwork image of his anger'.[43] The Catholic Eucharist melds with the vodoun ceremony of *manger les morts* in 'Eating the Dead';[44] a Rastafarian ceremony is evoked in 'Negus',[45] and a Baptist meeting in 'The Stone Sermon'.[46] In 'Shepherd', the celebrant in the Jamaican Pocomania ritual experiences the 'dumb-speaking god' of the African 'Tano',[47] and the repeated 'dumb' of silence merges with the 'dumb' of the speaking drum.[48] For

> the gods still have their places;
> they can walk up out of the sea
> into our houses[49]

The final sequence focuses on Carnival and steel band music, itself a vivid illustration of the syncretic creativity of the Caribbean, emerging from a history of poverty and deprivation. In Carnival, Tizzic, a representative of the Caribbean underprivileged, experiences a moment of release, but as soon as Carnival ends, is poor again. A slow, meditative passage takes the motif of *Vèvè*, patterns made in sand in the vodoun ceremony when 'the Word becomes/ again a god and walks among us',[50] directing back to Carnival, where violence is transformed into celebration, and where Christian and African Gods combine, the dancers

> making
> with their
>
> rhythms some-
> thing torn
>
> and new[51]

Like Brathwaite's trilogy, Derek Walcott's drama, *Dream on Monkey Mountain* (1970)[52] is an example of what Gordon Rohlehr has called 'ecstatic possession as a metaphor of a descent into the unconscious mind of the individual and the group' in Caribbean literatures.[53] It opens with Makak, an old black charcoal-seller, in prison for drunken behaviour. Earlier, on the mountain, he had had a vision of a white goddess who called him by his secret African name; he is the descendant of lions and kings. Transformed by his new-found faith, Makak comes down from the mountain, now a warrior and prophet, healing the village sick. But he is betrayed by his materialistic partner Moustique and by his own delusions of power. Back on the mountain, carried away in a dream, he executes all real and imaginary white figures, and finally the white apparition, the source of his vision, crying 'Now, O God, I am free'. There is immediate blackout and the bars descend: he is again the old drunken charcoal-seller, in prison. In the printed text, Walcott quotes from Frantz Fanon, the account of a state where the psychotic patient hallucinates voices alternating praise and insult. 'This is defence, but it is also the end of the story. The self is dissociated, and the patient heads for madness'.[54]

But the experience of watching the play conflicts with such an interpretation. The powerful central scene of healing, where Makak's faith saves a villager dying of snake-bite,[55] takes place at Quatre Chemin [four roads] market, implying the presence of Damballa, the Afro-Haitian god of the cross-roads, where the cabinet maker Basil in appearance resembles Baron Samedi, the guardian of the door between life and death in the vodoun ceremony. Walcott transforms the play's debt to Genet's drama of polarised racial identity, *Les nègres* [*The Blacks*] (1959),[56] into Trinidad folk-tale. Makak is Creole for monkey; his companions Tigre, Souris and Moustique also represent animals, returning them to archetypal identities. Only Lestrade ('astride' two cultures), agent of a bastardised authority, lacks the vitality of fable. Makak's final massacre of all whites is dance drama, projected into the realm of the imagination, not an actuality but a ritualised act of self-emancipation, a cutting free from the internalised categories of 'black' and 'white'. In the Epilogue, the white apparition has become a mere mask in the corporal's hand. At Quatre Chemin market Makak touched a power flowing from Africa, and he has now pierced through illusion. 'The branches of my fingers, the roots of my feet, could grip nothing, but now, God, they have found ground'.[57] He returns to the mountain, 'to the green beginning of this world'.

Walcott's play can be compared with Dennis Scott's play *An Echo in the Bone* (1974). This enacts a Pocomania 'Nine-Night' ceremony – a wake in which the dead return to make their farewell with the living. The villagers mourn Crew, a black labourer, who has killed Mr Charles the white plantation owner, and is now assumed to be drowned. In a state of possession, the villagers re-enact scenes from the past. They are on a slave ship, where a rebellious slave has his tongue cut out, a resonant act, for the drummer in the ceremony, who plays him, is a mute. Other scenes also set up 'echoes' which reverberate into the present: slave girls are humiliated and sold in a Kingston market; an estate owner hunts an escaped slave, is wounded, and is himself spared by two Maroons. In the present, the landowner Mr Charles diverts water from Crew's land in revenge for Rachel, Crew's wife, refusing to sleep with him, and his murder echoes the cycle of plantation history. But the ceremony is also a purgation. 'No matter what is past, you can't stop the past from drumming, and you can't stop the heart from hoping', Rachel declares.[58] And to the intensifying rhythms of the drums, the wake ceremony passes into joyful celebration.

Such works emerged directly from growing awareness of Caribbean popular religious practices. In the 1970s Erna Brodber gathered material for a sociological study of rural Jamaica, and also became aware of an apprehension of history mediated not through printed records, but through ritual and the oral tradition. This forms the basis for her novel, *Myal* (1988), whose title refers to the Jamaican cult of psychic possession. Brodber sees this in both its religious and cultural aspects, and as both invoking the souls of the ancestors and 'stealing' the spirits of the living. The story starts in the St Thomas area in 1919, after savage repression of the Morant Bay rebellion which took place there in 1865, and before movements towards national independence. In his grove, Mas Cyrus contemplates a cosmic disruption in all created being, from the mango trees and the caterpillars under their bark to the devastating storm clouds. This crisis is centred on Ella-O'Grady Langley, who 'had tripped out in foreign' [fallen into an alien psychic state]. A light-skinned girl of Jamaican/Moorish/ Irish blood, by education she is 'English', and she brilliantly recites Kipling. But she is profoundly sick in spirit, without roots, the victim of colonial history and present denial of the people's culture, where the well-meaning Jamaican-born Methodist pastor, William Brassington, campaigns against national language and dress.

Meanwhile, in the village, Anita, aged fifteen and entering puberty, is attacked by a stone-throwing poltergeist. Like Ella, she is the victim of her education, but is in particular danger from Mas Levi, a village leader who has gained authority and wealth by hard work and self-control, and is now sexually impotent, using Obeah to leach Anita's sexual vitality. As the two 'spirit-stealing' stories interweave, the leaders of the village combine against the forces of alien possession. Ras Silas, the Rastafarian 'Ole African', and the cultist leader Miss Gatha are aided by the psychically gifted English-born wife of the Methodist pastor, Maydene Brassington. The extraordinary climax to the novel is the spiritual contest for Anita's life between Mas Levi, holed over his privy with his Obeah books, and the cultists in their frenzied ritual. At the end Anita revives and Mas Levi is found lifeless, trouserless, bunched up like a spider, hugging a mutilated doll. Ella, too, is exorcised, and becomes a teacher, bringing a new communal consciousness for a new generation of Jamaicans. She 'decolonises' an English children's story of animals subordinated to the farmer, changing it to a Jamaican folk-tale in which animals have totemic identities. This looks back to Brodber's alternative version of the Anita/Levi story, in which Miss Gatha had been given a totemic identity as Mother Hen, Maydene Brassington was White Hen, and 'Ole African' became Willy, a dog 'with nose to the ground . . . no one knows the secrets of the earth better than he'.[59] Ella thus subverts the very story within which she herself has been conceived, returning prose narrative to a native Jamaican story-telling tradition.

Spiritual repossession of the past was one approach to exorcising the trauma of slavery, and the area has become a fruitful field for Caribbean writing. After *Season of Adventure*, Lamming returned to the plantation era in his difficult and complex novel, *Natives of my Person* (1972), writing of a slave ship without slaves, searching to understand the attitudes that lay behind slavery itself. The *Reconnaissance* is on an expedition to create an ideal community on the islands of the Black Rock. It is captained by the Commandant, a synthesis of historical figures such as Hawkins and Drake, and the mythical, Prospero and Ahab, but also contemporary 'Captains' of the Caribbean such as Eric Williams, the Prime Minister of Trinidad, and Forbes Burnham in Guyana. Like Shakespeare's Magus, the Commandant desires to create a brave new world in the Caribbean, while ignoring the rights of Caliban. His crew is also composite and symbolic. Some are called by name, others by function – Priest, Surgeon, Steward or Powder Maker – a 'Ship of Fools' comprising in miniature the society it left behind. In their hopes, they indicate the idealism and adventure of the earlier voyagers, just as their inadequacies and betrayals inevitably undermine them. The novel is imaginatively alive with Lamming's reading of Hakluyt and sixteenth- and seventeenth-century sea voyages, and the ship travels the slave trade triangle from Limestone and Antarctica, to Benin, and then westwards across the Atlantic towards the islands of the Black Rock. But the Commandant's spiritual failure is manifest: he has taken no account of the human basis for his colony, the Africans, and has no understanding of the absent partners of the expedition, the women, whom the crew regard as either idols or whores. The novel ends with a gleam of hope as the wives, who have reached Black Rock first, wait in their ship 'The Penalty' for their men. 'We are the future they must learn' says the Lady of House, the Commandant's partner, in the last words of the book.[60]

Other writers have approached the slave era using other stategies.[61] Caryl Phillips's accomplished novel *Cambridge* (1992) takes a linguistic perspective, finely exploiting the textures of eighteenth-century prose to dissect its moral attitudes. Emily Cartwright, a gentrified Englishwoman freshly arrived in the Caribbean, writes sentimentally of the slave longing for 'noonday rest neath the shade of Afric's huge trees with family and friends about him, their voices raised in gentle song'.[62] Her evasive prose reveals moral obliquity. Because she fears she 'might ruin the pleasantness of the day'[63] she avoids attempting to avert Cambridge's tragedy. Cambridge, like Harriet Beecher Stowe's Uncle Tom, is stalwart, grey haired and reads the Bible; like another anti-slavery hero, Olaudah Equiano, he has been freed and converted but, unlike Equiano, he returned to Africa as a missionary and was re-enslaved. Brown, the plantation overseer, sexually abuses Cambridge's common-law wife Christiana: Cambridge impulsively strikes Brown, who dies, and Cambridge is hanged. The issue of the book is Cambridge's real identity, again a stylistic crux. Originally named Olumide, he becomes a palimpsest of imposed identities – slave, missionary, black Tom, David Henderson, Cambridge. In his final confession he declares:

> He [Brown] struck me one with his crop, and I took it
> from him, and in the resultant struggle the life left his body.
> I then fell to my knees and prayed to my God to forgive
> me for my wretched condition.[64]

But was it murder or accidental death? Is Cambridge's prayer one of true repentance, or only a bitter lament for his 'wretched condition' as a slave? Is 'my God' Christian or African? The stiff language both communicates and hides, a formal mask covering a secret self untouched by the white world that attempted to possess him.

David Dabydeen's *Turner* (1994) starts from a painting. At its centre is J.M.W. Turner's 'Slavers Throwing Overboard the Dead and Dying' (1840), in which the bodies of the redundant slaves, discarded to lighten the ship against a hurricane, become fragmentary incidentals within the sublime seascape. The scene is given added significance by its context, a 1783 legal wrangle in which insurers admitted liability for sick, but not murdered, slaves. As a descendant of the enslaved black races, Dabydeen attempts to reinhabit the body of a shackled, disappearing slave as his alter ego, Mau, imaginatively recreating a mythos of his life. But he is prevented by 'Turner's hand gripping my neck,/ Pushing me towards the edge . . .',[65] as Dabydeen himself, an Asian Guyanese, experiences an identity culturally frustrated by Europe.

In contrast *The Longest Memory* (1996), by Dabydeen's Guyanese compatriot Fred D'Aguiar, confronts the physical immediacy of slave narrative recreated in recollection. It centres on the savage beating to death of Chapel, a young, intelligent slave whose attempted escape has been foiled by his own father Whitechapel, an old and trusted 'boss' slave. The violent act encapsulates the nature of plantation society itself. Whitechapel is of the old order, his slave mentality fostered by an intimate bond with his master, who has given him his own name. But his son Chapel ('Whitechapel' without the 'white'), who has illicitly learnt to read, is of a new generation, and the working relationship of the old feudal plantation system has passed to the naked racial prejudice of the overseer, who once raped Whitechapel's wife. In flogging Chapel to death, he is unaware that he is murdering his own son. D'Aguiar's subsequent novel, *Feeding the Ghosts* (1997), directly addresses Dabydeen's *Turner* in its account of Mintah, a slave girl thrown into the sea by slavers, but who clutches the wooden hull to survive: poised between reality and dream, her story is a redemptive 'feeding the ghosts' of the past, a preservation of the Caribbean identity in the destructive sea of history by the power of the imagination. Its theme can be seen as a recapitulation of this chapter.

Notes

1. Richard Allsopp, *Dictionary of Caribbean English Usage* (Oxford, 1996), p. 270.

2. Derek Walcott, *Omeros* (London, 1990), p. 143.

3. George Lamming, *Castle*, p. 57.

4. Derek Walcott, 'Laventville', *The Castaway* (London, 1965), pp. 32–5.

5. Denis Williams, *Image and Idea in the Arts of Guyana*, Edgar Mittelholzer Memorial Lectures, Georgetown, National History and Arts Council, 1969; quoted Micheal Gilkes. *The Caribbean Syzygy*, PhD thesis, Univ. of Kent at Canterbury, 1973, p. 95.

6. *Children of Kaywana* (1952), *The Harrowing of Hubertus* (1954, retitled *Kaywana Stock*, 1959) and *Kaywana Blood* (*The Old Blood*, 1962).

7. Ibid., p. 43.

8. Edgar Mittelholzer, *Kaywana Stock* (1960), p. 22.

9. Ibid., p. 488.

10. Ibid., p. 137.

11. Edgar Mittelholzer, *Kaywana Blood* ([1958] London, 1960), p. 329; Frank Birbalsingh, 'Edgar Mittelholzer: Moralist or Pornographer?', *Journal of Commonwealth Literature* 7 (July 1969), pp. 88–103.

12. Bill Carr, 'A Complex Fate', *The Islands in Between*, edited by Louis James (London, 1968), p. 101.

13. Ibid., p. 147.

14. Andrew Salkey, *A Quality of Violence* ([1959] London, 1978), p. 7.

15. Ibid., p. 206.

16. See C.L.R. James, *Black Jacobins*, ch. XIII.

17. Frantz Fanon, *The Damned*, p. 46.

18. Derek Walcott, 'A Far Cry from Africa', *Public Opinion* (Jamaica) 15 September 1956, p. 7; reprinted *In a Green Night* (London, 1962), p. 18.

19. Denis Williams, *Other Leopards* (London, 1963), p. 19.

20. Ibid., p. 170.

21. Derek Walcott, 'The Muse of History', *Is Massa Day Dead?*, ed. Orde Coombs, (Garden City, NY, 1974), pp. 1–28.

22. Ibid., p. 155.

23. Lamming's experience had been foreshadowed by Alejo Carpentier on his visit to Haiti in 1943. See the discussion of Carpentier's 'On the Marvellous Real in America' in relation to Haiti, above pp. 112–13.

24. '*Vèvè*: symbolic chalk (or flour) marks made on the ground by the priest at the start of the *vodoun* ceremony'. – Kamau Brathwaite.

25. George Lamming, *Season of Adventure* ([1960] London, 1979), p. 29.

26. Edward Brathwaite, 'Timehri', *Savacou* 2 (1970) p. 38.

27. Kamau Brathwaite, 'The African Presence in Caribbean Literature', reprinted in *Roots*, p. 192.

28. Kamau Brathwaite, *Roots*, p. 194.

29. Edward Brathwaite, *The Arrivants* (Oxford, 1973), p. 4.

30. Ibid., pp. 12–16.

31. Ibid., pp. 42–5.

32. Ibid., pp. 62–9.

33. Ibid., p. 64.

34. Gordon Rohlehr, *Pathfinder* (Tunapuna, Trinidad, 1981), p. 104.

35. *The Arrivants*, pp. 62–9

36. Ibid., p. 97.

37. Maureen Warner-Lewis, *Notes to 'Masks'* (Benin, 1977), pp. 44–7; Gordon Rohlehr, *Pathfinder*, pp. 156, 157.

38. *The Arrivants*, p. 146.

39. Ibid., p. 157; cf. p. 91.

40. Ibid., p. 250.

41. Ibid., pp. 225–9.

42. Ibid., pp. 244–7.

43. Ibid., p. 243.

44. Ibid., pp. 219–21.

45. Ibid., pp. 222–4.

46. Ibid., pp. 254–7.

47. Ibid., p. 153.

48. Ibid., p. 187.

49. Ibid., p. 190.

50. Ibid., p. 266.

51. Ibid., p. 270.

52. Text published, with an important 'Overture', in Derek Walcott, *Dream on Monkey Mountain and Other Plays* (London, 1972).

53. Gordon Rohlehr, *The Shape of That Hurt and Other Essays* (Port-of-Spain, 1992), p. 66.

54. *Dream on Monkey Mountain*, p. [211].

55. Ibid., pp. 243–55.

56. Moustique cites Fanon's *Black Skin, White Masks* (1952) when, about to be lynched by the villagers, he argues that all belief is illusion. 'All I have is this [*shows the Mask*], black faces, white masks!' Ibid., p. 271.

57. Ibid., p. 326.

58. Dennis Scott, *An Echo in the Bone* (1974), Act II, in Errol Hill (ed.), *Plays for Today* (Longman, 1985), p. 136.

59. Erna Brodber, *Myal* (London, 1988), p. 38.

60. George Lamming, *Natives of my Person* (London, 1972), p. 351.

61. Other significant novels of the slave era include Orlando Patterson's *Die the Long Day* (1972) and John Hearne's *The Sure Salvation* (1981).

62. Ibid., p. 63.

63. Ibid., p. 113.

64. Ibid., p. 167.

65. David Dabydeen, *Turner* (London, 1994), p. 21.

Chapter 12
India in the Caribbean

Derek Walcott has recounted how, to his astonishment, he came by chance upon a full-scale dramatisation of the Hindu *Ramayana* epic being performed by the inhabitants of Felicity, a small village bordering the Caroni plain in Trinidad.

> Here in Trinidad I had discovered that one of the greatest epics in the world was seasonally performed, not with that desperate resignation of preserving a culture, but with an openness of belief that was as steady as the wind bending the cane lances of the Caroni plain.[1]

A notable feature of Caribbean writing in English has been the segregation of Asian literature and culture. By 1950, East Indians made up between a third and a half of the population in Trinidad and Guyana, and held both economic and political power within the community,[2] yet they had made relatively little impact on the country's cultural life. As indentured labourers, Asians settled in separate villages, often in conditions approaching slavery, creating 'little Indias' with their own religious and cultural identity. Socially, they were neither 'white' nor 'black', though Sam Selvon, as an Asian child growing up in Trinidad in the 1930s, found that 'White people came first, then Indians, then Blacks'.[3] The main early Asian compositions appear to have been songs on the hard plight of the coolie workers,[4] and it was the coming of Asians to the burgeoning cities of Port-of-Spain and San Fernando that brought the beginnings of Asian West Indian literature. In 1929 Seepersad Naipaul, father to V.S. and Shiva, moved to Port-of-Spain to become roving reporter for the local newspaper, *The Trinidad Guardian*, the island's one paid outlet for creative writing. The paper was edited by Gault MacGowan, a newcomer to Trinidad, who was fascinated by its bizarre variety: 'Voodoo in backyards, obeah, prisoners escaping from Devil's island, vampire bats'.[5] Seepersad enthusiastically shared MacGowan's sensational interests. From reportage, Seepersad's writing developed into fiction. His elementary education was backed by a Brahmin's reverence for learning, and his stories reflect an immediate experience of Creole East Indian life. The locally published *Guruveda and other Indian Tales* (1943), edited by V.S. Naipaul for an English edition in 1976,[6] still repays reading for the crisp style and crafted economy of the stories. Although he viewed village life with an urban eye, with a view to its backward decadence, the sketches made Asian village life available to imaginative writing, and for his son Vidiadhur offered 'a sense of the order and special reality (at once simpler and sharper than life) that written words could be seen to create'.[7]

The first novel of Asian West Indian life was Edgar Mittelholzer's *Corentyne Thunder* (1941). Set on the coastal plains of Guyana, the story evokes an atmospheric pastoral world in which a motherless Indian family, the farmer Ramgololl and his daughters Beena and Katree, exist at one with the landscape, and the 'thunder' of the title brings together the brooding weather and the village drums. In a neat parable, Beena steals old Ramgololl's hoarded savings to pay for a lawyer to save her young lover Jannee from a murder charge; discovering his loss, Ramgololl dies heartbroken and the (guilty) Jannee goes free, 'but the whole Corentyne remained just the same'.[8] The villagers' unsentimentalised harmony with nature is contrasted with that of the observer, the educated Geoffry, Mittelholzer's alter ego, alienated and contemplating suicide.

The first major Asian West Indian writer was Sam Selvon, who, leaving the semi-rural San Fernando to go to school in the city, felt himself 'as Trinidadian as anyone could claim to be, quite at ease with a cosmopolitan attitude, and I had no desire to isolate myself from the mixture of races that comprised the community'.[9] In his early work, his awareness of his rural background persists. 'Cane is Bitter', an early story from *Ways of Sunlight* (1957), poignantly recounts the village homecoming of Romesh. Although critical of the backward condition of the community, he joins in the cane harvest, recovering the pleasure of rhythmic physical work alongside his brother. But his parents have arranged a wedding with the young daughter of a neighbouring farmer. When he refuses, it becomes clear that he could never return to the village. The story keeps sympathy for both ways of life. Like the crops, society is in cyclical change, and the story ends with sun burning down on the rustling cane. But the last Caribbean story in *Ways of Sunlight*, 'A Drink of Water',[10] returns us centrally to the Asian peasant experience, focusing on the family of the labourer Manko in the village of Las Lomas, in the Trinidad Great Drought. The sun is 'a yellow furnace in the sky', crops and animals are dying, and the villagers pray to the rain god Parajan.

A villager called Rampersad strikes water, and Manko tells his boy Sunny that blessing comes from the earth as well as from the sky. But, urged by his wife, Rampersad surrounds his well with barbed wire, selling the water to the villagers by the bucketful. Manko and Sunny, when their savings are gone and their mother lies dying of illness and thirst, attempt to steal water. Discovered, they face disaster, but a miracle happens. A cloud covers the moon, and Parajan's life-giving rain sheets down on the village. This parable of man's exploitation of nature's bounty was developed in *The Plains of Caroni* (1970), written during Selvon's visit to the island in 1969. This uncharacteristically stark novel explores the changes that independence had brought to Trinidad. There was an air of jaunty confidence on the island. Skyscraper-like buildings have been built, cars replace pedestrians, and black people have taken their place in industry and administration. Yet the surface panache is fragile: beneath, 'there was always the hope that whatever was unwelcome could be adjusted; or the people fooled themselves they were free to accept or reject, or create a new government if things became unbearable'.[11]

Among the rural communities, independence also brings change. The labourer Harrilal sells the family land in Wilderness to the expatriate sugar company, and becomes employed as their overseer. His new wealth, husbanded with peasant care by his wife Seeta, buys a large concrete house, a massive cream-coloured car, and sends their son Romesh to the University of the West Indies to study agricultural biology. Harrilal persuades his elder brother Balgobin to become his neighbour. But Balgobin is a labourer of the older generation, his whole identity bound up with 'Poya', his razor-honed cutlass. When the company introduces a mechanical cane harvester, and he faces the loss of his way of life, he secretly attacks the gleaming machine in a state of drunken hallucination, severing the fuel lines and gutting it with fire.[12] Romesh is sent by the company to detect the arsonist, and in finding him discovers his real father, for he had been the secret love child of Seeta and Balgobin. Balgobin dies, and caught in an agricultural riot, Romesh is only saved by the presence of his white girlfriend, Petra. As Balgobin's body is cremated with the traditional rites, the young couple prepare to leave Trinidad. Though not Selvon's finest novel, its writing has a focused seriousness, an uncompromising exploration of the crises facing his childhood's culture. In contrast, *Those that Eat the Cascadura* (1972) is a slighter, nostalgic novel, in which an English visitor finds love and healing among Indian girls working the coffee plantations of the interior. Other Asian Caribbean writers besides Selvon have explored ambivalent relationships to town and country, none more sensitively than Ismith Khan in his short story 'A Day in the Country', describing a town boy's visit to his village relatives.[13]

Although published within a decade of Selvon's *A Brighter Sun*, Ismith Khan's evocative *The Jumbie Bird* has received relatively little notice. This largely autobiographical novel explores generations of Pathans settled in the centre of Port-of-Spain. The grandfather, Kale Khan, retains his warrior identity, fiercely resenting British colonialism, and looking to Hindustan as his homeland. But he is out of place. He drives his wife, the independent Binti, to support herself by selling coal, and emotionally crushes his peacefully natured son, Rahim. He can relate only to his grandson, Jamini, through whose eyes the story is largely seen. When Kale Khan stick-fights at the annual *Shia* Muslim festival Hossay, however, repressed feelings for his Rahim affect his sight and, faltering, he is struck dead. Released, his son finds happiness making traditional Indian jewellery. A vivid evocation of Khan's childhood Port-of-Spain, the novel is both social observation and symbolic. Woodford Square, laid out like a Union Jack and over-looked by the statue of Sir Ralph Woodford who introduced indentured labour into Trinidad, is the refuge of the derelict and unemployed, providing a natural symbol of the colonial legacy. The eerie cry of the jumbie bird [owl] intimates death, contrasting with the grandmother's worn and shining coal scoop, an image of endurance burnished by suffering.[14] Jamini finds both alienation and a sense of personal release in the city. Khan's later novels, however, showed increasing pessimism. In *The Obeah Man* (1964) the holy man Zampi, 'one of the breeds of the island that has no race, no caste, no colour',[15] stands out against the depravity of Port-of-Spain with its disorderly carnival and stick-fighting. Much of the novel is set in a bar dominated by a sagging plaster effigy of Britannia. A still darker novel, Khan's *The Crucifixion* (1987), explores the plight of a guru who discovers that he is the victim of self-delusion.

As Jeremy Poynting has observed,[16] writing of rural Asian life has continued to reflect the sufferings of the peasant. In Peter Kempadoo's *Guiana Boy* (1960) and *Old Thom's Harvest* (1965) the decadence of the disintegrating plantation is relieved by the vitality and independence of picaresque characters like Uncle Tombi. The villages and rural communities of *Fireflies* (1970) and the *Chip-Chip Gatherers* (1973), by V.S. Naipaul's brother Shiva, reflect almost universal despair. Desolation reaches a surrealist intensity in Sonny Ladoo's *No Pain Like This Body* (1972), a startlingly intense account of a poor Hindu family in a rice-growing area of an imaginary eastern Caribbean island. In the claustrophobic community, domestic violence, hunger, illness and death combine in a landscape dangerous with snakes, red ants and scorpions, and drenched with the August rains. The story, dignified by the peasants' spirit of survival, shows a literary genius frustrated by Ladoo's tragic death at the age of twenty-eight. The leading Asian writer of country life, however, is Rooplall Monar, born on a plantation in Demarara, Guyana, and one of the few Asian writers who has experienced agricultural labour at first hand. He has spent his life working among the people of the east coast as journalist, estate book-keeper, teacher and traditional healer, and the life of the east coast peoples permeates his writing. His work is uneven, but as a master of the spoken idiom his best work creates humane, sharply focused sketches that reveal with unrivalled empathy the conditions and beliefs of the Indo-Guyanese plantation folk. They contain detailed records of their family and power structures, their relationships with overseers and authority, and peasant customs, illuminated by humour and an eye for the idiosyncrasies of the peasant character. The short stories of *Backdam People* (1985), his poems, *Koker*(1987) and his fine novel *Janjhat* (1989), all portray estate life from the 1930s to the 1950s; in the less successful *High House and Radio* (1992), the old barrack-room estates break up, giving the people greater freedom and better living conditions, but leaving them to face the loss of old certainties, and the pressures of a cosmopolitan Guyana.

Of the younger writers, David Dabydeen's *Coolie Odyssey* (1988) has attempted to do in miniature what Brathwaite did for the African diaspora, a medley of poems set in Guyana and Britain, deliberately contrasting in tone, subject and style, yet linked by a common core of Asian identity intensified by the pressures of emigration. His novel, *The Counting House* (1966), goes back to the Asians in nineteenth-century Guiana, moving between the Caribbean and India, to focus on the struggles of a peasant couple who migrate to British Guiana to find fresh land but find plantation life tangled in a web of commercial greed and continuing violence. The influence of traditional Hindu beliefs has persisted in West Indian Asian writing, and has become muted. Lakshmi Persaud has lovingly evoked the Hindu customs of her childhood Trinidad in *Butterfly in the Wind* (1990). Sasenarine Persaud adapted concepts of incarnation from the *Gita* to frame the spiritual quests of the boy Dalip in *Dear Death* (1989), and of the teacher Raj in *The Ghost of the Bellows Man* (1992), of which Persaud wrote:

> The novel reaches for the soul of the protagonist – a soul
> reaching to catch a soul – in a Hindu, and Indian way
> which makes the entire world Indian – and this fashions the
> style and form of the novel.[17]

Hindu faith and the Carib bone flute from her childhood Guyana come together to create the central image in Mahandai Das's fine collection of poems *Bones* (1988), where out of dry despair the bone becomes the fragile instrument of reincarnation:

> play gentle, love
> my frail reed's
> single stem
> can scarcely hold
> this rhapsody.[18]

Such writing claims ties with Indian culture rather than with India itself. In her poem 'If I came to India', Das muses on which India she would identify with – Gandhi's, the Deccan, Tibet? Harischandra Khemaj's *Cosmic Dance* (1994) develops Hindu concepts of self and karma in a socio-political thriller set in contemporary Guyana. If Asian West Indians were late in finding their voice, they now write from within an identity that is fully Caribbean.

Notes

1. Derek Walcott, *The Antilles. Fragments of Epic Memory* (London, 1993), p. 7.

2. Leo Lowental, *West Indian Societies* (1972), pp. 61–3, 145.

3. Sam Selvon, 'Epilogue – three into one can't go, East Indian, Trinidadian' [1979], reprinted in *Foreday Morning* (Harlow, 1989), p. 212.

4. Jeremy Poynting, *Literature and Cultural Pluralism: East Indians in the Caribbean*, PhD thesis, University of Leeds, 1985.

5. V.S. Naipaul, 'Foreword' to Seepersad Naipaul, *The Adventures of Guruveda and other Stories* (London, 1976), p. 14.

6. Seepersad Naipaul, ibid.

7. Ibid., p. 19.

8. Edgar Mittelholzer, *Corentyne Thunder* ([1941] London, 1970), p. 229.

9. Samuel Selvon, *Foreday Morning*, p. 213.

10. Samuel Selvon, *The Ways of Sunlight*, pp. 112–21.

11. Samuel Selvon, *The Plains of Caroni* (London, 1970), p. 10.

12. Ibid., pp. 87–97.

13. *Colorado Quarterly* (Autumn 1962), pp. 121–35; reprinted in *From the Green Antilles*, ed. Barbara Howe (London, 1966), pp. 48–62.

14. Ismith Khan, *The Jumbie Bird* ([1961] Harlow, 1985), pp. 183–4.

15. Ismith Khan, *The Obeah Man* (London, 1964), p. 11.

16. Jeremy Poynting, *From Sugar Cane to the Suburbs: Images of Diversity and Change in Indo-Caribbean Fiction*, University of Warwick Occasional Papers in Caribbean Studies, no. 1 (Warwick, n.d.).

17. Sasenarine Persaud, *The Ghost of the Bellow's Man* (Leeds, 1992), p. 132.

18. Mahandai Das, 'Flute', *Bones* (Leeds, 1988), p. 46.

Part V
On the Frontiers of Language

I went out to map the land and the land mapped me.
Wilson Harris[1]

Words are but the surface appearance of the deeper echoes of song, dance and eternal rhythms. Words are necessary. You must hear them. But there are times when it is not important to listen closely. Only their resonance is needed, their concrete existence and deeper urges are awakened.
Edouard Glissant[2]

This section considers ways in which Caribbean writers have reached out to their history, culture and environment, and have found themselves changed in the process.

Chapter 13
Things as They Are: V.S. Naipaul

When in 1989 Vidiadhur Surajprasad Naipaul was decorated with the Trinity Cross, Trinidad's highest honour, the wheel had come full circle. Nearly forty years earlier he had left the island to take up a scholarship to University College, Oxford, relieved to escape from a hot, small, remote and restrictive colony, to the centre of his imaginative world. He later recalled how, in an over-heated bedsitter in England, he had been 'awakened by the nightmare that I was back in tropical Trinidad'.[3] His first novels of Trinidad life, *The Mystic Masseur* (1957) and *The Suffrage of Elvira* (1958), prompted George Lamming to accuse him of writing 'castrated satire': 'Naipaul, with the diabolical help of Oxford University, has done a thorough job of wiping [his West Indian identity] out of his guts'.[4] In these novels Naipaul's disgust is indeed visceral: like Ramlogan's food shop in *The Mystic Masseur*, Trinidad looks as if it had been gone over, every morning, 'with a greased rag'.[5] The novel in fact shifts uneasily between sympathetic irony and satire. Ganesh Ramsumair, an incompetent 'masseur' in a Trinidad village, tricks his way to fame as a Hindu mystic, then to the Presidency of the Fuente Grove Institute of Hindu Culture, reaching supreme political status as 'G. Ramsay Muir, M.B.E.'. But, as Naipaul notes, 'The history of Ganesh is, in a way, the history of our times':[6] Ganesh is an impostor, but one created by a bogus society, and even shows potential as a genuine healer. He is asked to exorcise a malign 'black cloud' hanging over the boy narrator's head since the death of his brother. In the ceremony, staged in Ganesh's darkened bedroom, he tells the boy, 'I believe in you, but you must believe in me too'.[7] In an act of faith, the boy does, and the troubling 'cloud' disappears.

The later account of Ganesh's political career, in contrast, is straight satire, and Naipaul shows even less ambivalence about *The Suffrage of Elvira* (1958), a bitter farce concerning an election in a remote Trinidad village, where an outsider, Surujpat Harbans, an elderly truck-driver, gains the seat, winning Muslim, Hindu and Negro votes by bribery, superstition and skulduggery, though the novel must be placed in the context of Trinidad's massively bungled first free elections of 1950. In 1962 Naipaul published *The Middle Passage: Impressions of Five Societies . . . in the West Indies and South America.* The project was framed by Victorian travelogues of the Caribbean, and opens with a quotation from J.A. Froude's *The English in the West Indies* (1887). Like Froude, Naipaul portrayed a Caribbean lacking dignity or significance: 'History is built around achievement and creation; and nothing was created in the West Indies'.[8] Although often seen as an attack on a decadent Caribbean, however, Naipaul also wrote in anger against Europe. He deplored the rapacity that continued to rob the area for tourism, and which debased calypso for commerce. As Derek Walcott, reviewing *The Middle Passage* in *The [Trinidad] Sunday Guardian*, noted, it was not so much the content as the 'style' that offended West Indians. Naipaul treated his subject to 'a supercilious pat on the head, or a friendly volley of insults'. Walcott also perceived that Naipaul's urbanity covered 'a chronic dispiritedness'.[9] His 'style' was in fact brittle. Although decorated for his literary craft,[10] Naipaul was later to write that 'language can be so deceptive. It has taken me much time to realize how bad I am at interpreting the conventions and modes of English speech'.[11] Under the urbane expression lay a painful void. In a British education

> the language was ours, to use as we pleased. The literature that came with it was therefore of peculiar authority; but this literature was like an alien mythology. There was, for instance, Wordsworth's notorious poem about the daffodil. A pretty little flower no doubt; but we had never seen it. Could the poem have any meaning for us?[12]

In a story published in *Miguel Street*, Naipaul described 'B. [Black] Wordsworth', who spent his life composing 'the greatest poem in the world',[13] but who died without writing a line. Naipaul may have had in mind Aldous Huxley's essay, 'Wordsworth in the Tropics', which claimed that the Romantic view of nature was irrelevant away from the benign English Lake District.[14] But 'B. Wordsworth's' vision is not questioned; what is lacking is a culture which recognised anything but the calypsoes by which he made his living. Alongside resentment over having to learn of daffodils, Naipaul cites his puzzlement over 'jasmine'. Only in later life did he discover that he had known the flower since childhood. He tried to associate name and reality. 'Jasmine, jasmine. But the word and the flower had been separate in my mind for too long. They did not come together'.[15] Yet as Naipaul's brother Shiva noted, 'until it was written about, it had no status; no fixed place in the ragbag of images and ill-assorted feelings that characterize a tropical, Trinidadian childhood'.[16]

Although attacked for lacking Selvon's popular sympathies, Naipaul as a writer in England broke his creative 'block' in the same way as Selvon, by turning to the Trinidad vernacular idiom. In 1955, looking for inspiration while sitting at a typewriter in the freelancers' room at the BBC, he found himself writing: 'Every morning when he got up Hat would sit on the banister of his back verandah and shout across, "What happening there, Bogart?"'[17] Without knowing where it would lead, he began writing the sketches later edited together as *Miguel Street* (1959). The book consists of what Selvon would call 'episodes' or 'ballads', evoking memories of the Naipaul family's neighbours in a working-class street of Port-of-Spain – Bogart, Hat, Big Foot – names which in the calypso tradition both dramatise and mock. The original 'Bogart' was a Punjabi, and the community was largely Asian, yet in the stories themselves names are the only given identity. Behind each character lay a mystery. How did the idle Bogart make any money? What did Popo, calling himself a carpenter, really make in his shop? In discovering the truth, the boy maps his world. In adult terms, it is one of futility and illusion. Bogart's splendid fable of keeping a brothel in British Guiana hid a bigamous relationship with a girl in rural Trinidad; Popo stole and painted furniture, claiming it as his own to tempt his wife to return. Yet the tension between fantasy and futility remains poignant and, within the terms of the boy's imagination, positive. When Popo becomes a real carpenter, the boy prefers the old Popo of 'the thing without a name', and he weeps for the dying B. Wordsworth, who has written nothing, because failure in itself has become poetic. 'I left the house, and ran home crying, like a poet, for everything I saw.' Only towards the end, when Hat goes to gaol for wife-beating, does he feel 'something inside me had died'. In the final story the boy narrator is sent away to school in England by his mother who says, 'You getting too wild in this place.' He leaves 'not looking back, looking only at my shadow before me, a dancing dwarf on the tarmac'.[18]

The 'dancing dwarf' intimates Naipaul's disembodied stance in the early novels, in which nothing prepared the reader for the warmth and complexity of *A House for Mr Biswas* (1960). Naipaul began writing it in a bleak, littered attic. 'Old furniture, "things", homelessness: they were more than ideas when I began writing.' Then he found two years of solitude in a 'quiet, friendly house in Streatham Hill'.[19] The movement is reflected in the novel itself as the life of Biswas, a figure closely modelled on his own father Seepersad,[20] moves from isolation towards order within a house of his own. Both malign Hindu karma and colonial deprivation preside over Biswas's birth: he is born with a sixth finger – a bad omen and a sign of malnutrition – and in the wrong decade, on marshland later found to be an oil field. Disaster haunts him. Warned against water, he is not taught to swim, so when he goes missing, his father drowns diving to find him. Terror of isolation seeps into later life. As his father drowned, 'Mr Biswas was alone in the dark hut, and frightened'.[21] Later on a bus he has a momentary glimpse of a boy in a white vest, standing by the road.

Mr Biswas could not remember where the hut stood, but the picture remained: a boy leaning against an earth house that had no reason for being there, under the dark falling sky, a boy who didn't know where the road, and that bus, went.[22]

An introvert, by turns dreamy and spikily aggressive, Biswas is an easy prey for Mrs Tulsi, who, with her son and henchman Seth, presides over the ill-defined Tulsi mercantile empire from the fortress of Hanuman House. To acquire his Brahmin blood for the clan, Mrs Tulsi traps him into marriage with Shama, a junior Tulsi daughter, and exploits him for bare food and keep. As Gordon Rohlehr has noted, 'on closer examination, Hanuman House reveals itself not as the coherent reconstruction of the clan, but as a slave society, erected by Mrs Tulsi and Seth who need workers to help rebuild their tottering empire'.[23] Fastidiously clean, Biswas's taste is appalled by the Tulsis' sticky, screaming babies,[24] and their rice and curry bubbling with grease.[25] At the climactic centre of the novel, Biswas breaks away to build a house of his own, but he finds himself back in the world of his childhood terrors, surrounded by hostile labourers. Instinctively Brahmin, he bathes obsessively,[26] sings Hindi songs[27] and prays 'Rama Rama Sita Rama, Rama Rama Sita Rama . . .'.[28] A Caribbean natural disaster confirms his personal one, and a hurricane destroys his house. The labourer who rescues him is looking for 'my poor little calf' in the floods, recalling his father's death when rescuers, searching the pool for Biswas, find a drowned calf.[29]

Yet Biswas has to discover that his identity lies not in a retreat into the past, but in facing things as they are. He does not break down. The second half of the novel changes in tone as Biswas frees himself from the Tulsi family, as the clan itself disintegrates into individualism. Buying an old colonial Great House (up 'Christopher Columbus Road'), the Tulsis plunder it for private gain. Cumulatively through the book, houses and their contents symbolise a search for order and human meaning. Where Hanuman House is choked with miscellaneous clutter gathered indiscriminately by the clan, Biswas preserves objects significant of each stage in his inner Odyssey – paint-brushes kept oiled and supple; a typewriter painted yellow; a hatstand, the sign of his aspiring gentility. Biswas and his family finally achieve a home. It is jerry-built, heavily mortgaged, but nevertheless offers a shelter against the void faced by 'unaccommodated man'. 'From now their lives would be ordered, their memories coherent'.[30] Words, like houses, create significance for Biswas. He devours any print to hand. 'I have read a lot', he tells the Sentinel editor, Mr Burnett, 'Hall Caine, Marie Corelli, Jacob Boehme, Mark Twain, . . . Samuel Smiles, . . . Marcus Aurelius, . . . Epictetus'.[31] He paints letters with sensuous delight: 'I could eat the Gill Sans R,' Burnett tells him, admiring one of his signs.[32] Literature becomes his defence against exterior reality. Repeatedly he starts a story called 'Escape' beginning, 'At the age of thirty-three, when he was already the father of four children . . .'. In this the hero, trapped into marriage and burdened with children, meets a slim girl dressed in white, who cannot bear him children:[33] the story is never finished. Hunched up in his plantation shack, threatened by the labourers, he consoles himself by reading *The Hunchback of Notre Dame*.[34] He later discovers the 'solace' of Dickensian satire.

> In the grotesques of Dickens everything he feared and
> suffered from was ridiculed and diminished, so that his own
> anger, his own contempt became unnecessary, and he was
> given strength to bear with the most difficult part of his
> day: dressing in the morning, that daily affirmation of faith
> in oneself, which at times was for him almost like an act of
> sacrifice.[35]

Yet behind satire and escapism lies another narrative. He writes a simple account, addressed to his recently dead mother, celebrating her tenderness when returning home as a child. Although edited in memory, the story gives access to a repressed, intimate relationship. Reading it to a writers' circle, unprotected by literary style, Biswas breaks down, leaves and is violently sick. The episode has a wider significance. *A House for Mr Biswas*, too, was painful to write, and after it was published Naipaul could not bring himself to read it for twenty years.[36] Yet it was a house of words accommodating a lost father, a rejected childhood: for Naipaul, too, life became ordered, memories coherent. It provided a humanist assertion from which he could turn to a global quest to see 'things as they are'.

The year *Biswas* was published, Naipaul visited India, his ancestral homeland. He found only the dirt, overcrowding and futility intimated in the title he gave his travelogue, *An Area of Darkness* (1964).[37] He returned to London 'facing my own emptiness, my feeling of being physically lost'. Yet, paradoxically, he now saw 'how close I had been to the total Indian negation', and recognised that with personal self-discovery 'it was slipping away from me' for ever.[38] While in Kashmir he wrote *Mr Stone and the Knights Companion* (1963), set in London, in which a middle aged, alienated librarian became an unlikely alter ego for his Asian exploration of Karmic negation. *The Mimic Men* (1967) straddles the Caribbean and Britain. In form it is metafiction. Ralph Singh lives an empty life in London, writing his memoirs. He is forty, and his active life is already past. Scenes of London in the snow become a trope for existence without colour, without vitality. He drifts in a world of immigrants, chance contacts of meaningless sex, the detritus of old Empire. He defines his theme as 'shipwreck'. 'I have used this word before. With my island background, it was the word that always came to me'.[39] He is marooned in London as he once was on his home island of Isabella. Isabella is the modern Caribbean, first created by European exploitation, now fragmented by commercial and political chicanery. Ralph's father, a schoolteacher and poor, is alienated from his mother's family who have become millionaires from bottling Coca-Cola for the local market. At school Ralph changes his name Ranjit Kripalsingh to Ralph R. Singh. Yet he sees Ralph as 'unimportant', while Ranjit remains his real 'secret name'.[40] Frustrated emotions provoke aimless violence, and Ralph is nearly killed in a drunken, confused scene by his half-brother Cecil. Ralph has fantasies of his Aryan ancestors riding across the snows of northern India. In contrast, his father becomes a politicised *sanyasi*, a priest among the island poor. Trapped within a colonised consciousness, Ralph knows nothing of his father's career, learning it from the English magnate Lord Stockwell. Stockwell describes it as the 'Highway Code', 'no good until you are on the road'. The phrase is recalled when Ralph, in loveless coupling with a fat prostitute, experiences a moment of 'timelessness, horror, solace. The Highway Code! Through poor, hideous flesh to have learnt about flesh; through flesh to have gone beyond flesh'.[41] The novel becomes a meditation on the relationship between 'reality' and the craft of fiction. As a co-lodger shifts his food around his plate to make it edible,[42] Ralph the writer placed his failed marriage before accounts of his childhood, or framed life in Isabella within his experience of London, seeking to give it meaning. 'So writing, for all its initial distortion, clarifies, and even becomes a process of life'.[43]

The work initiated Naipaul's experimentation with the arrangement of historical narratives. *The Loss of El Dorado* (1969) juxtaposes the quest for El Dorado from 1595 to 1813 against Thomas Picton's later attempt as military Governor of Trinidad to foment rebellion in the Spanish Caribbean, intimating that the area, the focus for European exploitation, had the effect of reducing all aspiration to squalid absurdity. *In a Free State* (1971) moves to explore the interface between journalistic 'fact' and creative fiction. The Prologue, taken ostensibly from Naipaul's diary of a voyage from Piraeus to Alexandria, introduces one who appears a 'romantic wanderer of an earlier generation',[44] but on closer view appears a tattered tramp. Terrorised by his 'respectable' fellow-passengers, themselves multi-national wanderers, he becomes a type for the uprooted characters in the three novella, linked by a common sense of dispossession, that follow. They concern Santosh an Indian in New York, an unnamed Asian West Indian in Trinidad and London, and the English Bobby and Linda who make a terrifying journey across a mid-African country in revolution. The closing journal entry describes Luxor, where, among the ruins of a lost civilisation, tourists watch an Egyptian guard slash at children scrambling for food, and soldiers at the station await defeat in the impending war on Mount Sinai.

In 1973 Naipaul had visited Trinidad to report on the trial of the Black Power leader Michael de Freitas ('Michael X.') for brutally murdering British Gale Benson and other followers in his commune – violence which set against the failure of the island's 1970 Black Power movement.[45] Out of these Naipaul wrote the novel *Guerillas* (1975), set in a bleak, arid landscape, a composite of Trinidad and Jamaica in which Michael X. becomes Jimmy Ahmed and Gale Benson becomes Jane. The confused racial identities (Michael X. was light-skinned, Jimmy in the novel is half Chinese; Benson wore African clothes and affected Muslim faith) is mixed with romantic idealism, sex, commercial exploitation and liberal politics, creating a violent cocktail of desire and illusion where sodomy, masochism and murderous sexual humiliation become the ultimate expression of lost direction. Jimmy Ahmed's self-image as Heathcliff and Jane's association with Jane Eyre point to the novel's ironic subtext in the Brontë romance, and link it to the seminal novel of Caribbean deracination, Jean Rhys's *Wide Sargasso Sea*.[46]

A Bend in the River (1979) again intercuts fiction and history, drawing on Naipaul's travelogues, 'A New King for the Congo'[47] and *A Congo Diary*, published in 1980. Taking as its central figure Salim, a deraciné Muslim, attempting to establish his business in a disintegrating central African country in which only the bush and the water hyacinths, clogging the waterway to the outside world, remain certain. The two narratives of *Finding the Centre* (1984) bring together 'A Fragment of Autobiography', in which Naipaul contemplates finding a literary vocation, with the testimony of Ivory Coast Africans searching to understand their predicament recorded in 'The Crocodiles of Yamoussoukri'. Both reveal aspects of 'the process of writing'.

> A writer after a time carries his world with him, his own burden of experience, human experience and literary experience (one deepening the other); and I do believe – especially after writing 'Prologue to an Autobiography' – that I would have found equivalent connections with my past and myself wherever I had gone.[48]

Sequential narrative is dissolved still further in *The Enigma of Arrival*. A Proustian pattern of reflections, it takes its title from a surrealist painting by de Chirico which intimates that arrival and journeying are one. Returning to the wharf to rejoin his ship, the traveller finds 'there was no mast above the walls of the wharf. No ship. His journey – his life's journey – had been made'.[49] The novel intercuts autobiography with travel, literary and artistic subtexts, and creative fiction, with a focus on Wiltshire, Naipaul's home for much of his life. He explores the inscription of its landscape in the paintings of Constable, and the writings of Cobbett and Richard Jeffreys. He considers its peoples. Moving from the life of the labourers in the section 'Jack's Garden' to the squirality in 'Ivy', England's history within the returning of the seasons leads him to a new understanding of his own roots in the cyclical cultures of rural India. In the epilogue, the cremation of his sister in Trinidad by a Hindu ritual no longer appears an alien event. Death, too, unites his family in the mystery of continuity and, as the book ends, the author leaves to begin writing it.

A Way in the World (1994) continues Naipaul's experiment with diverse forms of narrative discourse. The opening section is an ostensibly factual account of one Leonard Side, a Muslim East Indian in Trinidad who both dresses corpses as an undertaker, and also decorates cakes with icing. The dual occupation disturbs the narrator, and points to our own unexplained incongruities. 'We cannot understand all the traits we have inherited. Sometimes we are strangers to ourselves'.[50] History, too, possesses mysterious lacunae. In 'A Parcel of Papers, a Roll of Tobacco, a Tortoise', a surgeon interrogates Christopher Columbus about his *History* in the light of Don José, an Arawak christened by the Spanish, using 'fiction' to reanimate forgotten 'truths' about early European contact with the Amerindian Caribbean. It is a significant development in Naipaul's art, for whereas, in his earlier work, the intuitive imagination was used to reveal Caribbean futility, it now becomes a means for identifying and embodying the reality of its lost communities. The final section returns to the present. It recounts the murder of Blair, a Trinidadian working as a Radical activist in East Africa. Naipaul renegotiates the themes of his earlier *The Loss of El Dorado*, but instead of the pessimism of his earlier writing, Naipaul now reads a hard-won hope in the endurance of humanity. If Blair had been asked:

> Does this betrayal mock your life? – the answer
> immediately after death would have been 'No! No! No!'[51]

Notes

1. Harris, reported by Pauline Melville, *Kyk-over-Al* no. 45 (December 1994), p. 65.

2. Edouard Glissant, *The Ripening* ([1958] London, 1985), translated by Michael Dash, p. 169.

3. V.S. Naipaul, *The Middle Passage* ([1962] Harmondsworth, 1969), p. 43.

4. George Lamming, *Pleasures*, p. 225.

5. V.S. Naipaul, *The Mystic Masseur* ([1957] Harmondsworth, 1964), p. 33.

6. Ibid., p. 18.

7. Ibid., p. 129.

8. Ibid., p. 29.

9. Derek Walcott, 'History and Picong . . . in *The Middle Passage*' (1962), reprinted in Hamner, *Critical Perspective on Derek Walcott*, pp. 17–18.

10. Naipaul's numerous prizes include the Booker Prize in 1971, and the David Cohen British Literature Prize in 1991. In 1990 he was knighted by the British Government for his literary achievements.

11. 'Jasmine', *The Overcrowded Barracoon* ([1972] Harmondsworth, 1976), p. 29.

12. Ibid., p. 24.

13. V.S. Naipaul, *Miguel Street* ([1959] London, 1974), p. 62.

14. Teaching English literature in Jamaica in the early 1960s, I also found my students indignant at Huxley's thesis. Wordsworth's experience, they argued, was as germane to the Jamaican Blue Mountains as it was to English Cumbria.

15. V.S. Naipaul, 'Jasmine', *The Overcrowded Barracoon*, p. 31.

16. Shiva Naipaul, 'The Writer Without a Society', in *Commonwealth* (Aarhus, 1972), edited by Anna Rutherford, p. 115.

17. V.S. Naipaul, *Finding the Centre* (1984), pp. 17–18.

18. V.S. Naipaul, *Miguel Street* ([1959] London, 1974), p. 222.

19. V.S. Naipaul, Foreword, *A House for Mr Biswas*, third edition ([1961] London, 1984), pp. 4–5.

20. See John Thieme, *The Web of Tradition* (1987), pp. 198–9.

21. V.S. Naipaul, *A House for Mr Biswas*, p. 28.

22. Ibid., p. 171.

23. Gordon Rohlehr, 'Character and Rebellion', in *A House for Mr Biswas*, reprinted in Robert D. Hamner, *Critical Perspectives on V.S. Naipaul* (London, 1979), p. 87.

24. V.S. Naipaul, *A House for Mr Biswas*, p. 138.

25. Ibid., p. 120.

26. Ibid., p. 188.

27. Ibid., p. 188.

28. Ibid., p. 262.

29. Ibid., pp. 29, 164.

30. Ibid., p. 523.

31. Ibid., p. 289.

32. Ibid., p. 291.

33. Ibid., pp. 311, 432.

34. Ibid., p. 239.

35. Ibid., p. 338.

36. V.S. Naipaul, 'Foreword' to *A House for Mr Biswas*, 1984 edition, p. 1.

37. V.S. Naipaul, *An Area of Darkness*, p. 30.

38. Ibid., p. 226.

39. V.S. Naipaul, *The Mimic Men* (London, 1967), p. 32.

40. Ibid., p. 113.

41. Ibid., p. 283.

42. Ibid., p. 273.

43. Ibid., p. 301.

44. V.S. Naipaul, *In a Free State* (London, 1971), p. 10.

45. 'The Killings in Trinidad', *Sunday Times*, 12 and 19 May 1974; reprinted in *The Return of Eva Peron* (London, 1980).

46. See Bruce King, *V.S. Naipaul* (Basingstoke, 1993), p. 111.

47. *New York Review of Books* 22 (June 26, 1975), pp. 19–25.

48. V.S. Naipaul, *Finding the Centre* (London, 1984), p. 11.

49. V.S. Naipaul, *The Enigma of Arrival* (London, 1987), p. 157.

50. V.S. Naipaul, *A Way in the World* (London, 1994), p. 4.

51. Ibid., p. 368.

Chapter 14

The 'True Substance of Life':[1]
Wilson Harris

Wilson Harris's fictional debut in 1960 with *Palace of the Peacock* has proved increasingly significant within the development of Caribbean literature. Harris himself has written some twenty-one novels, besides a major body of essays, lectures and critical works, by the end of 1997.[2] These have uncompromisingly developed his premise that West Indian literature should transform reality, rather than being 'a vested interest in a fixed assumption and classification of things'.[3] His fiction to date falls broadly into five interlinked cycles, with transitional works: the geographically based 'Guyanese Quartet' (1960–93); the 'dramas of consciousness' written between 1965 and 1970; outward-looking explorations of global identity (1972–82); and the 'Carnival Quartet' produced from 1985 to 1990. Two recent novels show Harris turning back to Guyana in a world perspective, and appear to indicate a new phase.[4]

Harris remains most easily accessible through his early writing. The volumes of the 'Guyanese Quartet' explore individual facets of that country's national character which make up Donne's crew in the already examined *Palace of the Peacock*. *The Far Journey of Oudin* (1961) focuses on the East Indian communities of the coastal plains who settled between the savannah and the coast. The commercial struggle between the wealthy landowner Mahommed, the inheritor of the old sugar plantations, and the ruthless, sexually impotent money-lender Ram, is interwoven with Ram's master–servant relation with his servant, Oudin, and the redemptive womanhood of Oudin's wife Beti. Despite passages of great poetic power, peasant socio-economic concerns failed to fire Harris's imagination. However, the remote Pomeroon area of Guyana provided a fertile setting for the psychic and political conflicts of *The Whole Armour* (1962). A community, a 'veneer of settlement against the encroachment of the sea and river and – above all – the jungle',[5] was also trapped between the Victorian and modern eras, in which the recluse Abram signals the old dispensation, while the outcast Cristo, possibly his son by the whore Magda, carries the future. Cristo, accused of murder, is hidden in Abram's hut. When Abram dies Magda forces her son to place his own clothes on Abram's rotting body and escape towards Venezuela, and she proclaims Cristo dead, holding a wild village 'wake'. Cristo however returns, appearing at night in the guise of a great jaguar, and meeting his love, Sharon. As the book ends, Cristo and Sharon, who has given birth to their son, are surrounded by the police, an image of the hope and peril facing the young nation of Guyana.

The Secret Ladder (1963) is partly autobiographical. Its central character is Fenwick, a government surveyor who, like Harris, explores the Canje river in order to remap the rivers and water tables of the interior. As Tim Cribb has demonstrated,[6] Harris's own task was to decipher a palimpsest of earlier maps and surveys of the interior, and measure the shifting balance of river, swamp and savannah on which the delicate ecology depended. In the novel the 'ladder' of the title is the gauge to the water level, but also a sensitive map of the emerging Guyanese identity, and the measure of Fenwick's rising spiritual awareness. Fenwick's mission focuses on a conflict between the developing coastal areas, requiring water for irrigation, and the natives of the interior, dependent on the river levels. Like Donne in Harris's first novel (Fenwick's boat is called 'Palace of the Peacock'), Fenwick also has to establish political authority over a racially mixed and discordant crew, while at the same time reconciling conflicts between European, African and Amerindian elements in his own ancestry. At the climax the surveying party confront a hostile community descended from escaped African slaves, and their leader, Poseidon. A classical name was often given to slaves, but 'Poseidon' also suggests the Greek child of Chronos [Time] and Rhea [Earth], and, more fundamentally, the life force of water that Fenwick surveys. Harris's poetic, hallucinatory prose here as elsewhere shifts constantly between levels of intuitive meaning.

> The strangest figure [Fenwick] had ever seen had appeared
> in the opening of the bush, dressed in a flannel vest,
> flapping ragged fins of trousers on his legs. Fenwick could
> not help fastening his eyes greedily upon him as if he saw
> down a bottomless gauge and river of reflection. He wanted
> to laugh at the wierd sensation but was unable to do so.
> The old man's hair was white as wool and his cheeks –
> covered with wild curling wings – looked like an unkempt
> sheep's back. The black wooden snake of skin peeping
> through its animal blanket was wrinked and stitched
> together incredibly.[7]

Both Fenwick and Jordan, his African deputy leader, recognise their affinity with Poseidon. Their meeting brings catastrophe as Poseidon dies in the confrontation and his followers flee. The tragedy, however, opens up the possibility of a new creative order in the violent, redemptive passion of Bryant for the woman Catalena, and Fenwick prepares to voyage on from 'an inquisition of dead gods and heroes'[8] into a new beginning.

Heartland (1964) is a transitional work. Its central character, Stevenson – a government inspector posted into the Guyanese jungles – looks back to Donne and Fenwick, and other characters from the *Quartet* reappear. The novel traces his search for a lost 'heartland' of identity, reaching a point of self-abandonment on the borderland between life and death, where he helps Petra, the deserted Arawak woman of *Palace*, deliver her child, recognising in her both lover and Muse. But at the end he pursues his quest through the 'crack in the floor or prison of the landscape'[9] through a decayed and menacing dream world towards presumptive death.

By the mid-1960s, political events in Guyana had destroyed Harris's hopes of national regeneration, and *The Eye of the Scarecrow* (1965) marks Harris's decisive shift towards a 'drama of consciousness'. The story introduces a recurrent Harris character, 'Idiot Namless', the neutral, objective observer, and also 'N.' who lacks all identity, recovering from amnesia caused by a car crash in the interior, which, in Harris's metaphysical imagination, would appear to stand for the people's encounter with colonialism. He is a 'scarecrow' like Yeats's 'tattered coat upon a stick',[10] an image both personal and social, for in 'N.'s' vision his Guyanese home town too is a 'scarecrow' of derelict tenements housing a destitute population, and the British Governor appears as a 'shirt cast over branches of wood and bone',[11] the effigy of a derelict empire. In the nine months of the narrative, the scarecrow can only recover flesh through the 'stubborn terrifying task' of poetic creation, 'the life-blood of *seeing*', a doorway into 'the original well of silence, that "silence" which language alone can evoke . . .'.[12] Related to the paradox of language generated by silence, the recovery of sight through blindness is explored in *The Waiting Room* (1967), in which Susan Forrestal awaits an eye operation to restore her vision. A transitional work, it leads to the major novel of Harris's mid-career, *Tumatumari* (1968).

In this work the central figure is again a woman, Prudence. In the novel's extraordinary opening, she hallucinates in postnatal depression that a floating mat of weed in the river is the head of Roi Solman, her husband; she cradles it and it becomes the premature child she lost three months before. She faints, and awakes in her bed, tended by Rakka the Amerindian servant who has found and rescued her. Out of this resonant and complex image the novel evolves. Her husband Roi Solman has indeed been decapitated in a fall into the rapids. Like Donne and Fenwick, Roi is a meeting point between the Western world and the folk of the interior, but the novel is precisely dated in modern Guyana, and Roi is an engineer working on a hydroelectric project. The Amerindian presence has dwindled to a ghost town at the foot of the falls. Yet his name Solman links him to the Indian sun god; he is the new 'Sun King' bringing light from the primeval power of the river and reforging links between people and environment that the Indians have lost. He takes the Indian Rakka as his mistress, and Prudence has a vision of a heroic battle in which Roi, in the midst of the waterfall, subdues a huge wild boar, symbolising his stand amid the maelstrom of history. Yet his attempt is flawed. He is failed by the Western investors in the dam, and by their technology, for he dies when his boat's propeller shears off. Above all, he is betrayed by his own insensitivity, shown in particular by his treatment of Prudence and the Amerindian Rakka, whom he beats and renders sterile. A sacrificial victim to his and others' failure, he is decapitated in the river he seeks to control.

It is Prudence (whose name intimates its Latin source, 'providens', foreseeing) who moves through five stages ever deeper into the mystery of the birth and death glimpsed in her first hallucination. 'Tumatumari' or 'talking rock' refers to the mysterious petrographs of the Guyanese interior, painted by unknown hands: it also links to the 'living stone', Peter the human rock, of Christian tradition. Within the rock well that Roi had tunnelled, Prudence finds herself in a 'theatre of memory', voyaging ever deeper into her inner consciousness. She senses her own kinship with 'the rock of the sun', the substance of life, her identity with the folk. Cracks in the rock open the way back into the experience of her father, the historian Henry Tenby, trapped in the 'Masks' of outward reality, a false vision of history that misunderstands and conceals the plight of the Guyanese poor. This long and complex section reflects Harris's own exploration of Guyanese history. It is simultaneously Prudence's exploration of her father's consciousness, and Tenby's movement into the mind of Prudence, his youngest daughter, bringing release from a love/hate relationship which was also their imprisonment within a false consciousness. The false 'mask' of surface reality becomes the 'eggshell' of new life. But there is no finality, only a new acceptance as Prudence lets herself slip 'step by step, hand over hand from the nervous precipice of breakdown into the bottomless pool of memory'.[13]

The *Tumatumari* cycle ends with *The Ascent to Omai* (1970) in which the main character Victor searches for Adam, his father, before himself dying on the cloudy mountain of Omai. It is a journey in which a guilty father–son relationship parallels the growth of the Guyanese nation. After this dark, complex work, *Black Marsden* (1972) introduces a note of comedy. The novel is set mainly in Scotland, where, flush from a win at the pools, Goodrich is entertained in Dunfermline Abbey by the mysterious Doctor Marsden and his motley crew of agents – Jenny Gordon, Knife and Harp. The story evinces a new lightness of touch, and an extension of subject, for its echoes of Hogg's *The Private Memoirs of a Justified Sinner* (1824) suggest parallels between the Scottish and Guyanese psyche.[14] The sequel, *Companions of the Day and Night* (1975), extends Goodrich's travels to Mexico. Harris is becoming increasingly concerned with the interplay of individual identity and artistic vision.

Companions reintroduces Idiot Nameless, the voice of neutral innocence, who becomes possessed by Mexican painting, sculpture and ritual, entering into the panorama of New World History from the invasion of the Spaniards to the present, and ending with a fall from the pyramid of the sun to his (symbolic?) death. Earlier Harris had contrasted creative art and reportage: towards the end of *Palace of the Peacock*, Da Silva confronts a twin brother with bones like splinters, his flesh wet drab newspaper and his hair like ink, 'a reporter who had returned from the grave with no news whatsoever of a living return'.[15] By *Da Silva da Silva's Cultivated Wilderness* (1977), the two Da Silvas have come closer, becoming both the artist and the objective reality he 'becomes', for 'one paints into one's flesh the mystery of the world's injustice'.[16] Da Silva da Silva's dual identity represents the process by which the writer 'cultivates' the 'wilderness' of experience into the fertile garden of his art.[17] In his painting he/they descend into a series of antagonistic figures and episodes, from the slave hero Cuffy with his links to the Haitian god Legba, to the explorer Magellan, revisioning history by reconciling oppositions into a new dimension of reality. The sequel, *The Tree of the Sun* (1978), takes the exploration further, using the processes not only of painting, but of sculpture, music, poetry and, finally, drama. Harris's central concern here is the deconstruction of and rehabilitation from sequential time. The book is prefaced with Eliot's lines, 'we are born with the dead', and the Arawak myth of the 'tree of the sun' that bridged earth and heaven. Tragedies of Inca and Arawak history are interwoven with those of Da Silva's near contemporaries, Francis and Julia Cortez, whose diary he edits. In a complex web of narrative in which Francis and Julia are recreated in Da Silva's imagination, Harris explores the power of imaginative understanding to regenerate within the very moment of loss.

Harris's more recent work has returned to a main source of his early poetry, the great archetypal myths of literature. The 'Carnival Trilogy' – *Carnival* (1985), *The Infinite Rehearsal* (1987) and *The Four Banks of the River of Space* (1990) – are based respectively on Dante's *Paradiso*, Goethe's *Faust* and Homer's *Odyssey*, yet the classical texts are used to revision our awareness of the present. Thus in *Carnival*, the Dante of Jonathon Wehl is led by his Virgil, Everyman Masters, through an Inferno of colonial history and the Purgatory of cleansed vision to reveal that 'the twentieth century was an age of realism that failed entirely to plumb the pagan in ourselves'.[18] In *The Infinite Rehearsal*, the bird-like Robin Redbreast Glass meets his *alter ego* as a Faust uncertain even of the nature of his temptation. 'The crucifixion's changing. Technology's changing. And quite frankly I'm not sure what investitures the devil now wears'.[19] In an age of Einstein's Theory of Relativity and the Quantum Theory, 'shape-shifting' is no longer the Anancy trickery of the imagination, but reflects scientific reality. In *The Four Banks of the River of Space*, Anselm's Odyssey through unimaginable dimensions is prefaced by a quotation from Nick Herbert:

> Quantum reality consists of simultaneous possibilities,
> a 'polyhistoric' kind of being . . . incompatible with
> our . . . one-track minds. If these alternative (and parallel)
> universes are really real and we are barred from
> experiencing them only by a biological accident, perhaps
> we can extend our senses with a kind of 'quantum
> microscope' . . .[20]

Resurrection at Sorrow Hill (1993) and *Jonestown* (1996) come full circle and return to the landscapes of the Guyanese Quartet. Like *Palace of the Peacock*, *Resurrection* is an expedition through time and space into the interior, but the centrifugal motif of the journey is countered by the centripetal focus on the Asylum for the 'Greats' at 'Sorrow Hill', a grave-yard near Bartica in the Guyanese interior, and one from which members of the Donne's crew in *Palace* had arisen. The mental hospital provides a 'theatre of the psyche'[21] in which historical characters such as Montezuma and Cortez, classical figures such as Tiresias, and Harris's own creations – Hope, the life/death Christopher D'eath, Butterfly and Daemon – interact and transcend the conflicts of Guyanese history. *Jonestown* too, based on the infamous commune created by James Warren Jones in 1977, probes areas of psychic disorientation within the Guyanese consciousness. Two of Jones's cultists were rumoured to have escaped the mass killing, and Harris, repeating the double vision of *Peacock*, recreates one as Francisco Bone, and his alter ego as Deacon, Jones's second in command, a skeleton figure of death and his mortal antagonist. In the narrative, Bone's story becomes a dream-book in which he and Deacon are transposed into the warring twins of the Mayan *Popul Vuh*, a myth set in a redemptive cycle where death is defeated by an offering of the blood-like sap of a sacred tree. In the dream sequences of the book, Bone, Deacon and the re-demptive figure of the Virgin (Marie) enter the cycles of myth, intimating that Jonestown was part of a recurring cycle of both destruction and healing in Guyana. In a moment of insight Bone sees beyond the 'dead' eyes of Deacon to the cosmic drama in which 'fiction' becomes simultaneously artifice and reality.

> The Play's the thing. The real world beyond all real worlds.
> *That is the innermost, outermost, vocation of trial and judgement*
> *in all fiction.*[22]

It is the quest that has underpinned all Harris's work, a search for 'the true substance of life' through the alchemy of the imagination. Thus in *The*

Ascent to Omai, Judge, half-asleep, soaring in an aeroplane, pieces together his memories in a wordless consciousness of the eternal present:

> *Language for him, therefore, was a vision of consciousness as if what one dreams of in the past is there with a new reality never so expressive before because nothing stands now to block the essential intercourse of its parts, however mute, however irrelevant.*[23]

Notes

1. 'Put it how you like', I cried, 'it's a fear of acknowledging the true substance of life.' Wilson Harris, *Palace of the Peacock* (London, 1960), p. 59.

2. See bibliography below, and *Wilson Harris: the Uncompromising Imagination*, edited by Hena Maes-Jelinek (Sydney, 1991), pp. 249–72.

3. Wilson Harris, *Tradition, the Writer and Society*, pp. 30–1.

4. See Joyce Spare Adler, 'A Wilson Harris Checklist', *The Review of Contemporary Fiction* 17, 2 (Summer 1997), p. 107.

5. Wilson Harris, *The Whole Armour* (London, 1962), p. 43.

6. Tim Cribb, 'T.W. Harris – Sworn Surveyor', *Journal of Commonwealth Literature* 19, 1 (1993), pp. 33–46.

7. Wilson Harris, *The Secret Ladder* (London, 1963), p. 23.

8. Ibid., p. 126.

9. *The Eye of the Scarecrow* (London, 1965), p. 89. Quoted by Hena Maes-Jelinek, *Wilson Harris* (Twayne, Boston, 1982), p. 62.

10. W.B. Yeats, 'Sailing to Byzantium', I. 9.

11. Ibid., p. 11.

12. Wilson Harris, *The Eye of the Scarecrow* (London, 1965), p. 97.

13. Wilson Harris, *Tumatumari* (London, 1968), p. 153.

14. See Alan Riarch, 'The Scottish Element in *Black Marsden*', in *Wilson Harris: the Uncompromising Imagination*, pp. 159–69.

15. Wilson Harris, *Palace*, p. 123.

16. Wilson Harris, *Da Silva da Silva's Cultivated Wilderness and the Genesis of the Clowns* (London, 1977), p. 12.

17. See Hena Maes-Jelinek, 'Faces on the Canvas', *WLWE* 22 1 (Spring 1983), p. 89.

18. Wilson Harris, *Carnival* (London, 1985), p. 109.

19. Wilson Harris, *The Infinite Rehearsal* (London, 1987), p. 236.

20. Wilson Harris, *The Four Banks of the River of Space* (London, 1990), p. [vi].

21. Wilson Harris, *Resurrection at Sorrow Hill* (London, 1993), p. 94.

22. Wilson Harris, *Jonestown* (London, 1996), p. 232.

23. Wilson Harris, *The Ascent of Omai* (London, 1970), p. 78.

Chapter 15

From Crusoe to Omeros: Derek Walcott

Where, for George Lamming, Caliban and Prospero offered images of the Caribbean predicament, Derek Walcott turned first to Robinson Crusoe. Explaining this 'figure' to an audience at the University of the West Indies in 1965, he warned that 'it is not the Crusoe you recognize', the romantic desert islander of fiction or tourist brochures. He is remote from Man Friday.[1] Walcott's Crusoe is the emptied, receptive self. He is Columbus, by accident discovering the New World; he is Adam in a second Eden, giving it names. Unlike Prospero, he is demotic, for

> Crusoe is no lord of magic, duke, prince. He does not
> possess the island he inhabits. He is alone, he is a craftsman,
> his beginnings are humble. He acts, not by authority, but
> by conscience.[2]

In *The Castaway* (1965), Walcott had explored the figure of Crusoe as artist. The sequence opens with the marooned poet stunned by heat and inactivity.

> Action breeds frenzy. I lie,
> Sailing the ribbed shadow of a palm,
> Afraid lest my own footprints multiply.[3]

In 'Crusoe's Island', outcast from a Christian God, he envies the unconscious radiance of 'Friday's progeny', the black children walking on the beach in the setting sun. Yet dereliction purifies:

> Godlike, annihilating godhead, art
> And self, I abandon
> Dead metaphors . . .[4]

In 'Crusoe's Journal', his exile becomes the point of artistic recreation.

> So from this house
> that faces nothing but the sea, his journals
>   assume a household use,
> We learn to shape from them, where nothing was
>   the language of a race . . .[5]

Crusoe collects driftwood and fires it into light and heat, a figure for the West Indian artist creating new literatures out of the cultural detritus of a fragmented history.

As a figure, Crusoe reflected but one side of Walcott's creativity, for his poetry, widely if inaccurately identified with a metropolitan 'literary' tradition, was being written alongside drama rooted and performed in the Caribbean. Appropriately, Friday enters the Crusoe trope within a play, *Pantomime* (1976), a brilliant two-hander which brings together both aspects of Walcott's talent. Harry Trewe, once an actor, is now proprietor of a run-down hotel on Tobago, in local legend the original of Crusoe's island. Bored, and looking to devise an entertainment for his guests, he starts to improvise on the Crusoe story with his black servant Jackson playing Friday. But he soon finds himself confronted by Defoe's racial stereotype. In Walcott's words, 'cracks appear [in the façade of the Englishman] and it is where these cracks appear that Jackson darts in and widens [until] we look into his room and see Trewe naked and exposed'.[6] Trewe attempts to stop the show, but Jackson insists it cannot be shrugged off so easily:

> You see, it's your people who introduced us to this culture:
> Shakespeare, *Robinson Crusoe*, the classics, and so on, and
> when we start getting as good as them, you can't leave
> halfway. So I will continue? Please?[7]

While Trewe remains trapped in his stereotype, Jackson, as a calypsonian, recreates his identity, by improvisation inventing practical ways of survival on the island. The play ends with Jackson's punning demand, 'Starting from Friday, Robinson, we could talk 'bout a raise?'[8]

By 1978, Walcott's poetic preoccupation was shifting from Crusoe to Odysseus, a move indicated in the title poem of *Sea Grapes* (1976):

> That little sail in light
> which tires of islands,
> a schooner beating up the Caribbean
>
> for home, could be Odysseus
> home-bound on the Aegean . . .[9]

Walcott himself was becoming something of an Odysseus. He had broken
with the Trinidad Theatre Workshop in 1976, and from the late 1970s his
life became increasingly divided between the United States, St Lucia and
Jamaica, with excursions to Europe. The poems in *Sea Grapes* (1976), *The
Star-Apple Kingdom* (1979) and *The Fortunate Traveller* (1982) reflect his
global travels: *The Arkansaw Testament* (1987) is divided between 'Here'
(the Caribbean) and 'Elsewhere'.

Travel is through cultures as well as space, shifting visual awareness
through a deepening awareness of literature and art. In *Midsummer* (1984)
the perceptions of Europe and America are mediated through the art of
Gauguin, Watteau, 'the yellow-rind light of Vermeer', and the 'rust-
edged' art of van Ruysdale: 'The Dutch blood in me is drawn to detail'.[10]
Walcott negotiates other times and voices – Hardy, Auden, Larkin; the
Americans Roethke, Brodsky, Bishop, Lowell. Caribbean and global
traditions meet. 'The Spoiler's Return'[11] brilliantly relates the 'picong' of
a legendary Trinidad Calypsonian[12] with European satire from Juvenal to
Lovelace.

Yet Walcott also returns to St Lucia asking, 'Come back to me/ my
language',[13] and emulating the 'accurate, honest' craft of unpainted St
Lucian carpentry.[14] If Odysseus is a figure of the global poet, he also takes
Walcott back into his roots in the Caribbean peoples. For the poetry of
'Homerus' (c. 850 BC), a poet of whom nothing is known, a name that
may include multiple authorships, predates Mediterranean city culture, and
comes directly from a folk imagination. *The Odyssey*, instinct with the sea,
islands and travelling, was the ultimate demotic epic. Shabine, the rough
'red nigger' [mixed blood] sailor who narrates 'The Schooner, *Flight*' is
Walcott's Odysseus. Shabine voyages northwards from Trinidad, leaving
family and parochial politics for the sea, his dreams and his poetry, declar-
ing 'I had no nation now but the imagination'.[15] He proclaims:

> I met History once, but he ain't recognize me,
> a parchment Creole, with warts
> like an old sea bottle, crawling like a crab
> through the holes of shadow cast by the net
> of a grille balcony; cream linen, cream hat.
> I confront him and shout, 'Sir, is Shabine!
> They say I'se your grandson. You remember Grandma,
> your black cook, at all?' The bitch hawk and spat.
> A spit like that worth any number of words.
> But that's all them bastards have left us: words.[16]

Shabine's flights of words intercut the ship's spatial passage, as in imagination he traverses Caribbean history from the Spanish genocide of the
Arawaks to the disaster of Federation. A climactic storm and ensuing calm

suggest baptismal drowning and rebirth as the voice of the people: 'either I'm nobody, or I'm a nation.'[17]

These themes are developed in Walcott's *Omeros* (1990) and *The Odyssey: a Stage Version* (1993). The first opens on a small Caribbean island divided between the world of the expatriate Major and Maude Plunkett, and the black poor of the fishing village. It has a looser relationship with Homer's original than Joyce's *Ulysses*, and its organising subtexts include Dante's *Divine Comedy*, whose terza rima form it shares. As in a Wilson Harris novel, connotations shift and develop – Helen is the village beauty, the island of St Lucia, and at times even her opposing self, the Irish expatriate Maud. In one dimension, Circe is history itself, bestialising islanders trapped in their past, and the island's historian, Plunkett, keeps pigs. The villager Philoctete like his classical forebear, suffers a malodorous sore, indicating the heritage of slave chains. But his wounding is shared by Major Plunkett, psychically damaged by white colonialism, and 'affliction is one theme/ of this work'.[18]

Voyaging is a central motif in the work. The poem opens with the epic account of shaping a canoe from a high forest tree. But it is to be a fishing boat: the journeys are local, and of the mind. Plunkett gains a 'son' not from his wife Maud but from his historical archives, a nineteen-year-old Midshipman who died in the Battle of the Saintes in 1782. The black fisherman Achille, rocked to sleep over a deep trough in the Atlantic, recovers the past through spiritual vision, travelling under sea and time to 'find his name and soul' in Africa:[19]

> He walked the ribbed sand under the flat keels of whales,
> under the translucent belly of the snaking current,
> the tiny shadows of tankers passed over him like snails
>
> as he breathed water, a walking fish in its element.
> . . .
>
> He woke to the sound of sunlight scratching at the door
> of the hut, and he smelt not salt but the sluggish odour
> of river. Fingers of light rethatched the roof's straw.[20]

The vision reconnects with the past of both Africa and the Caribbean. He recognises island customs in an African village festival; reawakening back home, he lies in the shade of a 'pomme-Arac', a tree of the Arawaks. Achille's journey is also the poet's, for like Donne's crew in *Palace of the Peacock*, the characters represent aspects of the author's own psychic and racial identity.

> Mark you, *he* does not go; he sends his narrator;
> he plays tricks with time because there are two journeys
> in every odyssey, one on worried water,

the other crouched and motionless, without noise.
For both, the 'I' is a mast; a desk is a raft
for one, foaming with paper, and dipping the beak

of a pen in its foam, while an actual craft
carries the other to cities where people speak
a different language, or look at him differently . . .[21]

Walcott, envisioning his own return to the States to visit his mother, finds something that 'enclosed my skin with an older darkness', and rediscovers the meaning of 'tongues of a speech I no longer understood'.[22] His Odyssey expands to include the massacred Indians in snow-bound North America; to Europe, where Walcott's father Warwick becomes Virgil to his son's Dante, exploring cultures which, mastered, 'carried me over the bridge of self-contempt'.[23]

But the trail runs cold, and Walcott's Odyssey begins and ends on the island. Here the acceptance of loss becomes part of the process of healing. With Shamanic powers from her African past, Ma Killman, keeper of the rumshop the NO PAIN CAFE, cures Philoctete's wound. The death of Maud releases Plunkett into the life of the community, and when Hector is killed in a crash, it breaks the abortive love triangle between him, Achille and Helen. Helen is pregnant with Hector's child, and Achille, returned from fishing, takes her a gift of dolphin meat in Hector's rusty tin. 'When he left the beach the sea was still going on'.[24] Through its exploration of the island, *Omeros* becomes a work ultimately about the Homeric quality of Caribbean life. For Walcott, Homer transformed his Aegean experience into the stuff of poetry, an imaginative achievement that opened the way for Walcott to do the same for his own islanded sea.

And Omeros nodded. 'We will both praise it now.'
But I could not before him. My tongue was a stone
at the bottom of the sea, my mouth a parted conch

from which nothing sounded, and then I heard his own
Greek calypso coming from the marble trunk . . .[25]

Such a vision is to discover 'that light beyond metaphor'.[26] For the ultimate Homeric skill is to dissolve all poetic figures, including that of the Homeric model itself.

Why not see Helen

As the sun saw her, with no Homeric shadow,
Swinging her plastic sandals on that beach alone,
as fresh as the sea-wind? Why make the smoke a door?[27]

Notes

1. Derek Walcott, 'The Figure of Crusoe' (1956), reprinted in *Critical Perspectives on Derek Walcott*, ed. Robert Hamner (Washington D.C., 1993), pp. 35–6.

2. Ibid., p. 37.

3. Derek Walcott, 'The Castaway', in *The Castaway* (London, 1965), p. 9.

4. 'Crusoe's Island', 'The Castaway', ibid., pp. 57, 10.

5. Ibid., p. 52.

6. Quoted by Christopher Gunness, 'White Man, Black Man', in Walcott, *Critical Perspectives*, p. 290.

7. Derek Walcott, *Remembrance & Pantomime* (New York, 1980), p. 124.

8. Ibid., p. 170.

9. Derek Walcott, *Sea Grapes* (London, 1976), p. 9.

10. Derek Walcott, *Midsummer* (New York, 1984), p. 27.

11. Derek Walcott, *The Fortunate Traveller* (London, 1982), pp. 53–60.

12. Theophilus Phillips; see Gordon Rohlehr, *Calypso and Society*, pp. 465–74.

13. Derek Walcott, 'St Lucie', *Sea Grapes*, p. 44.

14. Derek Walcott, 'Cul de sac valley', *The Arkansaw Testament* (New York, 1987), p. 9.

15. Derek Walcott, 'The Schooner, *Flight*', *The Star-Apple Kingdom* (London, 1980), p. 8.

16. Ibid., pp. 8–9.

17. Ibid., p. 5.

18. Derek Walcott, *Omeros* (New York, 1990), p. 28.

19. Ibid., p. 154.

20. Ibid., pp. 142–3.

21. Ibid., p. 291.

22. Ibid., p. 167.

23. Ibid., p. 187.

24. Ibid., p. 325.

25. Ibid., p. 287.

26. Ibid., p. 271.

27. Ibid., p. 27.

Chapter 16

The Poet as Seer:
Kamau Brathwaite

As a child, the then Edward (now Kamau) Brathwaite skidded a pebble from the beach outside his home in Newstead, Barbados, across the water. In his mind, 'the stone had skidded arc'd and bloomed into islands/ Cuba and San Domingo/ Jamaica and Puerto Rico/ Grenada, Guadeloupe Bonaire . . .'.[1] He was to write that 'all I have written since, if sense, comes out of this genesis',[2] a stone 'blooming' into islands, a defining moment of his creative imagination.[3] The epiphany radiated back to the creation of the Caribbean area out of coral and volcanic magma, and forward to present time and space, shaping, as it did for Wilson Harris, 'a mythology that marries us to rock and hill'.[4] In 1972 the adult Kamau stood on the same beach and again skidded a stone, and found inspiration for a second trilogy.[5]

Brathwaite's *Arrivants* trilogy, already examined, swept across Africa and the worldwide diaspora of the black peoples. *Mother Poem* (1977), *Sun Poem* (1982) and *X-Self* (1987) focus on his home island. The trilogy, as Brathwaite's sister Mary has written, 'are replete with echoes of childhood'[6] and of Brathwaite's parents, the mother 'warm, loving, almost overpowering', with a fierce ambition for her children's education, the father reserved, quietly evading her heated harangues.[7] Yet the poems are not autobiographical in the manner of Walcott's *Another Life*. *Mother Poem* in particular explores the lives of the common people from whose hardships Brathwaite himself had been largely protected. Chapel religion seduces a bereaved mother, literally, when she searches for consolation, and finds 'parson replaced husband'.[8] Western education becomes embodied in Chalkstick the teacher, leaning in at the mother's window, promising her son would be 'a *lux/ occidente*' in scholarship, but confining him in colonial culture, 'accepting another black hostage/ of verbs'.[9] The exploitation of plantation life literally grinds the father, a labourer whose hand becomes crushed in the sugar mill:

> the crunched bone was juicy
> to the iron: there was no difference
> between his knuckle joints

and ratoon shoots: the soil
receives the liquor with cool flutes:
three fingers are not even worth a stick
of cane . . .[10]

But 'mother' is also Barbados, limestone, honeycombed with life-giving
water. 'My mother is a pool',[11] 'she is his secret limestone cavern'.[12] She
has been raped and ravaged by commercial exploition, 'all the peaks, the
promontories, the coves, the glitter/ bays of her body have been turned
into money . . .'.[13] 'Nametracks' associates her with language in a dialogue
between the archetypal 'muddah/mud', who holds the child's true identity
or 'nam', and the voice of the (male) colonial oppressor. In this section
Brathwaite uses the trope of the game 'O'Grady says', with its verbal
repetition, to dramatise the effects of British education. 'Ogrady', 'the
man who possesses us all', imposes speech which embodies the colonial
experience – 'stick', 'ice', 'whip', 'kill', 'scream'. Both meaning and
intonation are harsh and invasive – 'say kill/not keel/ogrady says'.[14] Standard English is set against the soft, visceral sounds of the mother, on the
borders between sense and feeling:

> she cum to me years like de yess off a leaf
> an she issper
> she cum to me years and she purr like a puss and she
>   essssper[15]

Through the section, Ogrady imposes his regime with increasing desperation, but never reaches to 'nyam' [eat] the islander's 'nam' [his secret
self]: 'but e nevver maim what me /mudda me name'.[16] Ogrady himself
becomes confused into using the speech of the oppressed – 'so I keel you'
– as, for the intended victim, the shocks of violence modulate, through
suffering, into the rhythms of a popular slave-based folk-song, asserting
the strength of the spirit to transcend even death:

> *back to back belly to belly*
> *uh doan give a damm*
>
> *uh dun dead a'ready*[17]

Appropriately, the electrifying impact of 'Nametracks' is best experienced
in an oral performance.

Other presences surface within the island experience. In 'Angel/En-
gine' the steam train becomes the possessing power of Shango in a Shouter
Baptist ritual.[18] Brathwaite himself experienced a 'hounfort' [possession
ritual] in a Barbadian village, where a woman cultist, leaving behind her

background of poverty and deprivation, spoke with the power of Damballa/
Shango, the god of the crossroads between life and death:

> who hant me
> *huh*
>
> who haunt me
> *huh*
>
> my head is a cross
> is a cross–
>
> road[19]

The sequence ends movingly with the mother's death, and her rebirth
through the imagination and the poet's memories

> so that losing her now
> you will slowly restore her silent gutters of word-fall
>
> slipping over her footsteps like grass
> slippering out of her wrinkles like rain . . .[20]

The punning title of *Sun Poem* shifts the focus to father/son relationships, and is prefaced with the names and birthdates of five fathers in
Brathwaite's family tree. The poem contains much of Brathwaite's most
personal writing, and intimately renders the Bajan speech of his childhood
in verse and rhythmic prose. Boyhood scenes, people and sense experiences are vividly evoked: sand, diving in the tinkling sea, the warmth of
the sun; debates with his nine-year-old sister; first love with a village girl;
cricket on the beach with the village boys; and a fight with Batto, the
village bully. Its first half is set on the benign west coast of Barbados,
looking towards the Caribbean and the Americas. But a journey across
the island discovers the wild Atlantic coast (the setting for much of *Mother
Poem*). It is the coast facing Africa across the Atlantic, and introduces the
theme of the island's African presence. The long central passage 'Noom'
[noon/name/doom] explores the boy's growing consciousness of the island's slave roots, dramatised in the legend of the loa [spirit] who crossed
under the sea from Africa to Barbados, but in despair fell from the cliff:
'"*he dead where yu stannin now*" said the cattlewash boys'.[21] Bussa, leader
of the island's most notable slave revolt, is invoked, but 'few of our
fathers were heroes'. The enduring courage of the people is embodied
undramatically in the woman 'Esse' [both 'Essie' and the Latin 'to be'],
facing bereavement and poverty with '*amen amen*'.[22] As Stewart Brown

has demonstrated, an organising motif of the poem is the rainbow, in both African and Christian/Judaic mythology the sign of reconciliation and harmony between man and gods,[23] progressing from the opening, 'Red Rising', to 'Indigone'. After 'noom' the cycle turns backwards, and a regression of fathers return to the timeless 'son/sun' of spiritual identity, continually dying and reborn:

> and my thrill–
> dren are coming up coming up coming up coming up
> and the sun
>
> new[24]

If *Sun Poem* shows Brathwaite at his most intimate, the last work in the trilogy, *X-Self* (1987), moves outwards in time and space, sweeping from the rise and fall of the empires of Greece and Rome to the stumbling America of Richard Nixon. 'X-self' is the problematic identity created by a fragmented world, the 'X' indicating the 'cross'-roads of choice, and also the unknown potential of Caribbean man. Mont Blanc, Shelley's white 'city of death ... flood of ruin',[25] stands as an emblem of the inhuman forces that rule the white world, bringing colonialism, napalmed Vietnam, the 'strangled cities' of the Third World. In opposition stand the 'symbol(s) of the spirit',[26] Lake Chad[27] and Mount Kilimanjaro, the highest peak in Africa. Brathwaite envisions a Blakean dialectic: in 'Dies Irie' the 'Irae' (wrath) of Celano's thirteenth-century dirge melds with 'Irie' the Rastafarian word for joy, for repression and expression coexist, and the once betrayed Toussaint L'Ouverture, now a tutelary god, sheds his liberating influence through Caribbean history in 'the narrow thread of silver' spun by the poet 'in the long time of sand'.[28] Creative forces coalesce, and the concept 'nam' unites man's secret name or soul with 'nyam' (Afro/Creole, 'to eat'), 'yam' (food originating in Africa) and 'nyame' (an African god).[29]

Modern consciousness becomes electronic as Brathwaite composes directly onto the screen of his Applemac computer, patterning words and phrases, assaulting the received conventions of words on the page. The wheel comes full circle as this 'writing in light' returns poetry to its original spontaneity, giving it the immediacy of the oral. Brathwaite has claimed that

> if Prospero creates a prison of language in which Caliban is trapped, Caliban's responsibility is to break his way out of it. The only way he can break his way out of it is to return to the language of his mother, Sycorax, and that is what these poems are trying to do.[30]

For 'dis obeah blox' [block/box][31] is a device by which 'prospero get curse/ wid im own/curser' [cursor].[32] The sequence climaxes with 'Xango', where Shango the pan-African god of thunder and power, and his partner the Afro-Haitian goddess of love and fertility, Erzuli, return the poem to the green world, where 'j/ p morgan is dead/ coca cola is drowned'.[33] The apocalypse is both cosmic and personal, with the reader invited to 'touch/ him/ he will heal/ you'.[34]

Brathwaite's plans for a third trilogy were interrupted by a series of personal disasters: the death of his wife Doris in 1986; the partial loss of his life-time's research when his house was destroyed by Hurricane Gilbert in 1988, and the shock of facing violent assault and robbery in Jamaica in 1990. That year he emigrated to New York. The period and its aftermath were marked by the 'dark night of the soul' recorded in *The Zea Mexican Diary* (1993), in the long poem, *Shar* (1992), and in *Trench Town Rock* (1994) respectively. The seven powerful, allegorical, computer-generated sequences of *DreamStories* (1994) reflected the stone-like impasse of the present-day Caribbean.[35] Yet stone both establishes and excludes. Brathwaite has not been alone among Caribbean writers in exploring the paradox of 'stone' as a symbol for the Caribbean predicament.[36] In *Mother Poem*, limestone Barbados is envisaged as the ground of Brathwaite's being. But his earlier 'Stone Sermon' had dramatised cultists encountering the dark rock of Caribbean history:

> the eye dumb
> the night done
> the stone born . . .
>
> faith a–dark
> faith a–dark
> hope a–drownded[37]

Despair and affirmation are bound together in the cycle of Caribbean history, and *Barabajan Poems*, published the same year, was a massive recapitulation of the early trilogies, which remain Brathwaite's unalienable contribution to West Indian writing.

Notes

1. Kamau Brathwaite, *The Arrivants* (Oxford, 1973), p. 48.

2. Kamau Brathwaite, *Barabajan Poems* (Kingston, Jamaica and New York, 1994), p. 119.

3. Mary E. Morgan, 'Highway to Vision: This Sea our Nexus', *World Literature Today*, 68, 4 (Autumn 1994), p. 664.

4. W.B. Yeats, quoted by John Hearne in 'The Fugitive in the Forest', *The Islands in Between*, edited by Louis James (Oxford, 1968), p. 140.

5. Kamau Brathwaite, *Barabajan Poems*, p. 117.

6. Kamau Brathwaite, *Sun Poem*, pp. 9–18, and passim.

7. Ibid., pp. 22–4.

8. Kamau Brathwaite, *Mother Poem* (London, 1977), p. 10.

9. Ibid., pp. 22–4.

10. Ibid., p. 53.

11. Ibid., p. 3.

12. Ibid., p. 115.

13. Ibid., p. 46.

14. Ibid., p. 60.

15. Ibid., p. 62.

16. Ibid., p. 64.

17. Ibid., p. 64.

18. Ibid., pp. 98–103; *Barabajan Poems*, pp. 172–202 and 369–76.

19. *Mother Poem*, p. 101.

20. Ibid., p. 117.

21. Edward Kamau Brathwaite, *Sun Poem* (Oxford, 1982), p. 52.

22. Ibid., pp. 84–5.

23. Stewart Brown, 'Sun Poem: the Rainbow Sign?', *The Art of Kamau Brathwaite* (Bridgend, 1995), edited by Stewart Brown, pp. 152–62.

24. *Sun Poem*, p. 97.

25. Percy B. Shelley, 'Mont Blanc' (1816), ll. 104, 107.

26. Kamau Brathwaite, 'Metaphors of Undevelopment', *The Art of Kamau Brathwaite*, p. 246.

27. Kamau Brathwaite, *The Arrivants*, p. 105.

28. Ibid., pp. 53, 101.

29. Brathwaite's note, *Mother Poem*, p. 121.

30. Nathaniel Mackey, 'An Interview with Kamau Brathwaite', in *The Art of Kamau Brathwaite*, p. 16.

31. Edward Kamau Brathwaite, *X-Self* (Oxford, 1987), p. 81.

32. Ibid., p. 85.

33. Ibid., p. 109.

34. Ibid., p. 111.

35. Gordon Rohlehr, 'Introduction' to Kamau Brathwaite, *DreamStories* (Harlow, 1994), pp. iii–xvi.

36. See, e.g. Wilson Harris, *Tumatumari* and passim; E.M. Roach, *Flowering Rock*; George Lamming, 'The Black Rock of Africa', *African Forum*, I, 4 (1966), pp. 32–5.

37. *Islands*, p. 99.

Chapter 17

The Meaning of Personhood:
Earl Lovelace

Earl Lovelace in *The Dragon Can't Dance* has a wry dig at a 'Professor of English' who writes a learned review of a calypso 'Tarzan Man', sung by one of the novel's main characters, Philo.[1] The Professor had seen it as a subtle subversion of European stereotypes; Philo thought it was a joke, for the Africans would have eaten Tarzan. The Professor's review is close enough to a celebrated essay on the Mighty Sparrow's 'Congo Man'[2] to caution anyone who attempts a purely academic analysis of Lovelace's writing. Like Selvon, Lovelace came from a Trinidad village, and writes out of a popular tradition, suspicious of intellectual sophistry. Where Selvon's demotic sensibility was cosmopolitan, Lovelace is regional and Trinidadian, tuned to the virile rhetoric and vision of the island's Shouter Baptist tradition. 'No one of us is born into the world', Lovelace has said. 'Every one of us is born into a place in the world, in a culture, and it is from that standpoint of that culture that we contribute to the world'.[3] At the centre of his work is an exploration of what he has termed 'person-hood . . . man's view of himself, the search as it were for his integrity',[4] focused specifically on the traditional culture of the Trinidad peoples.

His first novel *While Gods are Falling* (1965) opened with the panoramic device which became characteristic of his fiction.

> You stand there on the top-floor landing of the three-
> storeyed tenement building on Webber Street, look out at
> the city of Port of Spain. Above the tangle of black electric
> wires, tops of taller buildings rise under the heavily clouded
> sky.[5]

The prosperous city centre is contrasted with the slums stretching to the south, and a collage of scenes and incidents follows. Selvon had used the device in *A Brighter Sun* to convey urban fragmentation; for Lovelace it intimates potential unity. 'What is wrong with this city?' asks the main character, 'What is this mystery here?'[6] Named Walter 'Castle' with a glance at the title of Lamming's first novel, his rural roots have been lost by a father who gambled away the family property. He can settle at nothing. His wife rallies him and asks

> 'What you want, Walter?'
> 'I just want to be a man,' he says, 'I just want to know and
>   to feel that I am a man . . .'

His unease is visceral. 'In this town', he comments, 'your balls get squashed out of your guts so fast',[7] and he even ponders 'What would happen if I cut out my balls?'[8] But he is concerned with more than male machismo. Walter's wife replies

> 'How you going to be that man, Walter? How? By
> running to the country on a piece of hard land with a hoe
> and a dirty sleeveless merino from mornin' 'till night; by
> running away from bosses and people; by leaving the
> world? O Jesus, Walter, you can't do that.'[9]

Re-establishing intimacy with his wife, estranged since she took up an independent career in the city, marks a new access of responsibility, and he ends by organising the community to care for street children, and defending a local boy falsely charged with murder. Apprentice work, the novel nevertheless marked the arrival of a distinctive moral vision in the Caribbean novel.

The Schoolmaster (1968) draws on Lovelace's experiences in the remote mountain areas of northern Trinidad where he worked for the Forestry Department. The village Kumaca is some eleven miles over precarious paths from the nearest town, Valencia, and Lovelace uses a folk-lore style to describe lives dominated by the seasonal cycle of small farming. Young Pedro and the self-taught Christiana fall in love, and their prospective marriage offers a bright prospect for the village. A road is being built to Valencia and to profit by modernisation the villagers build a school, and Christiana becomes assistant teacher. But the head teacher is Warrick, a young man brought in from the city, a moral void behind blank spectacles. One night he rapes Christiana in the schoolroom. She becomes pregnant and, fearing to lose Pedro, commits suicide. Warrick breaks his neck trying to escape from the village. Yet the village does not fall apart, and the tragedy offers them a basis of new awareness with which they can face the coming of the road. 'The land in Kumaca is rich and would bring good yams, and there is a school there now . . .'[10]

Lovelace's early work was however only preparation for *The Wine of Astonishment* (1982), which, although published second, was his third-written novel. The story is told by Eva, wife of Bee, leader of the Spiritual Baptists or Shouters in the village of Bonasse. Her strong Creole woman's voice, vibrant with Biblical cadences, embodies the warmth and courage she and the community personify. Her church looks back to African traditions. 'The church is the root for us to grow out of', says Eva, 'Africa in us, black in us'.[11] Banned by the British in 1917,[12] Shouters embodied a tradition of popular resistance to colonialism. Lovelace sets his story at a turning point in Trinidad history. The Second World War is ending, and as the Americans leave Trinidad, the island moves towards independence. Ivan Morton, the local boy, is elected to the assembly. But, having turned Catholic to qualify for a scholarship, he now moves into a smart house in the city suburb with a light-skinned mulatto, turning his back on the Baptists when they become tyrannised by the sadistic police. Deprived of their rituals, they find themselves spiritually impotent. The defiance of Bolo, the village strongman, fails and, beaten and humiliated, he turns his aggression on the community. Having kidnapped two girls, he is shot by the police, dying in a crucified position, arms outstretched. The cult is later legalised, but the Shouter Baptists never recover their original spirit. However, Bee watches children playing in the street and feels

> the music that those boys playing on the steelband have
> in it the same spirit that we miss in our church: the same
> spirit; and listening to them, my heart swell and it is like
> resurrection morning.[13]

The novel established Lovelace's distinctive style and his central themes: the problem of heroism in a Trinidad where frustration turns energy to violence;[14] the creative power of its popular culture, and the paradox of regeneration through the very loss of old traditions.

The Dragon Can't Dance (1979) is a direct sequel to the *The Wine of Astonishment*, and its three contrasting main characters, Aldrick, Fisheye and Philo, also have roots in the Shouter Baptist tradition. Their power has passed on to the pan-island celebration of Carnival, which the novel explores with an accuracy that has been used for research.[15] Yet there is nothing academic in the energising rhythms that pulse through Lovelace's prose.

> Dance! Dance! Dance! It is in dancing that you ward off
> evil. Dancing is a chant that cuts off the power from the
> devil. Dance! Dance! Dance! Carnival brings this dancing to
> every crevice on this hill.[16]

The story is set on a poor area of Port-of-Spain, Calvary Hill, where the history of the closely-knit community is sewn into the Carnival dragon mask worn by the novel's main protagonist, Aldrick.

> He worked, as it were, in a flood of memories, not trying
> to assemble them, to link them into a linear meaning, but

letting them soak him through and through; and his life
grew before him, in the texture of his paint and the angles
of his dragon's scales, as he worked.[17]

His neighbours on the Hill look to him to lead them and express their
identity. Yet in the very act of accepting this role, Aldrick is becoming
imprisoned within his mask. It is only when he shouts his defiance from
the back of a police van high-jacked on impulse that he begins to rediscover the true nature of 'the Dragon Dance'. Lovelace does not reject
Carnival, but by the end a new voice of the people has emerged in Philo,
a calypsonian. Philo creates his 'mask' not through paint and cloth, but in
self-dramatisation within the ambivalent rhetoric of his calypsoes. Once
rejected by the Hill, at the end he accepts an invitation into the bedroom
of Miss Cleotilda, the Hill's ageing Carnival Queen, Carnival King at
last. Aldrick hopes for a renewed identity with a young and vivacious
partner, Sylvia.

Although *Dragon* is set in Port-of-Spain, Lovelace has remained committed to his rural roots in Matura, and when his community play *My
Name is Village* was produced in the capital, it kept its local actors. The
twelve sketches of *A Brief Conversion* show the variety of Trinidad country life, and its subjects range from a fair-ground strong man, a fire-eater
and stick-fighting, to conversations in a village barbershop. The nature of
'personhood' remains the central theme. The title story finely balances
the father's loss of freedom in giving up stick-fighting for his family,
against his son finding the courage to physically stand up to the school
bully. The focus is largely but not exclusively male. The lead character in
his play *Jestina's Calypso* [1978] rudely reverses the male expectation that
a woman is chosen for her looks, and wants a man's protection. 'But they
ain't make the man yet, with the love yet, and the courage and the
beauty to get me. So kiss my arse', cries Jestina.[18]

Salt, which won the Commonwealth Writer's Prize for 1997, turns to
the nature of Trinidad society as a total community. 'Salt' is an emblem
for the slave experience and its consequences. It embraces the oceanic
Middle Passage from Africa to the Caribbean, the salt sweat of the slaves,
the 'salary' [Latin for salt] of indentured labour, and the human integrity
by which the descendants of slaves become 'the salt of the earth'. The
novel evokes the great sweep of Trinidad's landscape and history, and is
written in a vibrantly oral style which can swing from biting irony, as
when Europeans are pitied for having to endure the heat in cork hats and
sweat while beating work out of their slaves, to dramatic confrontations
between conflicting sections of the community. Characteristically, Lovelace
creates a dialogue between two contrasting personae. George Alford, like
the earlier Bee or Aldrick, is thoughtful but perplexed, uncertain of his
roots, stumbling in his attempts to discover his responsibility to both self

and the wider society. Alienated from his folk roots, he triumphs by persistence, as, in an earlier episode, when finding himself unpicked by a village cricket team, he establishes himself in the role of the umpire. An awkward but obstinately determined schoolmaster, Alford slowly makes his mark and is elected to a seat in the new island Parliament. The novel closely follows Trinidad history, and the National Party with its autocratic leader is clearly recognisable as Eric Williams's PNM.

Alford's career is counterpointed to that of Bango – like Lovelace's earlier characters Bolo and Fisheye he is one of the people, acting on impulse, lost in the Babylon of modern Trinidad, yet impelled by blind instinct to reconstruct the present out of the past immanent within Trinidad popular culture. Bango is a worker who annually organises a Quixotic freedom march among the villagers in instinctive protest against the island's failure to face the true meaning of emancipation from slavery. Behind him is a culture of resistance going back to the early black leader of the slave revolt, Guinea John, who, a magician like the Haitian Macandal, 'put two corn cobs under his armpits, and flew away to Africa, taking with him the mysteries of levitation and flight . . .'.[19] Closer in history is Bango's grandfather Jo-jo, who, at the time of slave emancipation in 1836, was offered 'freedom' and found nothing had changed. Nor had the situation essentially changed by the time of Trinidad's achievement of independence in 1962. The white Creole Adolphe Caradon represents the new generation of plantation owners, and the plight of the dispossessed Africans has been indeed complicated by the influx of indentured Indians, with legal rights to the land the Africans had worked. Jo-jo's anger in 1836 is repeated in the present when Bango is offered compensation in land by Alford, now an establishment figure, and refuses it, seeing it as an evasion of responsibility, of the need to confront the real issues of independence. 'I don't want people to be sorry for me'.[20] He wants not charity, but a recognition of Trinidad history, and its people's rights as human beings.

The process of true social regeneration is a complex one, and left unfinished in the narrative. It demands Alford's recognition of his forgotten spiritual roots, a process begun when, as a child born dumb, he found speech through contact with the village healer. It is a shared inheritance which provides a tenuous but unbroken ligament between Alford and Bango. If the novel dramatises Alford's need to reconnect with his African past, as a Trinidadian he must establish his community with the island's Africans and Indians, Chinese and Europeans, all of whom play a part in the novel, realigning their histories within a new national identity. Equally important is the growth in understanding between the male and female characters, and in the novel's movement towards communal understanding, both Bango's wife Myrtle and Alford's fiesty partner Florence play significant roles. Lovelace's complex, panoramic novel comes to its climax in an Independence Day celebration, part political rally, part Carnival.

This offers no solution, but moves forward by recognising a need for change, an awareness voiced significantly by Florence:

> Then I saw it clearly. The tragedy of our time is to have lost the ability to feel loss, the inability of power to rise to its responsibility for human decency. . . . I was thinking that if what distinguishes us as humans is our stupidity, what may redeem us is our grace.[21]

In Lovelace's use of Florence's personal 'I' to end the book, the collective consciousness of the novel crystallises into the island's future 'personhood'.

> Once more I worked my way through the crowd up to the front where Miss Myrtle was now at the side of Bango . . . making me feel that this march of his was for all our own lives and had to be carried on, even if it took us to the very end of time. I got in beside them.[22]

Notes

1. Earl Lovelace, *The Dragon Can't Dance* (London, 1979), p. 231.

2. Gordon Rohlehr, 'Sparrow and the Language of Calypso', *Savacou* 2 (September 1970), pp. 94–5.

3. Earl Lovelace, 'Engaging the World', *Wasafiri* 1, 1 (Autumn 1984), p. 4.

4. Daryl Cumber Dance, *Fifty Caribbean Writers*, p. 277.

5. Earl Lovelace, *While Gods are Falling* (London, 1967), p. 7.

6. Ibid., p. 9.

7. Ibid., p. 15.

8. Ibid., p. 73.

9. Ibid., pp. 73–4.

10. Earl Lovelace, *The Schoolmaster* (London, 1979), p. 224.

11. Earl Lovelace, *The Wine of Astonishment* ([1982], London, 1983), p. 133.

12. The Shouters Prohibition Ordinance of 1917; lifted 1951.

13. Earl Lovelace, *The Wine of Astonishment*, p. 146.

14. Lovelace's treatment of the emergence of the gangster-hero in West Indian popular culture can be compared with Gordon Rohlehr's discussion of the Jamaican, *The Harder They Come*, in *My Strangled City* (San Juan, Trinidad, 1992), ch. 5.

15. See Keith Warner, *The Trinidad Calypso* (Washington, D.C., 1982); Angelita Reyes, 'Carnival Ritual Dance of the Past and Present in Earl Lovelace's *The Dragon Can't Dance*', *World Literature Written in English* 24 (Summer 1984), pp. 107–20.

16. Earl Lovelace, *The Dragon Can't Dance* (London, 1979), p. 14.

17. Ibid., p. 36.

18. Earl Lovelace, *Jestina's Calypso* (London, 1984), p. 41.

19. Earl Lovelace, *Salt* (London, 1996), p. 3.

20. Ibid., p. 163.

21. Ibid., p. 259.

22. Ibid., p. 260.

Chapter 18
From Castle to Kumbla: Women's Writing in the Caribbean

The 'Castle' of the title to George Lamming's *In the Castle of my Skin* represents the carapace within which 'G' develops his individuality. Twenty-seven years later, in *Jane and Louisa Will Soon Come Home*, Erna Brodber used the term 'kumbla' for the covering, both protective and isolating, within which Nellie grows to womanhood. 'Kumbla' is Brodber's nonce-word, based on the Jamaican 'coobla', a small calabash. The shift from Lamming's rigid image, with its literary associations with Walcott and Joyce,[1] to a secret word taken from the folk experience, organic and growing in meaning with Nellie,[2] points to wider developments in the Caribbean literary imagination. These changes partly reflect the impact, since the 1970s, of Caribbean women's writing. This development is striking. Out of the sixty West Indian novelists listed in Kenneth Ramchand's 1903–67 bibliography, only six were women, credited with one title each, although the imbalance would have been less for poets. By contrast, in 1988 an international Conference at Wellesley College brought together some fifty women Caribbean writers and critics.[3] This explosion of women's writing in some ways parallels the male-dominated 'phenomenon' of West Indian writing in the 1960s.

This has been the effect of wider shifts affecting all sections of Caribbean society. In the black communities, the legacy of slavery had created a pattern of absent fathers in which the mother or grandmother was the sole parent and provider. Yet, as Olive Senior has written, the 'myth' of the strong black matriarch 'disguises the fact of her powerlessness in the wider society'.

> The majority of working women are in low-paid, low status jobs such as domestic service, and women, especially young women, experience the highest rates of unemployment. Women have little share in the formal power structures, although they are the ones who are the domestic managers. Caribbean women shoulder the most tremendous burdens.[4]

Many decades after emancipation, Honor Ford Smith, researching the life of black communities in Jamaica in the 1970s, still found little concern for women's rights or their education.[5] Even for middle-class Creoles the main routes to publication, higher education, journalism, or a life of economic independence, were generally confined to men. But political independence brought the beginnings of more liberal attitudes to women in society, and a broadening of the educational base.

Merle Hodge won a scholarship from Trinidad to the University of London, where in 1967 she completed an M.Phil thesis on French Caribbean poetry, and translated the work of Radical French Guyanese poet, Leon Damas. In 1970 she published *Crick Crack Monkey*. Hodge later wrote, 'I do not think that I knew the word *feminism*, and I may have been only vaguely aware of such a thing as a woman's movement.'[6] Nevertheless, her novel marked a turning point in Caribbean women's writing. She introduced a new perspective and vitality into what had become the well-used device of the child growing up between two cultural worlds. Simon Gikandi has argued that while male West Indian writers such as Lamming and Naipaul were modernists who transferred 'the authority of power and utterance in the Caribbean from the Colonizer to the black male, then a feminist renaming of experience implies the revision of modernism, even the outright rejection of its totalizing tendencies'.[7] Whereas the earlier writers privileged a (male) authorial point of view, Merle Hodge and successive women writers were concerned 'with a subject that is defined by what de Laurentis calls "a multiple, shifting, and often self-contradictory identity, a subject that is not divided in, but rather at odds with, language"'.[8]

This is seen in the different perspectives embedded in Hodge's novel. Tee and her brother Toddan, whose mother is dead and their father abroad, have their childhood divided between life with the raucous Tantie, who lives in a remote Trinidad country village, and Beatrice their maternal 'city' aunt. Tantie is illiterate, and dependent on favours from a shadowy succession of 'uncles', but also hugely warm-hearted. Her ebullient language tumbles across the page. Delighted to get custody of the children she crows,

> 'Well she know big-shot, yu know, big-shot in all kinda
> government office, Father-priest and thing – so she get this
> paper. But we wipe we backside with she paper – we send
> the chirren to get some town-breeze, and in that time I get
> a statement from Selwyn – you should a seen the bitch face
> in the Courthouse! Eh! she face look like if she panty
> fall-down.'[9]

The style of Tantie's speech invades the narrative voice itself. 'Tantie's company was loud and hilarious and the intermittent squawk and flurry of mirth made me think of the fowl-run when something fell in the midst of the fat hens.'[10] The children also spend holidays with their grand-mother at Pointe Espoir, where the kitchen is fragrant with cooking 'guava-cheese and guava-jelly, sugar-cake, nut-cake, bennay-balls, toolum, shaddock-peel candy, chilibibi . . .'

> Ma's land was to us an enchanted country, dipping into
> valley after valley, hills thickly covered with every
> conceivable kind of foliage, cool green darknesses, sudden
> little streams that must surely have been squabbling past in
> the day when Brar Anancy and Brar Leopard and all the
> others roamed the earth outsmarting each other.[11]

In contrast, in the city Aunt Beatrice, who speaks with 'a firm voice like high-heels and stockings',[12] is neurotically respectable. She calls Tee 'Cynthia Davis', and her brother 'Codrington'. Yet while hating 'the Bitch', Tee is drawn to respectability. She find herself escaping into books 'which transported you always into Reality and Rightness, which were always to be found Abroad',[13] inventing an English 'double', Helen. 'Helen' despises Tantie's way of life, and even carnival becomes alienated by its 'unmistake-able niggeryness'.[14] Yet the narrative does not privilege 'Tee' or 'Helen', leaving the choice between its competing voices open. The story ends when her father, presumably at Tantie's prompting, sends air tickets for her and Toddan to join him in England. Written some twenty-five years later, Hodge's children's novel *For the Love of Laetitia* (1995) brings the story full circle. It tells how the twelve-year-old Laetitia Johnson wins a scholarship to a city school, but finds the town regime cold and oppressive, leading her to rediscover her true place within the village community.

The success of *Crick Crack Monkey* was followed by a surge of women's writing. In 1977 the Caribbean Artists Movement published a special issue of *Savacou* on 'Caribbean Woman', including both history and lit-erature, and a short bibliography of West Indian women's writing. That year in Jamaica the 'Sistren [sisterhood] Collective' was formed to en-courage women to narrate and improvise plays out of their working lives, part of a 'make-work' initiative of the Manley Government. Directed by Honor Ford Smith of the Jamaica School of Drama, their performances and workshops achieved striking success in Jamaica and throughout the Caribbean and, visiting Europe in 1983, 'Sistren' became part of the global women's movement. A remarkable collection of their life stories was published in 1986.[15] In the Caribbean itself, women writers were making contact across languages and territories. The Caribbean Associa-tion Feminist Research and Action (CAFRA) was founded in 1985, celebrated by the publication of Ramabai Espinet's major collection of Caribbean women's verse, *Creation Fire* (1990).

While this writing is as diverse as the women writing it, it is possible to identify particular emphases. The Jamaican poet and short-story writer Olive Senior has noted that Caribbean women 'don't act as if they're victimised. They're very positive, no matter how poor they are.'[16] A vivid example of this courage, insight and humour is Mama King in Beryl Gilroy's *Frangipani House* (1985), who, in infirm old age, refuses to accept isolation in a claustrophobic nursing home, breaks out, endures the dangers and vitality of slum life, and finally recovers her place in the community. Reflecting their increasing involvement in Caribbean society and politics, women's writing has tended to shift the focus in literature from the alienated individual to embrace the community as a whole.

Zee Edgell's *Beka Lamb* (1982) is set in Belize in the turmoil before the country's independence in 1981. Beka's *bildungsroman* is centrally concerned with the identity of the emergent nation. Beka's father, struggling in his business, wants to preserve the colonial connections. His anxieties are projected onto Beka, and his brutal bullying contributes to her breakdown. She becomes a compulsive liar and fails at school. The story, told in flashback, follows Beka's recovery. As Bev Brown has pointed out, the novel focuses on the Caribbean 'seed matriarchs', whose historical vision and creative energies preserved the strength of political survival.[17] This is seen in Beka's militant Greatgrannie Straker, who is rooted in both African and Carib cultures.[18] We learn that Beka 'shure resembles her',[19] and at her greatgrannie's wake she falls asleep on her bed, experiencing a peace that intimates a spiritual affinity between the generations. Toycie is an older working-class girl who was herself abandoned by her parents and brought up in poverty. With her roots in the vital life of the underprivileged, she gives Beka the nurture denied her by her tense, middle-class parents. But Toycie becomes pregnant by the son of a merchant family. She is abandoned by her child's father and with equal callousness expelled from the Convent just before she can take her exams. She has a breakdown, and dies during a hurricane. Yet by her life Toycie has enabled Beka to survive. When Beka wins the island essay prize she remembers the days they spent swimming in childhood, and feels Toycie's presence.

> Concentrating on the memory she relived the times they
> floated, fingers linked and spluttering with delight, upon the
> choppy aquamarine sea beneath the pier.[20]

Her cultural schizophrenia healed, Beka can now play her part in Belize society. *Beka Lamb* was followed with two powerfully written novels in which Edgell completed a trilogy celebrating the contribution of different classes of women to Belize's independence. *In Times like These* (1991) focuses on an educated expatriate woman returning to Belize from

England; the protagonist of *The Festival of San Joaquin* (1997) is from the lower *Mestizo* class.

Renu Juneja has drawn attention to the writing of Paule Marshall, a Barbadian by birth though domiciled in the United States,[21] noting that Marshall has taken her first three novels, *Brown Girl Brownstones* (1959), *The Chosen Place, the Timeless People* (1969) and *Praisesong for a Widow* (1983) as 'a trilogy describing, in reverse, the slave trade's route back to the motherland, the source'.[22] Marshall's partly autobiographical first novel was set in New York, where the young Selina Boyce is caught between the nostalgia for Barbados felt by her father, unable to succeed in city life, and her mother's fear of the poverty of the island villages. *The Chosen Place* is a major novel, broad in scope and concern. It is set on the Bournehills Estate on an island partly Barbados, partly the whole Caribbean, where Merle Kibona's identity is complicated by her training in England, a failed marriage to an African, and her involvement with an American social research unit who are attempting to lift the 'backward' villagers into the modern age. Merle's background aligns her with Western 'progress', but she instinctively identifies with the 'timeless' villagers who, in their annual carnival, embody the continued presence of Ned Cuffee, the leader of an historical slave revolt. *Praisesong* moves from the communal celebration of Carnival to the recovery of self through memory and ritual. The sixty-four year old widow, Avey Johnson, explores memories of her great-aunt with her tales of slaves from South Carolina who walked back over the sea to Africa. In the final sections Avey visits Carriacou, an island in the Grenadines, and by sharing in the ritual dances through which the island's blacks reestablish contact with their past, becomes physically and psychically reintegrated with her repressed ancestral identity.

If *Praisesong* emerged from a black American consciousness of the Caribbean, Erna Brodber's early work is rooted firmly in Jamaica, although her more recent *Louisiana* (1994), too, looks to North America. She originally intended to write *Jane and Louisa Will Soon Come Home* as a case study of the dissociative personality to help social work students in Jamaica.[23] For conventional narrative Brodber substitutes the shifting voices of recollection and dream, both subjective of a hidden village life.

> Yes. It is difficult to find us. Mountains ring us round and
> cover us, banana leaves shelter us and sustain us, boiled,
> chips, porridge, three times a day.[24]

Physical experience is haunted by the presence of ancestral spirits. 'Our dead and living had no stone casements . . . Life is scary when you talk about it.'[25] Hints of danger evoked the image of the 'kumbla' protecting the secret identity of the young Nellie, and the focus shifts from the community to her personal crisis. Nellie, now eleven, is approaching the shame of 'the hidey-hidey thing',[26] her periods and sexual puberty. The first experience of sex disgusts: 'one long, nasty snail, curling up, straightening out to show its white underside that the sun never touches.'[27] She feels a terror of unbeing, and the swirling narrative intimates the approach of breakdown. She remembers her father's folk-tale of Anancy shouting his innocence, only to be answered by confusing echoes. 'Nothing. Twirling madly in a still life. Poor Nancy. Poor me.'[28] Folk wisdom is rooted both in fear and resilience. In a second story Anancy tricks Brother Dryhead (Death) by repeatedly sending him his son Tacuma in different disguises: survival requires adapting one's kumbla. Nellie becomes aware of the voices of her extended family, the village. Aunt Becca, who lost her cultural identity in the process of marrying to become 'respectable', provides one model; Aunt Alice, who lacks work or family but remains emotionally liberated, is her opposite. A dream of Aunt Alice[29] directs Nellie towards healing under the direction of Baba, a childhood friend, now grown up and unrecognised. Baba smells of lime, intimating asceticism and cleansing. Carolyn Cooper has emphasised the way he connects Nellie with Afro-Caribbean healing. 'This obeahman of an anancy' grounds Nellie in her cultural past, and exorcises her possession by Aunt Becca.[30] Refusing her the easy options of sex or self-pity, Baba points her towards her psychic rediscovery of community. In a vision she sees

> 'the myriad pieces of crystal litter around this base . . . I saw them stand still. They were people, I had sensed them but I could still not discern faces or limbs.'[31]

The final sections show Nellie returning to her extended family, the village, rhythmically reassembled in the traditional quadrille dance of the title, itself a creative symbiosis of African and European traditions, in which the outsider waltzes into a protective circle, imaging healing.[32] As the novel ends she dreams of bearing a fish, an Afro-Jamaican sign for fertility. But she is not yet ready to bear a child. 'Good bye Aunt Becca. We are getting ready.'[33]

Radically different in approach, the work of Jamaica Kincaid, born in Antigua as Elaine Potter Richardson, also explores the psychic re-integration of a young Caribbean woman. The ten surreal prose poems collected in *At the Bottom of the River* (1984) form existential explorations of a young woman's being. 'Blackness' becomes an image of both nothingness and pure self; 'Wingless' explores identity without objective reality. Central to the work is her mother, 'the fertile soil of my creative life'[34] with whom she shares an extraordinary love/hate relationship. In the final section the father, a carpenter, builds a house, enabling the narrator herself to enter the river of life and, awakening, discover her true substance. 'I claim these things then – mine – and now feel myself grow solid and complete, my name filling up my mouth'.[35] In one section the mother becomes a maternal reptile internalised by a monstrous daughter, but the end presages harmony: 'My mother and I live in a bower made from flowers whose petals are imperishable.'[36] Kincaid's second work, *Annie John* (1985), explores the same experience of mother and daughter in prose ostensibly as lucid as the earlier work is surreal. The protagonist Annie is caught between two worlds, and her friendship with the genteel Gwen, and with the dirty-nailed, tree-climbing 'Red Girl', reflect two sides of her personality. She horrifies her teacher by writing beneath a picture of Columbus in chains, 'The Great Man Can No Longer Just Get Up and Go'.[37] Yet her education provides her with escape, and she dreams of being Charlotte Brontë, living alone in Belgium.

The book's surface 'realism' is deceptive. Kincaid has noted, 'to be honest, I don't really think I make these distinctions between dreaming and waking'.[38] In an early passage she compares seeing a dead friend with looking through a stereoscopic 'Viewmaster' when it has ceased to create three-dimensional images,[39] using metaphors of imaging to interrogate the nature of reality. The figure is repeated when, aged fifteen, Annie has a nervous breakdown. Hallucinating, she washes out the family photographs, leaving only her own face. 'In the picture of my mother and father, I had erased them from the waist down. In the picture of me wearing my confirmation dress, I had erased all of myself except my shoes.'[40] She is finally healed by her maternal grandmother from another island, who nurses Annie day and night until, mysteriously, the illness ends with season's rains. Implicitly, Annie is saved by her grandmother's traditional healing. But at seventeen she leaves Antigua for Barbados, then England. *Lucy* (1990) takes up the story, with a girl's emigration from the Caribbean to Canada to work as an *au pair*. As her mother tells her, 'Lucy' is from 'Lucifer', and Kincaid's edgy prose probes Lucy's rebellion in another postcolonial world, still compromised by her unresolved relation with her mother: Lucy is unable to open her mother's letters for fear she cannot handle her longing. This appears to reflect a repression within Jamaica Kincaid herself. In an interview with Selwyn Cudjoe she admitted that she omitted important areas of her childhood world from her writing, sometimes subconsciously. 'I was very interested in [obeah] – it was such an everyday part of life, you see.' Yet 'until you mentioned it, I had never realised it had any particular role' in island life.[41]

The Autobiography of My Mother (1996) begins 'My mother died the moment I was born',[42] and the absence of a mother/daughter relationship allows a new objectivity into Kincaid's account of her island. The colours, scents and touch of the island world become now foregrounded in a rhythmic, poetic prose, which includes as factual Kincaid's childhood memory of seeing a spectral woman in the water beckoning a boy to his death. The mother is restored. If Annie John washed out her mother's photograph, each section of *The Autobiography* is prefaced by a fuller reproduction of her photo, until at the end the full-length image reappears. Yet the narrative is both about roots and uprooting. The mother's first name, Xuela, came from her Carib grandmother. Yet the link is lost, for her child was found abandoned in a convent doorway. Her father, the black village policeman, is a colonial presence, a ruthless capitalist, exploiter of the villagers, and incapable of love. He trades his daughter with a business associate as a servant and to be used for sex. She becomes incapable of sustaining relations. She marries Philip whom she does not love, an English doctor whose hobby is growing European plants in the tropics, and she passionately loves Roland, a black stevedore who is married and promiscuous. By the end, infirm and sterile, she awaits the only certainty, death. Her childlessness problematises the title – who is the *my* of *The Autobiography of My Mother?* The riddle emphasises the isolation of the mother. But it may also indicate Kincaid's loss. Insofar as the 'mother' comes into existence in the book, it implies the unreality of its Westernised author.

Ancestral recovery has been a central theme in women's writing. Lorna Goodison's poem 'Guinea Woman' imaginatively explores the moment when

> Great grandmother's royal scent of
> cinnamon and escallions
> drew the sailor up the straits of Africa.[43]

Grace Nichols's *I is a long-memoried woman* grew out of her dream of an African girl swimming, garlanded, from Africa to the Caribbean.[44] The poetic cycle moves between Africa and the West Indies slave plantations, bringing a deepening understanding of her identity. It culminates in poems of resistance in which the now emancipated woman takes her place beside figures of black resistance such as Nanny the Maroon warrior priestess:

> but
> the power to be what I am/a woman
> charting my own futures/ a woman
> holding my beads in my hand[45]

'Nanny' (or 'Ni') as a resistance leader against the British in the early 1700s has provided a focus for militancy in West Indian women's writing, bringing into prominence a figure whose name remains in the ruined 'Nanny Town' concealed deep in the Jamaican mountains, but previously shadowy in Jamaican folk history. While male leaders like Cudjoe were renowned principally as warriors, Nanny has been celebrated as being also priestess and cultural organiser of the Maroon community.[46] Goodison's poem 'Nanny' celebrates her transmission of healing arts from Africa:

> I was schooled in the green-giving ways
> of the roots and the vines
> made accomplice to the healing acts
> of Chainey root, fever grass and vervain.[47]

Nanny lies at the heart of the novel *Abeng* (1984) by the Jamaican-born novelist Michelle Cliff. 'Abeng' was a conch shell whose womb-like shape has given it feminine connotations. Blown both by plantation overseers to call slaves to work, and by the Maroon armies to mobilise resistance, it represents both sides of Clare Savage's cultural identity, for her great-grandfather was Judge Savage, a planter who burnt his slaves alive rather than emancipate them, while her maternal ancestry goes back to the Maroons. Clare divides her life between her Kingston parents and her grandmother Miss Mattie who lives a traditional life in the hills. In a central episode Clare impulsively fires her grandmother's gun, with disastrous results, and she is banished back to the city. Through her friendship with the dark-skinned Zoë in particular, she comes to recognise that the act linked her to both repression and rebellion: all Jamaican history is within her, although 'she had no idea that everyone we dream about we are'.[48] The sequel *No Telephone to Heaven* (1987) begins with a present-day massacre of a middle-class Jamaican family by their black servant, on an island where beauty is inseparable from cruelty, and political action is trapped in historical cycles of violence. The title indicates that the black population should not look to the God of the missionaries, but to themselves, and the novel ends as Clare, returned to her grandmother's house, waits, with a party of present-day rebels, as the helicopter gunships circle in.

The 1983 invasion of Grenada by the United States sent shock-waves through the Caribbean community. Dionne Brand, a Trinidadian living in Toronto, made it the focus of her angry poem sequence, *Chronicles of a Hostile Sun* (1984). Her novel, *In Another Place, not Here* (1996), powerfully interweaves feminist and political concerns in the relationship between two Grenadian women, the dispossessed Elizete and the politically active Verlia tragically culminating in the American invasion. The invasion also had a powerful effect on Merle Collins, who grew up in Grenada and worked there until 1983. She dedicated the militant poems of *Because Dawn Breaks* (1985) 'to the Grenadian People'.[49] Her first novel *Angel* (1987) traces three generations of politically active Grenadian women to the culminating crisis of the American invasion. 'Angel', the name of her black protagonist, itself renegotiates a missionary ethos where angels are white. While studying at the University of the West Indies, the Black

Consciousness celebrations of 1968 start her on a Radical career that culminates in membership of the Grenadian New Jewel movement, and the novel builds up to a climax in the American invasion, in which Angel is nearly blinded.

The manner of the telling is as important as the content. Collins, a talented performance poet, gives *Angel* a strong oral base in the Grenadian idiom. Angel's political quest is framed within the choric and questioning voices of her family and community, while the narrative as a whole is counterpointed against traditional proverbs, creating the effect of a folk epic in which Angel's courage becomes identified with that of the Grenadian people:

> You not no egg, girl!
>
> You caan break so easy![50]

Women's writing in the Anglophone Caribbean has joined with women's movements across the region, and Merle Collins's more recent *The Colour of Forgetting* (1995) shows the impact of 'magical realism' in works of writing from the French and Spanish Caribbean, as found in the Guadeloupe novelists Simone Schwartz-Bart[51] and Maryse Condé.[52] Yet while women's writing has continued to be technically adventurous, it has continued to challenge neocolonial presences from basic, body-centred truths. Grace Nichols's *The Fat Black Woman's Poems* (1984) and *Lazy Thoughts of a Lazy Woman* reject Western stereotypes of femininity with wit and humanity. Marlene Nourbese Philip's verse/prose *Looking for Livingstone* (1991) wittily revisions a black Caribbean woman encountering the archetypal British male explorer, in the process showing the impossibility of communicating a postcolonial experience in the coloniser's language. Yet beneath the polemic lies a private Odyssey reaching beyond words towards personal touch and human intuition:

> through its blackness I touched something warm familiar
> like my own hand human something I could not see in the
> SILENCE reaching out . . .[53]

Women writers have redressed the imbalanced authority of the isolated, intellectually fixated male found in much early Caribbean writing. Their assertion of the role of mother and grandmother has also been an affirmation of the wider community, bringing the tough resilience of women in Caribbean history to sharpen a keen political awareness. In the end, the success of the movement of Caribbean women's writing is to be seen in its integration with Caribbean literature as a whole, as women take a central place in its developing achievement.

Notes

1. Derek Walcott, *Epitaph for the Young* (Bridgetown, Barbados, 1940), p. 6. The context suggests links with the Martello Tower that opens Joyce's *Ulysses* (1922); and the (black) 'ivory tower' of the artist.

2. See Frederic G. Cassidy, *Jamaica Talk* (London, 1961), pp. 84, 400; Carolyn Cooper, 'The fertility of the gardens of woman' (review article), *New Beacon Review* 2/3 (November 1986), pp. 139–47.

3. Kenneth Ramchand, *The West Indian Novel and its Background* (London, 1970), pp. 274–86; *Caribbean Women Writers*, edited by Selwyn R. Cudjoe (Wellesley, Mass., 1990).

4. Anna Rutherford, 'Interview' with Olive Senior, 1986, *Kunapipi* 7, 2 (1986), pp. 16–17.

5. Honor Ford Smith, *Sistren* (London, 1986), pp. xix–xx.

6. Merle Hodge, 'Challenging the struggle for sovereignty', in Selwyn R. Cudjoe, ed., *Caribbean Women Writers*, p. 208.

7. Simon Gikandi, 'Narration in the Post-Colonial Moment: Merle Hodge's *Crick Crack Monkey*', in *Past the Last Post* (New York and London, 1991), edited by Ian Adam and Helen Tiffin, p. 14.

8. Ibid., p. 14; Teresa de Laurentis, 'Feminist Studies/Critical Studies: Issues, Terms and Contexts', ed. Teresa de Laurentis (Bloomington, 1986), p. 9.

9. Merle Hodge, *Crick Crack Monkey* (London, 1970), p. 57.

10. Ibid., p. 4.

11. Ibid., p. 26.

12. Ibid., p. 8.

13. Ibid., p. 89.

14. Ibid., p. 125.

15. SISTREN with Honor Ford Smith (ed.), *Lionheart Gal: Life Stories of Jamaican Women* (London, 1986). See also Carolyn Cooper, *Noises in the Blood* (London, 1993), ch. 5.

16. Olive Senior, 'Interview', *Kunapipi* 7, 2 (1986), p. 17.

17. Bev E.L. Brown, 'Mansong and Matrix: a Radical Experiment', *Kunapipi* 7, 2–3 (1985), pp. 68–79.

18. Ibid., p. 70.

19. Ibid., p. 73.

20. Zee Edgell, *Beka Lamb* (London, 1982), p. 171.

21. Renu Juneja, *Caribbean Transactions. West Indian Culture in Literature* (London, 1996).

22. Paule Marshall, 'Shaping the World of my Art', *New Letters* 40, 1 (1970), p. 107. Quoted by Juneja, p. 53.

23. Evelyn O'Callaghan, 'Re-discovering the Natives of my Person', *Jamaica Journal* 16, 3 (1983), p. 6.

24. Erna Brodber, *Jane and Louisa Will Soon Come Home* (London, 1980), p. 9.

25. Ibid., pp. 12, 14.

26. Ibid., p. 120.

27. Ibid., p. 28.

28. Ibid., p. 38.

29. Ibid., p. 39. 'Alice' also suggests 'Alice in Wonderland', an ambivalent image.

30. Carolyn Cooper, 'Afro-Jamaican folk elements in Brodber's *Jane and Louisa Will Soon Come Home*', in *Out of the Kumbla*, pp. 279–88.

31. Ibid., p. 76.

32. Carolyn Cooper, 'The Fertility of the Gardens of Women', *New Beacon Review* 2/3 (November 1986), p. 140.

33. Ibid., p. 147.

34. Selwyn R. Cudjoe, 'Jamaica Kincaid. . . . : An Interview', in *Caribbean Women Writers*, p. 222.

35. Jamaica Kincaid, *At the Bottom of the River* (London, 1984), p. 82.

36. Ibid., p. 61.

37. Jamaica Kincaid, *Annie John* (London, 1985), p. 78.

38. Selwyn R. Cudjoe, 'Jamaica Kincaid', p. 230.

39. Jamaica Kincaid, *Annie John* (London, 1985), p. 11. Kincaid's early training was in photography.

40. Ibid., p. 120.

41. Selwyn R. Cudjoe, 'Jamaica Kincaid', p. 229.

42. Jamaica Kincaid, *The Autobiography of my Mother* (New York, 1996), p. 3.

43. Lorna Goodison, *I am Becoming my Mother* (London, 1986), pp. 39–40.

44. Grace Nichols, 'Home Truths', *Hinterland*, ed. E.A. Markham (Newcastle-on-Tyne, 1989), p. 298.

45. Grace Nichols, *i is a long-memoried woman* (1983), p. 79.

46. See *General History of the Caribbean*, vol. III (London and Basingstoke, 1997), pp. 181–2.

47. Lorna Goodison, *I am Becoming my Mother*, p. 44.

48. Michelle Cliff, *Abeng* (1984), p. 166.

49. Merle Collins, *Because Dawn Breaks!* (London, 1985), Introduction by Ngugi Wa Thiong'o.

50. Merle Collins, *Angel* (London, 1987), p. 285.

51. Schwartz-Bart's *Ti Jean L'horizon* (1979) was translated as *Between Two Worlds* in 1981.

52. Maryse Condé's *La Vie Scelerte* (1987) was translated as *The Tree of Life* in 1992.

53. Marlene Nourbese Philip, *Looking for Livingstone* (1991), p. 75.

Postscript

The pleasure and paradox of my own exile is that I belong wherever I am.

George Lamming[1]

Caribbean Writing as World Literature

There are few more vividly local West Indian novels than George Lamming's *In the Castle of my Skin*. Yet the global experience of growing up under colonialism in the novel's lifeblood made it at once local and universal. In Kenya, Ngugi wa Thiong'o read it, and recognised Lamming's world as his own. 'And suddenly I knew a novel could be made to speak to me', he wrote, 'could, with a compelling urgency, touch chords deep in me'.[2] The chords reverberate in Ngugi's own first novel, *Weep not Child* (1964). In France, Sartre chose the novel as one of the significant texts of the mid-century, reprinting it in his series, *Les Temps Modernes*. The historical context of the Caribbean has given it a unique position in world literature. Both intimately implicated in the hegemony of colonial culture, yet separate from it, Caribbean authors have been uniquely placed to 'write back' against Western imperialism, where the truest hate comes out of knowledge and love. Black consciousness in the United States found its catalyst in the writing of a Jamaican, Marcus Garvey, and the movement drew inspiration from a lengthy roster of eminent West Indians, including Claude McKay, Eric Walrond, Richard B. Moore, and Walter Adolphe Roberts. Expelled from the United States for their Marxist beliefs, C.L.R. James and George Padmore played a part in the pan-African movement: Padmore died in Ghana, Nkrumah's personal adviser on African affairs. Francophone Caribbean authors sparked the new African literatures. The concept of négritude, developed in the politics and poetry of Leopold Senghor in Senegal, grew from Césaire's Martinican *Cahier*, and Senghor's epoch-making anthology, *Anthologie de la nouvelle poésie nègre et malagache de langue française* (1948) was dominated by poets from the West Indies. Anglophone West Indians, too, featured in the important cultural magazine *Black Orpheus* when it was founded in Nigeria in 1957. Frantz Fanon drew on his childhood experience of Martinique in formulating concepts of colonialism and race whose impacts were world wide.

As we noted at the beginning of this study, the global significance of the Caribbean makes it peculiarly difficult to define. This study comes to an uncertain halt on the shadowy borders between Caribbean writing in English, and black British, black United States and black Canadian writing. My distinctions have been necessarily arbitrary. Where does one place the Canadian writers Marlene Nourbese Philip or Dionne Brand; or British-based authors such as Caryl Phillips, John Agard, Archie Markham, Beryl Gilroy or Joan Riley? Caryl Phillips, born in St Kitts but brought up in England, writes as a second-generation immigrant. In his *The Final Passage* (1985), Leila emigrates from a small Caribbean island with her husband Michael and a small child. As the title suggests, the voyage completes the triangle of the 'middle passage' of the slave trade, the ships returning to Britain with a reprocessed cargo of cheap black labour. When the sensitive Leila faces madness in a cold, lonely bedsitter, it is the final stage in a cycle of psychic dispossession, and catching sight of herself in a mirror, she 'looked like a yellowing snapshot of an old relative, fading with the years'.[3] Yet Phillips also found himself out of touch with his parents' Caribbean,[4] a situation dramatised in his novel *A State of Independence* (1986), where Bertram returns to his home island and finds it Americanised and alien. In Austin Clarke's *The Prime Minister* (1977), John Moore goes back to a government post in his independent home island, only to become caught in a web of corruption within which he nearly loses his life. Leaving it he muses mordantly that 'the land is beautiful, the only truly beautiful thing about this country'.[5] The theme is repeated in Neil Bissondath's compelling novel of a doctor returning from Canada to the economically corrupted Caribbean island of 'Casquemada' in *A Casual Brutality* (1988).

Yet exile has become, for writers like Lamming and V.S. Naipaul, a form of homecoming, a location within the 'free state' of the modern. Deprived of roots, West Indians become citizens of the world. In 1956, Selvon's *The Lonely Londoners* heralded 'colonisation in reverse', as the immigrants set about creating a Caribbean London.[6] Caryl Phillips's *The European Tribe* (1987) is a travelogue which revisions Britain as seen through West Indian eyes, and in his screenplay *Playing Away* (1986), an English village is colonised by a West Indian cricket eleven from Brixton. Fragmented experience itself can become the paradoxical basis for identity. In his wickedly sharp first novel *The Intended* (1991), David Dabydeen intercuts memories of childhood Guyana with those of his youth in London among Asian and West Indian friends, and their readings of

Conrad's *Heart of Darkness* relocate Marlow's voyage upriver in search of Kurtz in the heart of London. Yet the novel is unified by the consciousness of alienation and out of the jumble of ethnic experience comes a new formulation of the expatriate community. It forms the basis for new movements in writing, and 'Black British' verse constitutes a third of the 1988 Paladin anthology, *The New British Poetry*.[7] England is no longer the only centre for expatriate Caribbean writing. As the colonial ties have loosened, West Indians have turned increasingly to the United States, and in particular to Canada.[8] Cyril Dabydeen's anthology *A Shapely Fire* (1987) featured the work of twenty West Indians writing in Canada, ranging from older generation figures such as Austin Clarke to new writers including Claire Harris, Marlene Nourbese Philip, Neil Bissoondath and Cyril Dabydeen himself. This writing interrogates Canadian life and receives back echoes of yet another colonial culture.

As Caribbean literature can no longer be limited to writing from the Caribbean area – if it ever could be – the question becomes more insistent, 'How can Caribbean writing be defined?' It has frequently been associated with rhythm, physical movement, a 'performance' literature with strong links between writing and the communal experience. A Caribbean identity was first associated with distinctive rhythms,[9] a feature reinforced by the tradition of Carnival, which, as Nourbese Philip observed,[10] West Indians have established wherever they have settled, recreating 'Mas' in the streets of Brooklyn, Montreal, Toronto and London's Notting Hill.

> What connecting Maisie and Totoben on the slave ship to Totoben and Maisie on University Avenue up in Canada is moving – the moving of their bodies. . . . Totoben and Maisie understanding and tasting the power of the cross-roads of Eshu-Elegbara and the power of anything happening; they breaking up space into rhythm which is time, and time and space making one.[11]

For Philip, the rhythms of Carnival maintain a continuity between expatriate West Indians and Africa, where the Masqueraders danced on the ritual cross-roads linking the living and the dead. As we have seen, for Wilson Harris, the connections may be with the cultures of South America, or the timeless archetypes of Europe. Edouard Glissant locates the Caribbean identity within the opacity of the complex Antillean experience itself. These and other definitions are not mutually exclusive. For Caribbean identity has emerged from a history of loss and uprooting, as a catalytic genius, creating literatures defined not by form but by the ability to transform. Caribbean arts have characteristically moved between cultures, and between the categories imposed by Western convention – between the written and the oral, materialism and a spiritual dimension, social realism and the magic of the imagination. The fragmenting post-colonial age has placed Caribbean writers, prime inheritors of colonial fragmentation, in a central position within world literature.

Notes

1. George Lamming, *The Pleasures of Exile* (London, 1960), p. 50.

2. Ngugi wa Thiong'o, *Homecoming* (London, 1972), p. 81.

3. Caryl Phillips, *The Final Passage* (London, 1985), pp. 204–5.

4. Caryl Phillips, 'The Legacy of Othello', in *Frontiers of Caribbean Literature in English*, ed. Frank Birbalsingh (London, 1996), pp. 183–97.

5. Austin Clarke, *The Prime Minister* (London, 1978), p. 191.

6. The phrase is Louise Bennett's – see 'Colonisation in Reverse', in *Jamaica Labrish*, pp. 179–80.

7. *The New British Poetry* (London, 1988), edited by Gillian Allbutt, Fred D'Aguiar, Ken Edwards and Eric Mottram.

8. See Victor Ramraj, 'West Indian Writing in Canada', in *West Indian Literature* (2nd edn, London, 1995), edited by Bruce King, ch. 9.

9. See above, pp. 23–4.

10. M. Nourbese Philip, *Race, Space and the Poetics of Moving* (Toronto, 1996), p. 4.

11. Ibid., pp. 4, 30.

Chronology

Date	Cultural/historical events	Literature
1791–4	Slave revolt in Saint-Domingue led by Toussaint L'Ouverture culminates in Jean-Jacques Dessalines proclaiming Haiti the first independent black Caribbean state	
1793		J.B. Moreton, *West Indian Customs and Manners*
1801–5		Lady Nugent, *Diaries*
1827		[Anon.] *Hamel the Obeah Man*
1833	Emancipation of slaves in British Caribbean	
1834		M.G. Lewis, *Journal of a West Indian Proprietor*
1838	Import of Asian indentured labour to British West Indies begins	
1865	In Jamaica the Morant Bay rebellion is brutally repressed and punished by Governor Eyre	
1869		J.J. Thomas, *Creole Grammar*
1883		'Tom Redcam', *Jamaica*
1912		Claude McKay, *Constab Ballads; Songs of Jamaica*
1912–13	E.G. de Lisser starts the Pioneer Press, Jamaica	de Lisser, *Jane: a Story of Jamaica*
1914	Marcus Garvey founds the Universal Negro Improvement Association (UNIA)	
1929		J.E. Clare McFarlane edits *Voices from Summerland* (Jamaica)
1929–36		*Beacon* and *Trinidad* (periodicals)
1933		Claude McKay, *Banana Bottom*
1936		C.L.R. James, *Minty Alley*
1937–8	Riots across the British Caribbean	
1939		Aimé Césaire, *Cahier* (Fr.)
1939–42	Second World War involves West Indian servicemen abroad. Major US military presence in Trinidad	
1941		Edgar Mittelholzer, *Corentyne Thunder*
1942		*Bim* started (periodical). *Caribbean Voices* broadcast from BBC (to 1959)

1948	Empire Windrush lands Jamaicans at Tilbury, beginning massive Caribbean immigration to Britain	
1949	First students enter University of the West Indies, Jamaica campus	V.S. Reid, *New Day*
1950		Edgar Mittelholzer, *Morning at the Office*
1952		Samuel Selvon, *A Brighter Sun*; Frantz Fanon, *Black Skins White Masks* (Fr.)
1953	Leonard Howell establishes Rastafarian commune at Pinnacle, outside Kingston	George Lamming, *In the Castle of my Skin*
1956		Samuel Selvon, *The Lonely Londoners*
1957		Errol John, *Moon on a Rainbow Shawl* (drama)
1958	Race riots in Britain	
1959	Castro comes to power in Cuba	
1953		Alejo Carpentier, *The Lost Steps* (Sp.)
1960		Wilson Harris, *Palace of the Peacock*
1961		V.S. Naipaul, *A House for Mr Biswas*; Frantz Fanon, *the Wretched of the Earth* (Fr.)
1962	Jamaica, Trinidad become independent	Derek Walcott, *In a Green Night*
1965	USA invade Dominican Republic	
1966	Barbados, Guyana become independent; Caribbean Artists Movement founded in London	Jean Rhys, *Wide Sargasso Sea*
1968	Caribbean Free Trade area formed	
1967–9		Kamau Brathwaite, *The Arrivants* trilogy
1970	Guyana becomes a Republic	Merle Hodge, *Crick Crack Monkey*
1971	First CARIFESTA held in Guyana	Trevor Rhone, *Smile Orange* (drama)
1973		Derek Walcott, *Another Life*
1979		Earl Lovelace, *The Dragon Can't Dance*
1980		Erna Brodber, *Jane and Louisa will Soon Come Home*

Date	Cultural/historical events	Literature
1983	USA invades Grenada	
1985	'CAFRA' founded to promote Feminist Research and Action	
1990		Derek Walcott, *Omeros*
1996		Earl Lovelace, *Salt*
1997		Pauline Melville, *The Ventriloquist's Tale*

Bibliographies

Place of publication is abbreviated as follows:

Ba. – Bridgetown, Barbados	NY. – New York
C. – Cambridge, England	O. – Oxford
Ge. – Georgetown, British Guiana/Guyana	POS. – Port-of-Spain, Trinidad
Ja. – Jamaica	To. – Toronto
K. – Kingston, Jamaica	Tr. – Trinidad
L. –. London	

Where a significant later edition appeared, its date is added after that of the first publication.

1. Encyclopaedias/bibliographies

The Year's Work in English Studies includes an annual bibliography. Bibliographies of Caribbean literature can also be found, irregularly, in *The Journal of Commonwealth Literature, Kunapipi* and *Callaloo.*

Allis, Jeanette B., *West Indian Literature: An Index to Criticism, 1930–1975* (Boston, 1981).

Benson, Eugene and L.W. Connolly (eds), *Encyclopaedia of Post-Colonial Literatures in English*, 2 vols (L. and NY., 1994).

Berrian, Brenda F. and Aart Broek, *Bibliography of Women Writers from the Caribbean* (Washington, DC, 1989).

Boxill, Anthony, 'A Bibliography of West Indian Fiction', *WLWE Newsletter*, no. 19 (1971), pp. 23–44.

Dance, Daryl Cumber (ed.), *Fifty Caribbean Writers: A Bio-Bibliographical Critical Sourcebook* (Westport, Conn., 1986).

Dance, Daryl Cumber, *New World Adams. Conversations with Contemporary West Indian Writers* (Leeds, 1992).

Dyde, Brian, *Caribbean Companion. The A to Z Reference* (L., 1992). (Includes writers, history, geography.)

Herdeck, Donald E. (ed.), *Caribbean Writers. A Bio-Bibliographical-Critical Encyclopaedia* (Washington, DC, 1979). (Covers all linguistic areas.)

Hughes, Michael, *A Companion to West Indian Literature* (L., 1979).

Lindfors, Bernth and Reinhard Sander (eds), *Dictionary of Literary Biography: Twentieth-Century Caribbean and Black African Writers. First Series* (Detroit, 1992).

McDowell, Robert (ed.), *Bibliography of Literature from Guyana* (Arlington, Texas, 1975).

Morris, Mervyn, 'Little Magazines in the Caribbean', *Bim* (1984), pp. 3–9.

Paravisini-Gebert, Lizabeth and Olga Torres-Seda, *Caribbean Women Novelists. An Annotated Critical Bibliography* (Westport, Conn., 1996).

Poynting, Jeremy, *East Indians in the Caribbean: a Bibliography of Imaginative Literature* (UWI, St Augustine, Tr., 1984).

Sander, Reinhart W., 'Short Fiction in West Indian Periodicals: A Checklist', *World Literature Written in English*, vol. 15 (November 1976), pp. 438–62.

University of the West Indies Library, *West Indian Literature. A Select Bibliography* (Mona, Ja., 1964).

2. Literary periodicals

Criticism and/or creative writing of the Caribbean features regularly in a number of periodicals, including the following: *Ariel*; *Commonwealth*; *The Journal of Commonwealth Literature* (JCL); *Kunapipi*; *Wasafiri*; *World Literature Today*; *World Literature Written in English* (WLWE).

The Beacon (1931–3, 1939) (occasional annual) (Tr.).

Bim (1942–73) (Ba.).

Caribana (Rome, Italy, 1991–)

Caribbean Quarterly (1949–) (Cumulative index, 1990) (Ja.)

The Caribbean Writer (1987–) (St Croix, Virgin Islands).

Focus (occasional annual, 1943, 1948, 1956, 1960) (Ja.).

Jamaica Journal (1967–) (Ja.).

Journal of West Indian Literature (1986–) (Ja.)

Journal of Caribbean Literature (Cedar Falls, Iowa, USA)

Kyk-over-Al (1945–61; 1984–) (Gu.).

New World Quarterly (1963–) (Ja.).

Savacou (1970–80) (L. and Ja.)

Tapia (Trinidad and Tobago Review) (1968–) (Tr.)

Trinidad (1929–30) (Tr.).

Voices (1964–6, 1969–70) (Ba.).

3. Historical and intellectual background

Barrett, Leonard E., Sr, *The Rastafarians*, revised edition (Boston, Mass., 1988).

Brathwaite, Kamau, *Roots* (Ann Arbor, 1993).

Coulthard, G.R., *Race and Colour in Caribbean Literature* (L., 1962).

Dabydeen, David, and Brinsley Samaroo (eds), *India in the Caribbean* (Warwick and L., 1987).

Goveia, Elsa V., *A Study on the Historiography of the British West Indies to the End of the Nineteenth Century* (Tacubaya, Mexico, 1956). (Ground-breaking study.)

Hall, Douglas (ed.), *In Miserable Slavery. Thomas Thistlewood in Jamaica, 1750–86* (L., 1989). (Annotated selections from diaries of slave-owner.)

Hennessy, Alistair (ed.), *Intellectuals in the Twentieth-Century Caribbean*, 2 vols (L., 1992). (Includes the Commonwealth, Hispanic and Francophone Caribbean.)

Hulme, Peter and Neil L. Whitehead (eds), *Wild Majesty. Encounters with Caribs from Columbus to the Present Day* (O., 1992).

Knight, Franklin W., *The Caribbean. The Genesis of a Fragmented Nationalism*, 2nd edn (NY., 1990).
Lowenthal, David, *West Indian Societies* (L., 1972). (Comprehensive, authoritative.)
Mintz, Sidney W. and Sally Price (eds), *Caribbean Contours* (Baltimore, 1985). (Socio-historical essays.)
Silverberg, Robert (ed.), *The Golden Dream. Seekers of El Dorado* (Athens, Ohio, 1967, 1985).
Thomas, J.J., *Froudacity. West Indian Fables Explained*, with an introduction by C.L.R. James ([1889] L., 1969).
Walmsley, Anne, *The Caribbean Artists Movement 1966–1972. A Literary and Cultural Study* (L., 1992).

4. The oral tradition, dictionaries, drama

A full bibliography of Caribbean drama in English, including critical work, can be found in Judy S.J. Stone, *Theatre*, below.

Allsopp, Richard (ed.), *Dictionary of Caribbean English Usage. With French and Spanish Supplement edited by Jeannette Allsopp* (O., 1996). (Definitive work; introduction; bibliography.)
Banham, Martin, Errol Hill, George Woodyard (eds), *The Cambridge Guide to African and Caribbean Theatre* (C., 1994).
Barrett, Leonard, *The Sun and the Drum. African Roots in Jamaican Folk Tradition* (K., 1976).
Brathwaite, Edward Kamau, *History of the Voice* (L., 1984).
Brown, Stewart (ed.), *The Pressures of the Text. Orality, Texts and the Telling of Tales* (Birmingham, 1995).
Cassidy, Frederic G., *Jamaica Talk. Three Hundred Years of the English Language in Jamaica* (L., 1961).
Clarke, Sebastian, *Jah Music. The Evolution of Popular Jamaican Song* (L., 1980).
Cooper, Carolyn, *Noises in the Blood. Orality, Gender and the 'Vulgar' Body of Jamaican Popular Culture* (K., 1993).
Connor, Edric (ed.), *Songs from Trinidad* (L., 1958).
Habekost, Christian, *Verbal Riddim: the Politics and Aesthetics of African-Caribbean Dub Poetry* (Amsterdam/Atlanta, 1993).
Hill, Errol, *The Trinidad Carnival: Mandate for a National Theatre* (Austin, Texas, 1972).
Hill, Errol (ed.), *Plays for Today* (Derek Walcott, *Ti-Jean and his Brothers*; Dennis Scott, *An Echo in the Bone*; Erroll Hill, *Man Better Man*) (Harlow, 1985).
Jekyll, Walter (ed.), *Jamaican Song and Story* ([1907] NY., 1966).
Kole Omotoso, *The Theatrical into Theatre* (L., 1982).
Lawton, David L., 'English in the Caribbean', in Richard W. Bailey and Manfred Gorlach (eds), *English as a World Language* (C., 1982), pp. 251–80.
Rohlehr, Gordon, *Calypso and Society in Pre-Independence Trinidad* (POS., 1990).
Sherlock, Philip (ed.,) *West Indian Folk Tales* (L., 1968).
Sherlock, Philip (ed.,) *Anansi, the Spider Man* (L., 1956).
Sistren, with Honor Ford Smith, *Lionheart Gal. Life Stories of Jamaican Women* (L., 1986).
Stone, Judy S.J., *Studies in West Indian Literature: Theatre* (L., 1994).
van Koningsbruggen, Peter, *Trinidad Carnival. A Quest for National Identity* (L., 1997). (Full bibliography.)
Warner, Keith, *The Trinidad Calypso* (L., 1982).

5. Major anthologies

Brown, Stewart (ed.), *Caribbean New Wave. Contemporary Short Stories* (O., 1990).

Brown, Stewart (ed.), *Caribbean New Voices 1* (Harlow, 1995).

Brown, Stewart, Mervyn Morris and Gordon Rohlehr (eds), *Voiceprint. An Anthology of Oral and Related Poetry from the Caribbean* (Harlow, 1985).

Burnett, Paula (ed.), *Penguin Book of Caribbean Verse in English* (Harmondsworth, 1986).

D'Costa, Jean and Barbara Lalla (eds), *Voices in Exile. Jamaican Texts of the 18th and 19th Centuries* (Tuscaloosa, 1989).

Donnell and Sarah Lawson Welsh, *The Routledge Reader in Caribbean Literature* (L. and NY., 1996)

Espinet, Ramabai, *Creation Fire. A CAFRA Anthology of Caribbean Women's Poetry* (To., 1990)

Figueroa, John (ed.), *Caribbean Voices* 2 vols (L., 1966, 1970).

Habekost, Christian (ed.), *Dub Poetry: 19 Poets from England and Jamaica* (Amsterdam | Atlanta 1989).

Howes, Barbara (ed.), *From the Green Antilles* (NY. and To., 1966). (A pioneering pan-Caribbean prose anthology, in English translation.)

Markham, E.A. (ed.), *Hinterland. Caribbean Poetry from the West Indies and Britain* (Newcastle-upon-Tyne, 1989).

McDonald, Ian and Stewart Brown (eds), *The Heinemann Book of Caribbean Poetry* (O., 1992).

Mordecai, Pamela (ed.), *From Our Yard. Jamaican Poetry since Independence* (K., 1987).

Mordecai, Pamela and Betty Wilson, *Her True-true Name. An Anthology of Women's Writing from the Caribbean* (O., 1989).

Morris, Mervyn (ed.), *The Faber Book of Contemporary Caribbean Short Stories* (L., 1990).

Salkey, Andrew (ed.), *Stories from the Caribbean* (L., 1965).

Salkey, Andrew (ed.), *Breaklight* (L., 1971).

Sander, Reinhard W. (ed.), *From Trinidad. An Anthology of Early West Indian Writing* (L., 1978).

6. Literary criticism

See also notes to individual authors and works in the main body of the text.

Baugh, Edward, *West Indian Poetry: a Study in Cultural Decolonization* (K., 1971).

Baugh, Edward (ed.), *Critics on Caribbean Literature* (L., 1978).

Birbalsingh, Frank, *Passion and Exile. Essays in Caribbean Literature* (L., 1988).

Birbalsingh, Frank (ed.), *Frontiers of Caribbean Literatures in English* (L., 1996). (Interviews.)

Brown, Lloyd W., *West Indian Poetry*, 2nd edn (L., 1984).

Chamberlin, J. Edward, *Come Back to Me My Language. Poetry and the West Indies* (Urbana and Chicago, 1993).

Chang, Victor L., *Three Caribbean Poets on their Work. E. Kamau Brathwaite, Mervyn Morris, Lorna Goodison* (Mona, Ja., 1993).

'Critical Approaches to West Indian Literature', Special Issue of *Caribbean Quarterly*, 38, 1/2 (March–June, 1982).

Cudjoe, Selwyn R., *Caribbean Women Writers. Essays from the First International Conference* (Wellesley, Mass., 1990).

Cudjoe, Selwyn R., *Resistance and Caribbean Literature* (Athens, Ohio, 1980).

Dabydeen, David (ed.), *A Handbook for Teaching Caribbean Literature* (L., 1988).

Davies, Carole Boyce and Elaine Savory Fido (eds), *Out of the Kumbla* (Trenton, NJ, 1990). (Major critical anthology on women's writing in the Caribbean.)

Gikandi, Simon, *Writing in Limbo. Modernism and Caribbean Literature* (Ithaca, 1992).

Gilkes, Michael, *The West Indian Novel* (Boston, 1981).

Griffith, Glyne A., *Deconstruction, Imperialism and the West Indian Novel* (K., 1996).

Griffiths, Gareth, *A Double Exile: African and West Indian Writing Between two Cultures* (L., 1978).

Harris, Wilson, *Tradition, the Writer and Society* ([1967] L., 1973).

James, Louis (ed.), *The Islands in Between* (L., 1968). (First published collection of Caribbean criticism.)

Jonas, Joyce, *Anancy in the Great House* (Westport, Conn., 1990). (On Lamming, Harris.)

Juneja, Renu, *Caribbean Transactions. West Indian Culture in Literature* (L., 1996).

King, Bruce (ed.), *West Indian Literature*, rev. edn (L., 1995).

McWatt, Mark (ed.), *West Indian Literature and its Social Context* (Cave Hill, Ba., 1988).

Moore, Gerald, *The Chosen Tongue. English Writing in the Tropical World* (L., 1969). (Compares Caribbean and African writers.)

Munro, Ian and Reinhard Sander (ed.), *Kas-Kas. Interviews with Three Caribbean Writers in Texas. George Lamming, C.L.R. James and Wilson Harris* (Austin, Texas, 1972).

Nasta, Susheila (ed.), *Motherlands. Black Women's Writing from Africa, the Caribbean and South Asia* (L., 1991).

O'Callaghan, Evelyn, *Woman Version. Theoretical Approaches to West Indian Fiction by Women* (L., 1993).

Pereira, J.R. (ed.), *Caribbean Literature in Comparison* (Mona, Ja., 1990).

Ramchand, Kenneth, *The West Indian Novel and its Background* (L., 1970).

Ramchand, Kenneth, *An Introduction to the Study of West Indian Literature* (K., 1976)

Richardson, Michael (ed.), *Refusal of the Shadow. Surrealism and the Caribbean*, translated by Michael Richardson and Krzysztovski (L. and NY., 1996).

Rohlehr, Gordon, *The Shape of that Hurt and Other Essays* (POS., 1992).

Rohlehr, Gordon, *My Strangled City and Other Essays* (POS., 1992).

Sander, Reinhard, *The Trinidad Awakening: West Indian Literature of the Nineteen-Thirties* (L., 1988).

Sakaana, Amon Saba, *The Colonial Legacy in Caribbean Literature* (L., 1987).

Smilowitz, Erika Sollish and Roberta Quarles Knowles (eds), *Critical Issues in West Indian Literature* (Parkersburg, Iowa, 1984).

Taylor, Patrick, *The Narrative of Liberation: Perspectives on Afro-Caribbean Literature, Popular Culture and Politics* (Ithaca, 1989).

van Sertima, Ivan, *Caribbean Writers. Critical Essays* (L., 1968).

Webb, Barbara, *Myth and History in Caribbean Fiction* (Westport, 1990).

Zamora, Lois Parkinson and Wendy B. Farris (eds), *Magical Realism. Theory, History, Community* (Durham, N.C. and L., 1995).

7. Selective bibliographies of eight writers

BENNETT, Louise, M.B.E. Poet, folklorist, performer. Born Jamaica, 1919. **Publications**: *Jamaica Labrish* (K., 1966); *Anancy and Miss Lou* (K., 1979); *Selected Poems* (K., 1982). **Criticism**: Mervyn Morris, 'On Reading Louise Bennett, Seriously', *Jamaica Journal* 1 (December 1967), pp. 69–74; Mervyn Morris,

'Introduction' to *Selected Poems*; Carolyn Cooper, *Noises in the Blood*, pp. 47–67; Daryl Cumber Dance, *New World Adams*, pp. 26–30; Dennis Scott, 'Bennett on Bennett', *Caribbean Quarterly* 14 (March–June 1968), pp. 97–101; Gordon Rohlehr, 'Literature and the Folk', in *My Strangled City*, pp. 52–85.

BRATHWAITE, Edward Kamau (Lawson Edward) Born Barbados, 1930. Poet, historian, critic. **Publications**: *The Arrivants: A New World Trilogy* (L., 1973) (combining *Rights of Passage* (1967), *Masks* (1968), *Islands* (1969)); *Contrary Omens: Cultural Diversity and Integration in the Caribbean* (Mona, Ja., 1974); *Mother Poem* (L., 1977); *Sun Poem* (L.,1982); *The History of the Voice* (L., 1984); *Jah Music* (K., 1986); *X-Self* (L., 1987); *Middle Passages* (Newcastle-upon-Tyne, 1992); *The Zea Mexican Diary* (Madison, Wis., 1993); *Roots* (Ann Arbor, 1973) (collected essays); *DreamStories* (Harlow, 1994); *Trench Town Rock* (Providence, 1994); *Barabajan Poems* (K. and NY., 1994). **Criticism:** Doris Monica Brathwaite, *A Descriptive and Chronological Bibliography (1950–1980)* (L., 1988); *World Literature Today*, 68, 4 (Autumn 1994) (special Brathwaite issue); Stewart Brown (ed.), *The Art of Kamau Brathwaite* (Bridgend, Wales, 1995) (critical essays, bibliography); J. Michael Dash, 'Edward Kamau Brathwaite', in Bruce King, *West Indian Literature*; Gordon Rohlehr, *Pathfinder* (Tunapuna, Tr., 1981) (fine analysis of *The Arrivants*).

HARRIS, Wilson. Novelist and critic. Born Guyana, 1921. **Publications**: Fiction – *Palace of the Peacock* (L., 1960); *The Far Journey of Oudin* (L., 1961); *The Whole Armour* (L., 1962); *Heartland* (1964); *The Eye of the Scarecrow* (L., 1965); *The Waiting Room* (L., 1967); *Tumatumari* (L., 1968); *The Ascent to Omai* (L., 1970); *The Sleepers of Roraima* (L., 1970); *The Age of the Rainmakers* (L., 1971); *Black Marsden* (L., 1972); *Companions of the Day and Night* (L., 1975); *Da Silva da Silva's Cultivated Wilderness and the Genesis of the Clowns* (L., 1977); *The Tree of the Sun* (L., 1978); *Angel at the Gate* (L., 1982); *Carnival* (L., 1985); *The Infinite Rehearsal* (L., 1987); *The Four Banks of the River of Space* (L., 1990); *Resurrection at Sorrow Hill* (L., 1993); *Jonestown* (1996). Essays – *Tradition, the Writer and Society* (L., 1967, 1973); *Explorations* (Mundelstrup, 1981); *History, Fable and Myth in the Caribbean and Guyana* (Georgetown, Gu., 1970; rev. version, Wellesley, Mass., 1995); *Fossil and Psyche* (Austin, Texas, 1974); *The Womb of Space: the Cross-Cultural Imagination* (Westport, Conn., 1983); Alan Riarch and Mark Williams (eds), *The Radical Imagination* (Liège, 1992). **Criticism:** Sandra Drake, *Wilson Harris and the Modern Tradition* (Westport, Conn., 1986); Michael Gilkes, *Wilson Harris and Caribbean Novel* (L., 1975); Hena Maes-Jelinek, *The Naked Design* (Aarhus, 1976); Hena Maes-Jelinek, *Wilson Harris* (Boston, 1982); Hena Maes-Jelinek (ed.), *Wilson Harris. The Uncompromising Imagination* (Sydney, 1991) (full bibliography); Kirsten Holst Petersen and Anna Rutherford (eds), *Enigma of Values: An Introduction* (Aarhus, 1975).

LAMMING, George. Novelist and critic. Born Barbados, 1927. **Publications:** Fiction – *In the Castle of my Skin* (L., 1953, 1970); *The Emigrants* (L., 1954); *Of Age and Innocence* (L., 1958, 1981); *Season of Adventure* (1970, 1979); *Water with Berries* (L., 1971); *Natives of my Person* (1972). Non-fiction – *The Pleasures of Exile* (L., 1960); Richard Drayton, and Andaiye (eds), *Conversations. George Lamming. Essays, Addresses and Interviews 1953–1990* (L., 1992); *Coming Coming Come. Conversations II* (Philipsburg, St Martin, 1995). **Criticism:** Mervyn Morrris, 'The Poet as Novelist', in Louis James (ed.), *The Islands in Between* (L., 1968), pp. 73–85; Ian Munro, 'The Theme of Exile in George Lamming's *In the Castle of my Skin*', *WLWE* 20 (Nov. 1971), pp. 51–60; Ngugi wa Thiong'o, 'George Lamming's *In the Castle of my Skin*', in *Homecoming* (NY., 1972); Sandra Pouchet Paquet, *The Novels of George Lamming* (L., 1982); Kirsten Holst Petersen, 'Time, Timelessness and the Journey Metaphor in George Lamming's *In the Castle of my Skin* and *Natives of my Person*', in Alastair Niven (ed.), *Commonwealth Writers Overseas* (Brussels, 1976), pp. 283–8; Helen

Tiffin, 'The Tyranny of History: George Lamming's *Natives of My Person* and *Water with Berries*', *Ariel* 10 (Oct. 1979), pp. 37–52.

LOVELACE, Earl. Novelist, short-story writer, playwright. Born Trinidad, 1935. **Publications:** Fiction – *While Gods are Falling* (L., 1965); *The Schoolmaster* (L., 1968); *The Dragon Can't Dance* (L., 1979); *The Wine of Astonishment* (L., 1982); *A Brief Conversion* (O., 1988). Drama – *Jestina's Calypso* (L., 1984). **Criticism:** Marjorie Thorpe, introduction to *The Wine of Astonishment*, C.W.S. edition (L., 1982), pp. vii–xiv; Angelita Reyes, 'Carnival . . . in Earl Lovelace's *The Dragon Can't Dance*', *WLWE* 24 (Summer 1984), pp. 107–20; Marjorie Thorpe, 'In Search of the West Indian Hero: a Study of Earl Lovelace's Fiction', in Smilowitz, *Critical Issues*; Norman Cary Reed, 'Salvation, self and solidarity in the work of Earl Lovelace', *WLWE* 1 (1988); Dance, 'Conversation', in *New World Adams*, pp. 145–57.

NAIPAUL, V.S. (Vidiadhar Surajprasad). Novelist, short-story writer, essayist. Born Trinidad, 1932. **Publications:** Fiction – *The Mystic Masseur* (L., 1957); *The Suffrage of Elvira* (L., 1958); *Miguel Street* (L., 1959); *A House for Mr Biswas* (L., 1961, 1983); *Mr Stone and the Knights Companion* (L., 1963); *The Mimic Men* (L., 1967); *A Flag on the Island* (L., 1967); *In a Free State* (L., 1971); *Guerillas* (L., 1975); *A Bend in the River* (L., 1979); *The Enigma of Arrival* (NY., 1987); *A Way in the World* (NY., 1994). Non-fiction – *The Middle Passage* (L., 1962); *An Area of Darkness* (L., 1964); *The Loss of El Dorado* (1969); *The Overcrowded Barracoon and Other Articles* (L., 1972); *India: A Wounded Civilization* (NY., 1977); *The Return of Eva Peron with The Killings in Trinidad* (NY., 1980); *A Congo Diary* (Los Angeles, 1980); *Among the Believers* (NY., 1981); *Finding the Centre: Two Narratives* (NY., 1984); *A Turn in the South* (NY., 1989); *India: A Million Mutinies* (L., 1990). **Criticism:** Anthony Boxill, *V.S. Naipaul's Fiction* (Fredericton, N.B. 1983); Robert Hamner, *Critical Perspectives on V.S. Naipaul* (Washington, DC, 1977, 1979); Hamner, *V.S. Naipaul* (NY., 1983); Kelvin Jarvis, *V.S. Naipaul: A Selective Bibliography with Annotations, 1957–1987* (1989); Renu Juneja, in *Caribbean Transactions*; Bruce King, *V.S. Naipaul* (L., 1993); Rob Nixon, *London Calling: V.S. Naipaul, Postcolonial Mandarin* (NY., 1992); Fawzia Mustafa, *V.S. Naipaul* (C., 1995); John Thieme, *The Web of Tradition* (Hertford, UK, 1987); Kenneth Ramchand, 'Partial Truths: A Critical Account of V.S. Naipaul's Later Fiction', in Smilowitz, *Critical Issues*; Gordon Rohlehr, 'The Ironic Approach. The Novels of V.S. Naipaul', in Louis James, *The Islands in Between*; Paul Theroux, *V.S. Naipaul* (NY., 1972); William Walsh, *V.S. Naipaul* (L., 1973); Timothy Weiss, *On the Margins: the Art of Exile in V.S. Naipaul*; Landeg White, *V.S. Naipaul. A Critical Introduction* (L., 1975). See also, special Naipaul issues of *Commonwealth* 6 (Autumn 1983); *Modern Fiction Studies* 30, 3 (Autumn 1984).

RHYS, Jean (Ella Gwendoline Rees Williams). Novelist. Born Dominica, 1890 (d. 1979). **Publications:** *The Left Bank and Other Stories* (L., 1927); *Postures* (L., 1928; as *Quartet*, NY., 1929 and subsequent editions); *After Leaving Mr Mackenzie* (L., 1931); *Voyage in the Dark* (L., 1934); *Good Morning, Midnight* (L., 1939); (the four first novels were republished in *Jean Rhys: The Early Novels* (L., 1984); *Wide Sargasso Sea* (L., 1966); *Tigers are Better-Looking, with a Selection from The Left Bank* (L., 1968); *Sleep It Off, Lady* (L., 1976); *Smile, Please: an Unfinished Autobiography* (L., 1979); Francis Wyndham and Diana Melly (ed.), *Jean Rhys: Letters 1931–1966* (L., 1984); Kenneth Ramchand (ed.), *Tales of the Wide Caribbean* (L., 1985). **Criticism**: Louis James, *Jean Rhys* (L., 1978); Thomas F. Staley, *Jean Rhys: A Critical Study* (L., 1979); Helen Nebeker, *Jean Rhys, Woman in Passage* (Montreal, 1981); Elgin W. Mellown, *Jean Rhys: a Descriptive and Annotated Bibliography* (NY., 1984); Teresa O'Connor, *Jean Rhys: the West Indian Novels* (NY., 1986); Carole Angier, *Jean Rhys: Life and Work* (Boston, 1990); Carol Ann Howells,

Jean Rhys (L., 1991). Veronica Marie Gregg, *Jean Rhys's Historical Imagination: Reading and Writing the Creole* (Chapel Hill, 1995).

SELVON, Samuel (Dickson). Novelist, short-story writer, playwright. Born Trinidad, 1923 (d. 1994). **Publications:** *A Brighter Sun* (L., 1952); *An Island is a World* (L., 1955); *The Lonely Londoners* (L., 1956); *Turn Again Tiger* (L., 1958); *I Hear Thunder* (L., 1963); *The Housing Lark* (L., 1965); *The Plains of Caroni* (L., 1970); *Those that Eat the Cascadura* (L., 1972); *Moses Ascending* (L., 1975); *Moses Migrating* (L., 1983); *Eldorado West One* (Leeds, 1988). **Criticism:** Kenneth Ramchand, 'The Lonely Londoners as a literary work', *WLWE* 21 (Autumn 1982), pp. 644–84; Susheila Nasta (ed.), *Critical Perspectives on Sam Selvon* (Washington, DC, 1988); Nasta and Anna Rutherford (eds), *Tiger's Triumph* (Armidale, NSW, 1995).

WALCOTT, Derek (Alton). Poet, dramatist, painter, critic. Born St Lucia, 1930. **Publications:** Poetry – *Epitaph for the Young* (Ba., 1949); *25 Poems* (POS., 1948); *Poems* (K., 1951); *In a Green Night* (1962); *The Castaway and Other Poems* (L., 1965); *The Gulf* (1969); *Another Life* (NY., 1873, 1982); *Sea Grapes* (NY., 1976); *The Star-Apple Kingdom* (NY., 1970); *The Fortunate Traveller* (NY., 1981); *Midsummer* (NY., 1984); *The Arkansaw Testament* (NY., 1987); *Collected Poems 1948–1984* (NY., 1986); *Omeros* (NY., 1990); *The Bounty* (L., 1997). Plays – *Henri Christophe* (Ba., 1950); *Drums and Colours*, in *Caribbean Quarterly* Special Issue 7 (June 1961); *Dream on Monkey Mountain and Other Plays* (*The Sea at Dauphin, Malcochon, Ti-Jean and His Brothers* (NY., 1970); *The Joker of Seville, and O Babylon!* (NY., 1978); *Remembrance, and Pantomime* (NY., 1980); *Three Plays* (*The Last Carnival, Beef, No Chicken, A Branch of the Blue Nile* (NY., 1986); *The Odyssey* (L., 1993). **Criticism:** Irma Goldstraw, *Derek Walcott: a Bibliography of Published Poems . . . 1944–1979* (St Augustine, Tr., 1979); Goldstraw, *Derek Walcott: an Annotated Bibliography of His Writings, 1944–1980* (NY., 1984); Stewart Brown (ed.), *The Art of Derek Walcott* (Bridgend, 1991); Robert D. Hamner (ed.), *Critical Perspectives on Derek Walcott* (Washington, DC, 1993) (bibliography); Bruce King, *The Theatre of Derek Walcott* (L., 1996); Terada, Rei, *Derek Walcott's Poetry: American Mimicry* (Boston, 1992).

Index

For main entries, numbers are in **bold**.
Notes are only listed where they contain bibliographical information, and are indicated by 'n'.